More Perspectives on
BioBusiness in Asia

For readers who already believe that the 21st Century will be the century of Asia and Biotechnology then this book puts meat on the bone. For those who do not yet appreciate what the future holds, this will go a long way to convincing them. In the coming decades, the world is going to see a combination of ingredients coming together to deliver a powerful force in the global economy: Asia + Entrepreneurship + Biotechnology. This book is an essential tool for those on the ground who will make this happen.

Hugh Purser, former Advisor,
National Science and Technology Board (Singapore)

A major overview of biotechnology today. The identification of opportunities and challenges is cleverly presented…there are lessons in the book for readers worldwide.

Prof Frank Gannon, Executive Director,
European Molecular Biology Organization

Political leaders, scientists and entrepreneurs throughout Asia are determined to use the region's natural resources and eager workforce to get in at the start of the life science revolution rather than play catch-up later. *BioBusiness in Asia* is an eminently readable front-lines guide to the region's current biotechnology activities and future challenges.

Dennis Normile, Japan/Asia Bureau Chief, Science

… extremely useful for students, investors and anyone currently involved in the biotech industry, at any level.

Dr Glenn Rice, Vice President, Biosciences Division,
Stanford Research Institute (SRI International)

A timely, perceptive, informative and highly readable book.

Timothy Rothermel, United Nations Development Programme

I could not put the book down and read it in a day. The ideas were so vivid; I felt that I was having a conversation with the author. One aspect that stood out was the wealth of relevant information that it contained… The author has quite elegantly separated the wheat from the chaff, and often with incisive frankness, even at the boundaries of controversy. No doubt this book will stir up a few hornets from their nests, but all with good reason, I'm sure.

Dr Gerrard Teoh, Consultant Hematologist, Singapore General Hospital

The book is interesting from many perspectives. For the novice it provides a unique background to our industry and its link with history; for the experienced it provides valuable knowledge and insights into an area of the world few of us are familiar with; and for all it weaves a delightful blend of philosophy and information that make for enjoyable reading.

Dr Abe Abuchowsky, President, Prolong Pharmaceuticals

Dr Shahi's strategic insights and abilities are amply demonstrated... His work has already strongly influenced molecular biology and biotechnology development in the Asia Pacific region!

Prof Jeongbin Yim, President,
Asia-Pacific Molecular Biology Network; and Director, Bio-Max (Korea)

A comprehensive review and a thorough analysis of the critical factors that shape BioBusiness in the Asia Pacific region.

Prof Nancy Ip, Biotech Research Institute,
Hong Kong University of Science and Technology

A refreshing, honest and much needed review of the issues and challenges facing the development of biobusiness in Asia today from an excellent perspective, one that's fully committed to its development in Asia... Should be read by anyone who is seriously committed to biotech development in Asia and indeed globally.

Guy Heather, Biotech Research Ventures

A wonderfully concise encapsulation of the potential social, economic and commercial implications of the biological revolution and how it will shape our future... correctly emphasizes not just the entrepreneurial and business opportunities that the life sciences present, but also the opportunity to fast forward/ accelerate the process (especially in the Asia-Pacific region)... and the reality that the smart marriage of Industry, Science and Government will be necessary in the translational effort to reap practical applications from the new knowledge in the life sciences.

Prof Keson Tan, National University of Singapore

This authoritative book contains a wealth of information on the latest development of biomedical sciences and their application to entrepreneurship.

Prof Lam Sai Kit, University of Malaya

A must read for policy-makers, entrepreneurs, investors and scientists... should be discussed across scientific, national, industry and sector borders, in a truly interdisciplinary way – and its many conclusions and suggestions implemented in concerted efforts without undue delay.

Dr Reto Callegari, Investment Banker

Truly essential reading for anyone who is trying to understand the world of biotechnology and its relation to healthcare, environmental life sciences and agrobiology.

Dennis Susay, Principal Consultant (Healthcare and Life Sciences),
Bentley Porter Novelli, South East Asia

...a highly impressive, informative work which gives significant qualitative and quantitative information on the life sciences in Asia... a "must have" guide to those seeking to build business in Asia.

David Collingham, Managing Director, Ruston Poole International

Breathtaking! One-stop shopping for Asia (and global) "BioBusiness" insight and analysis – both broad and deep. A superb contribution to everyone, whether new to the topic or experienced, who is interested in Asia's BioBusiness opportunities. A tour d'force!

Prof Jack G. Lewis, Marshall School of Business,
University of Southern California

Dr Shahi heralds the dawn of the life sciences revolution in this exciting and well-written book about biobusiness opportunities in Asia... assesses the life sciences landscape in the post-genome era with a practised eye. It's a must-read for anyone interested in biobusiness in Asia and defines research and development priorities for the Asia-Pacific.

Trish Saywell, journalist,
Far Eastern Economic Review and the Asian Wall Street Journal

...covers a very broad array of material in a clear and well-organized way, with excellent use of tables and graphics. The best book on biotech business in Asia that I've seen.

Prof David Finegold, Keck Graduate Institute

A balanced and comprehensive overview of Asia's burgeoning biobusiness sectors, and the challenges and opportunities presented. The industry should find this report, and Shahi's comments on the management and productivity of R&D, of particular interest.

Ian Haydock, SCRIP (Japan)

A useful reference for people who are thinking of getting into Biotech investments. It gives a general perspective of the challenges, opportunities and issues related to doing biobusiness. The book is a good first stop for would-be investors.

Inderjit Singh, leading Technopreneur and Member of Parliament (Singapore)

A very comprehensive and well written piece of work... an excellent guide for businesspeople but also policymakers. In addition, it's fun to read!

Michael Buschle, Chief Scientific Officer, Intercell AG

...should be of particular interest to investors from outside the region. I particularly like the flow, the constant information, charts and emphasis on the region. Dr Shahi is without doubt the protagonist of the biotech industry for Southeast Asia... this book proves beyond doubt that Gurinder is the first port of call for any biotech entrepreneur wanting to explore Asia's potential.

Phil Fersht, former regional Director, Life Sciences, IDC (Asia-Pacific)

Captures a vast and diverse subject in a structured, easy-to-comprehend book which appeals to a wide audience.

Janson Yap, Principal, Process/Life Sciences Industries,
Deloitte Consulting (South East Asia)

… written in a very clear, witty and fluent manner, providing an excellent introduction to modern biology, to biology-related business and the special role of Asia in the global arena of biological research and biotechnological development.

Prof Benny Geiger, Weizmann Institute

This book has revealed to me the extent of biotechnology and made me feel lucky to be in Asia. If you are interested in the biotechnology business, it contains valuable insights and guidance for entrepreneurs.

Jeff Pinkham, Entrepreneur-in-residence, MSC Ventures (Malaysia)

… puts forth a convincing case that the region has the necessary skills and business acumen to be a world leader in the life science revolution… Both complimentary and critical, Dr Shahi provides a blueprint for the advancement of several different biotech-related industries; gives insight on Asia's present positioning vs. the United States and Europe; and expresses the priorities he feels are vital to accelerate the pace of Asian biobusiness.

Joseph J Hoess and Hong Wai Mei, ABN-AMRO Bank (Asia)

… this book contemporaneously mirrors the mapping to provide the blueprint for BioBusiness. …an enlightening and well-presented fountainhead of knowledge on BioBusiness. The buzzword is finally put in perspective!

Tarn Sien Hao, Haw Par Group

… essential reading for anyone who wants to make sense of the buzz on biotech, and who wants a well-researched perspective on business opportunities in the Asian biosciences sector. Non-scientists will appreciate the chapter on "Life Sciences and Biotechnology 101" and the glossary of technical terms expressed in plain English.

Susan de Silva, Partner, ATMD Law (Singapore)

An excellent primer for those attempting to understand the BioBusiness environment – the first book to look at all the vectors that determine a 'successful BioBusiness'. Highly recommended!

Dr Vikram J.S. Chhatwal, Apollo Hospitals Group

… a tour de force. It should be read by investors, scientific entrepreneurs and all those wishing to understand this emerging area.

Dr Matthew Cullen , Co-President, McKesson Asia-Pacific

This is really a great effort and permeated by the author's passion and vision for Asia.

Dr Giorgio Roscigno, President, Foundation for Innovative New Diagnostics

BioBusiness in Asia

How Asia can Capitalize on the
Life Science Revolution

Gurinder S. Shahi

Singapore   London   New York   Toronto   Sydney   Tokyo   Madrid
Mexico City   Munich   Paris   Capetown   Hong Kong   Montreal

Published in 2004 by
Prentice Hall
Pearson Education South Asia Pte Ltd
23/25 First Lok Yang Road, Jurong
Singapore 629733

Pearson Education offices in Asia: *Bangkok, Beijing, Hong Kong, Jakarta, Kuala Lumpur, Manila, New Delhi, Seoul, Singapore, Taipei, Tokyo, Shanghai*

Printed in Singapore

4   3   2   1
07   06   05   04

ISBN 0-13-062045-9

Showing an ancient Chinese ideographic character meaning "together" or "并/bing", dating to the Shang Dynasty (1800 – 1200 BCE), the cover signifies the opportunity and need for people throughout the Asia-Pacific region (and beyond) to work synergistically to maximize potential and create lasting value in the global marketplace.

*When it comes to the future, there are three kinds of people:
those who let it happen, those who make it happen,
and those who wonder what happened.*

John M. Richardson, Jr.

This book is dedicated to all who are not afraid to dream of the profound implications of the life science revolution for every aspect of our lives, and who want to play a part in translating the dream to reality.

The best way to predict the future is to invent it.

Alan Kay

Contents

Foreword

*It is far better to proactively seek to influence
the direction of change than to sit on our hands and
be "surprised" when change inevitably comes.*

Gurinder Shahi

I have worked with Dr Gurinder Shahi for many years now in the context of our efforts together to establish and operationalize the Asia-Pacific International Molecular Biology Network (A-IMBN). We share common perspectives on the way forward for building a viable and vibrant life science and biotechnology sector for the region.

Gurinder's unique mix of cultural experience and technical capabilities has fascinated me since I first met him. I sometimes describe him as a "mystery" man, even an enigma: A man of the East who has been trained in the best Western tradition; a turban-wearing Sikh who professes to be a freethinker; a physician who views the practice of medicine from a social and public policy perspective; a scientist who sees his role as helping to unclog the atherosclerotic translation pipeline from scientific insight into practical application; a manager, communicator and entrepreneur who sometimes sounds like an ivory-tower academic. He questions, he challenges, he inspires, he provokes – earning himself many friends and, as anyone who has ever worked to change the *status quo* will appreciate, the occasional detractor.

To avoid criticism, do nothing, say nothing, be nothing.

Elbert Hubbard

There are few who understand the Asia-Pacific, and the opportunities and challenges in the life sciences and biotechnology for the region, so well.

BioBusiness in Asia is a watershed book that provides both insight and a framework for action. Not only do Gurinder and the BioEnterprise Asia team document our experience to date in the life sciences and biotechnology (in the region and internationally), they lay out an exciting vision of what could be possible – not just in relation to increasing our effectiveness in translating new knowledge to practical application, but also in terms of increasing our success in building both the infrastructure and capabilities for life science entrepreneurship and industry development in Asia. *BioBusiness in Asia* essentially provides a blueprint for what countries in the Asia-Pacific region (as well as other developing regions) could do, and how they might operate, if they are to strategically apply modern knowledge and insights to solve age old problems and developmental challenges.

There is growing evidence that we are reaching critical mass, in the Asia-Pacific region, in life science and biotechnology development. We have already achieved much in building up a base of knowledgeable scientists and centers of excellence that are equal to the best in the world. There is also growing commercial interest and recognition of the potential of the biobusiness-related sector. How things evolve depends, to a large extent, on how we choose to operate as individuals and as societies.

Useful insights in *BioBusiness in Asia* include:

- BioBusiness is already BIG business – accounting for nearly US$10 trillion worldwide (generating over 25% of global GDP, and employing more than 40% of the global labor force).
- The bulk of BioBusiness activity today is commoditized and relatively low value-added.
- New innovations in the life sciences and biotechnology (which generated about US$40 billion in revenue in 2001) still account for less than 0.5% of the BioBusiness economy, but have the potential to revolutionize the entire BioBusiness landscape.
- There is substantial scope to greatly increase the efficiency of the life science innovation process – and to greatly reduce the risk and the time for life science technology and product development. This book shows you how.
- Those companies, countries and regions that will be most successful in capturing the value of BioBusiness opportunities will be the ones that most effectively bring together a confluence of 4 "smarts" – smart people, smart ideas, smart money, and smart alliances and partnerships.

While Asia is clearly a relatively late starter in the life science revolution, starting late does have its advantages:

- Players in the region can learn from the mistakes of those who started earlier, and, hence, shorten their learning curves.

- Technologies, processes and business models are more mature and better validated today than they were at the start of the life science revolution – hence reducing execution risk and increasing prospects for success.
- The existence of companies with innovative products and services, and validated technology platforms, creates opportunities for collaboration and value creation through partnering and strategic alliances for product, market and technology development.

Asian countries need to find their own solutions to the myriad problems and challenges that the region faces – while we should obviously learn from the experience of the US and Europe, we should not blindly imitate approaches and strategies. For example, there is much to be gained from translating low value and commoditized "Valley" BioBusiness opportunities into higher value-added "Summit" opportunities in the region, even as we work in common with more developed regions to translate "Cloud" opportunities into "Summits" (for more details on the BioBusiness landscape conceptual framework developed and used in this book, see Figure 4.1, pg 48 and Chapter 4).

For best results, there should be close alliance involving government, academia, industry and investors working together to maximize innovation and value creation. There is also need to overcome our natural tendencies to compete so we work together to build real value – both across and within nations (and regions).

This is a book with a practical message. Read it, and consider how you can proactively apply its insights and recommendations. In true scientific tradition, the reader is entirely free to either accept or reject arguments and opinions expressed.

Regardless of whether or not you agree with the thrust of the book, we look forward to engaging in constructive dialog – and to finding mutually meaningful ways of working together as individuals, organizations, companies and governments to help create a BioBusiness future that will bring meaningful value to the lives of people in the region and beyond.

Working together, we can achieve far more than we ever could working apart!

Professor Kenichi Arai, MD, PhD
Founding President of Asia-Pacific IMBN
Former Director of the Institute of Medical Science,
University of Tokyo

Preface

May you live in exciting times.

Ancient Chinese Curse

We are living today in exponential time. In every sphere of human activity, new knowledge and insights are being generated at such an incredible pace that few, if any, can keep up. The Internet and new approaches to telecommunications are changing the way we communicate and our expectations of turnaround time for service and its delivery. The life science revolution is changing our perceptions of ourselves, our health, our diseases, and of our relatedness to the world around us.

The future is coming at us at an ever-increasing pace – whether we are ready for it or not.

On the social front, massive changes have been underway for decades as societies in Asia and around the world have unshackled themselves from the chains of colonialism and ideological dogmatism, and as societies have modernized and come to terms with growing urbanization, industrialization, the rapidly changing status and expectations of women, and increasing globalization. On top of everything else, we have had to live through economic, social and political transition and turmoil; with the fear and pain caused by terrorism and the threat of biological weapons and weapons of mass destruction (real or imagined); and with coping with Nature's own genetic engineering experiments in the form of new and emerging infectious diseases (including HIV, Ebola, West Nile fever, SARS, and the constant threat of pandemic influenza).

Humankind has undergone many major transitions throughout our history (and our pre-history). The recent period of economic and social upheaval and rapid change is simply the latest in a long line of many such transitions. Witness the changes that our human ancestors must have experienced with the discovery of how to use tools and weapons for hunting, defence and offence; the agricultural revolution that enabled a shift to controlled human cultivation of plants and the domestication of animals; and the industrial revolution which led to accelerated urbanization and the creation of such wealth that those societies and individuals that benefited from it have since largely been able to live substantially beyond the basic survival mode of traditional hunter-gather societies or agrarian communities.

Transition can be painful and difficult – or it can spell tremendous opportunity to transform our societies and create sustainable progress and growth for those who know what they are doing, and why.

The massive explosion of new information, insights and capabilities enabled by the Internet and the telecommunications revolution has already had far-reaching consequences on every aspect of human existence. Coming close on its heels, and building on the data capture and analysis base provided by new advances in information and communications technology, the life science revolution is completely transforming our understanding of life and our place on this earth as we come face-to-face with the implications of the mapping of the human genome; and as we deal with issues and concerns that new innovation and technological advances inevitably bring: such as cloning; transgenic organisms; new applications in nanotechnology; and the potential to develop new and previously unknown biomaterials.

Already, the insights from the mapping of the blueprint of life in our genomes are mind-numbing and revolutionary – and greatly shake human perceptions regarding our previously imagined exalted place in the hierarchy of life. Over 80% of our genetic make-up appears to be of microbial origin – likely the result of both our own single-celled roots and of previous visitors and invaders of our ancestral bodies that left traces of themselves in our genes. But even more startling is how closely we are connected with each other and with other species – we share over 80% of our genes with the mouse, over 98% with the chimpanzee, and over 99% with other humans. We even appear to share 50% of our genes with the bananas we eat!

This book intertwines three strands of particular interest: new knowledge, insights and capabilities from the modern life sciences and biotechnology and how they promise to transform the BioBusiness[1] landscape; opportunities and challenges for driving technology innovation, bioentrepreneurship and value creation; and consideration of the opportunity and need for socio-economic growth and development of the Asia-Pacific region (and other less developed parts of the world).

---

[1] BioBusiness, as defined in this book, refers to social, economic and commercial activity depending on application of biology and life processes. See Chapter 1, and Box 1.1, pg 2.

Among other things, *BioBusiness in Asia* seeks to provide an integrated strategic framework for addressing opportunities and challenges in BioBusiness, and a clear sense of how we might go about capturing a piece of the economic and social value that the life science revolution will undoubtedly create.

Acknowledgements

I am a part of all that I have met.

John Milton

This book builds on a lifetime of experiences, observations, insights and lessons learnt from mistakes (lots of them!). I have been truly blessed in that I have had the opportunity to meet and interact with so many wonderful and remarkable people in the course of an unconventional career as student, soldier, physician, scientist, lecturer, activist, analyst, international technocrat, consultant and entrepreneur. Building on this, I have also gained from being son, brother, classmate, colleague, mentor, advisor and friend to an even more remarkable cast of characters.

BioBusiness in Asia is the result of synergistic collaboration, partnership and open sharing of ideas and experiences from throughout the Asia-Pacific region and beyond.

There is simply not sufficient space to adequately express my sincere thanks to all who have contributed in one way or another to the insights and observations contained in this book.

The secret to creativity is knowing how to hide your sources.

Albert Einstein

Nevertheless, I would be doing a grave injustice if I failed to mention the following:

- The National University of Singapore and Harvard University School of Public Health provided the opportunity to learn, research, and teach the fundamentals of healthcare and the life sciences; and to wake up to the revolutionary opportunity and potential for new advances in biological sciences and biotechnology to fundamentally change the world as we know it.
- The Rockefeller Foundation, the United Nations Development Programme, the World Health Organization and the International Vaccine Institute enabled partnership and interaction with some of

the brightest and most inspiring minds working across disciplinary boundaries to solve issues and challenges in international public health and development. In particular, I must acknowledge the lessons I learnt from Al Binger, Bob Lawrence, Peter Goldmark, Scott Halstead, Timothy Rothermel, Frank Hartvelt, Seung-il Shin, Margaret Catley-Carlson, John La Montagne, Demissie Habte, GP Talwar, JW Lee, Shigeru Omi, Barry Bloom, Seth Berkley, and Tord Kjellstrom.

- My many colleagues, mentors and friends associated with the Asia-Pacific International Molecular Biology Network (Asia-Pacific IMBN), a leading organization dedicated to promoting molecular biology and biotechnology in the region. Of particular note are Kenichi Arai (Japan), Jeongbin Yim (Korea), Louis Lim (Singapore), Nicos Nicola and John Mattick (Australia), Gong Zuxun (China), Lin Jung-Yaw (Chinese Taipei), Nancy Ip (Hong Kong), Obaid Siddiqi (India), Sangkot Marzuki (Indonesia), Benny Geiger and Yoram Groner (Israel), Chong-Lek Koh (Malaysia), Warren Tate (New Zealand), and Jisnuson Svasti (Thailand). Frank Gannon, Executive Director, EMBO, has been a wonderful advisor and friend – and played a key role in facilitating our early efforts with the Asia-Pacific IMBN. I am ever indebted for the opportunity to play a part in helping to bring this cherished dream of scientific leaders and visionaries (in the region and beyond) to reality.

- My colleagues and friends associated with BioEnterprise Asia who worked with me to lay the groundwork for this organization, and for our initiatives together. These include (in alphabetical order): Michael Berger, David Bligh-Smith, Boey Tuck Khiong, Ben Chung, Thomas Ginzel, Goh Wan Ha, Hari Gurunath, Victor Li, Priya Rath, Sharan Sambhi, Nirman Sodhi, Anita Suresh, and Sabrina Wee. Rupa Bose, Dawn Chan, Chan Yiulin, Eric Lam, Phil Masters and Azlyn Supingi all played key roles in helping to develop some aspect or other of our early programs and efforts.

- Hugh Purser, Lee Chee Wee, Shabbir Moochhala, NP Das, Barry Levy, Howard Frumkin, Nicole Lee, Hazelle Lam, Michael Richardson, Bruno Rossi, Nicholas Seah, Davey Raj, Jerry Kokoshka, Ravinder Manocha, Inderjit Singh, Ti Kiang Heng, Maninder Shahi, Beh Swan Gin, Bhrigubir Singh, Dato (Dr) M Jegathesan, Ezehan Kamaluddin, Pavandip Wasan, Datuk Yahya Baba, Peter Brazier, Mohd Azwar Mahmud, Saibal Chowdhury, Suria Aziz, Simon Tay, Edison Liu, Zahir Ismail, Ramona Volkert, Nick Ashby, Kulwinder Singh, Garry Prior, Eric Mun, Nor

Shahidah Khairullah, Arthur Lahr, Aamir Nordin, Peter Saunders, Anand Govindaluri, Kevin Keane, Sanne Melles and a host of others who helped me understand what we need to have in place to make the biggest difference to policy-makers, entrepreneurs and investors as they take the risks critical to building true value for our societies.

- I would like to express my heartfelt appreciation to the many leading experts from around the world who took the time and effort to review the draft manuscript for the book and to share their thoughtful advice and suggestions for improving it and making it more pertinent to the reader. I learnt much from them, and greatly enjoyed our discussions and thought-provoking exchanges.

- Most of all, I am grateful to my parents, Sohinder and Inderbir, for their unwavering faith, confidence, love and guidance; to Chen, my partner in life; and to Sonia, Savrina, Zuvin and Zadeev, my young teachers and friends to whom the future belongs. They have tolerated a near virtual father and showered him with unconditional love and affection despite all his obvious failings – and helped him understand why everything we are doing, and seeking to do, is so worthwhile.

A Note to the Reader

BioBusiness in Asia has been written so the interested reader with little or no prior formal knowledge and understanding of the life sciences will have little difficulty in following its thrust.

The book is organized into four sections:

Section A. BioBusiness: The Big Picture
Section B. Opportunities in BioBusiness: Implications for Asia
Section C. Issues and Challenges in BioBusiness
Section D. Capturing the Value

Section A lays out a framework for understanding the BioBusiness landscape and considers what it takes to go about making things happen.

Section B addresses opportunities in different BioBusiness sectors (specifically healthcare, biomedical sciences, agriculture, environmental and industrial BioBusiness) and considers how different countries in the region stack up.

Section C focuses on BioBusiness-related challenges, dilemmas (including the moral, ethical, environmental and social issues and concerns) and needs that should be addressed even as we work to build a solid foundation for future growth and development, and work to create world-class institutions and corporations.

Section D begins to outline an action agenda for catalyzing BioBusiness development and value creation in Asia (for the region as a whole, and for key stakeholders including the innovator/entrepreneur, the policy-maker and the investor).

Some readers may choose to go through the book sequentially; others to dip randomly into areas of special interest to them. The book is designed to accommodate different reading styles: each chapter builds on material from prior chapters but effectively stands on its own – starting with a "Summary" section, and concluding with a "Key Points" box outlining the main take-away messages of the chapter.

To guide and facilitate understanding of the exciting new developments in the life sciences and biotechnology, a brief, slightly technical, overview chapter on "Life Sciences and Biotechnology for BioBusiness 101" (Chapter 2) is included, together with a glossary of common abbreviations and terms.[1]

This book will be of interest to all who want to understand the life science buzz, and to see how it is likely to affect our lives – our food, our health, the clothes we wear, the energy we burn, our environment. It will also appeal to students of business and management who want to get a handle on the commercial and public policy opportunities and implications of the life science revolution. Finally, it will likely interest the journalist, the scientist, the entrepreneur, the investor and the policy-maker who want to keep ahead of the curve in understanding the trends in relation to the "next big thing" that is coming at us faster than we realize.

---

[1] Feedback from reviewers of the pre-print manuscript suggests that Chapter 2 is probably the single most challenging chapter for the naïve reader with little or no background in biology – one non-technical reviewer reported that while it took a bit of effort to work through the material in this chapter, the understanding and perspective it provided substantially enriched her experience of reading the rest of the book.

Chapter 1
Introduction: Why BioBusiness? Why Asia?

To know what one knows, and to know what one is ignorant of:
that is true science![1]

Confucius

Summary

This chapter describes the growing importance of BioBusiness in the age of biology, and explains how the arena stands to be transformed by our growing knowledge and expertise base in the life sciences and biotechnology. It goes on to examine the range of problems and issues confronting the Asia-Pacific region, and the opportunity that the region has to apply the new tools of biotechnology to help solve these problems and to capture long-term value.

Why BioBusiness?

The 19th century can be described as the *age of chemistry*. Progress in the 20th century was fueled largely by exciting developments in the physical and engineering sciences, and in information and communication technology. One could, therefore, describe this as the *age of physics*. The 21st century promises to be the realm of exciting new insights and developments in the life sciences and biotechnology that will revolutionize the BioBusiness landscape as we know it – the *age of biology*.

The term "BioBusiness", as defined in this book, refers to social, economic and commercial activity depending on application of our understanding of biology and life processes. The BioBusiness arena includes both traditional and modern agricultural, manufacturing and service sectors founded upon insights involving the biological or life sciences (see Box 1.1).

---

[1] Reviewer Tarn Sien Hao points out that "true science" in the original Chinese script for this quote can also be literally translated to mean "true knowledge".

1

Box 1.1   The BioBusiness Spectrum

BioBusiness includes commercial activities associated with virtually every aspect of human endeavor.[2] For the purpose of this book, BioBusiness is taken to encompass:

Biomedical BioBusiness
- Healthcare
- Pharmaceuticals
- Biomedical biotechnology
- Herbal and traditional medicine
- Medical devices
- Diagnostics

Agri-veterinary BioBusiness
- Agriculture
- Fisheries and aquaculture
- Animal husbandry
- Forestry and lumber
- Agri-biotechnology
- Recreational animal industry (pets, racehorses, etc.)

Food-related BioBusiness
- Food processing
- Food biotechnology
- Food services

Environmental and Industrial BioBusiness
- Management of biodiversity
- Environmental bioremediation
- Waste management
- Environmental biotechnology
- Marine biotechnology
- Industrial biotechnology

Other BioBusiness Activities
- Bio-IT and the application of information and communication technology in the life sciences
- Bioengineering
- Nanotechnologies as applied to the life sciences and biotechnology
- Life science and biotechnology education
- Life science and biotech research and development
- Life science and biotech contract services (for example, contract research and contract manufacturing)

---

[2] In its broadest sense, one might legitimately include the sex trade as a valid BioBusiness activity given the very biological imperative it serves. Similarly, the cosmetics and beauty industries, and the restaurant and food retail industries can also clearly be seen to build on the life sciences. Nevertheless, to avoid unnecessary controversy or distraction, we have chosen **not** to include these very interesting sectors in the current assessment (see also Box 3.1, pg 39).

Since the dawn of civilization, BioBusiness has contributed far more substantially to economic activity in human societies than is generally recognized – whether one speaks of agriculture, healthcare, food processing or the application of modern biotechnology for therapeutic or diagnostic use. BioEnterprise Asia estimates that BioBusiness-related activities employ some 40% of the global labor force, and account for 25% or more of global wealth generation in Gross Domestic Product terms (in 2001, this amounted to over US$9 trillion; see also Table 3.1, pg 38).

While the BioBusiness sectors have traditionally been relatively low value-added and slow to embrace technological advances (the bulk of global BioBusiness workers today are engaged in subsistence-level agriculture or in low-wage, labor-intensive jobs in developing countries), new insights and developments over the last several decades promise to transform the BioBusiness landscape (see also Figure 4.1, pg 48).

This is where the modern life sciences (including molecular biology) and biotechnology[3] come in. The modern biotechnology industry is still relatively small (accounting in 2001 for less than 0.5% of BioBusiness activity; see Table 3.1, pg 38), but is a very rapidly growing and increasingly important BioBusiness sector – the sale of modern biotechnology products, services, and technology solutions is estimated to have generated about US$25 billion in the US alone during 2001, and close to US$40 billion worldwide. BioEnterprise Asia projects that the world market for modern biotechnology-related products, services, and technologies is likely to exceed US$150 billion by 2010 (growing at a rate of about 15% annually).

While the rate of growth of the modern biotechnology sector is interesting in itself, the underlying reason why the modern life sciences and biotechnology are attracting so much interest and investment is their potential to catalyze a fundamental revolution across the BioBusiness arena and beyond.

BioEnterprise Asia estimates that 50% or more of the GDP of most countries today will be impacted by innovations in the life sciences and biotechnology through, for example, the development of:

- New tools for biomedical diagnosis or treatment
- Innovations in terms of new and improved crops
- New biofuels as substitutes for fossil fuels
- New biomaterials to replace plastics or textiles

---

[3] Molecular biology can be defined as the science based on our understanding of life processes at the molecular level. Biotechnology refers to the application of our understanding of life processes for social, commercial or industrial use (see also Chapter 2, pg 13).

- More efficient industrial processes
- New approaches to protecting our environment and replenishing damaged land and marine resources
- New technologies for mining
- Bio-based computing and information management capabilities
- New biodefence systems to protect against and combat the threat of bioterrorism

Clearly, some BioBusiness activities bring higher economic returns than others, and some new developments will bring returns sooner than others (see also Chapter 4). There is, therefore, need to differentiate between low value-added or "commoditized" opportunities (traditional or "Valley" opportunities); high growth and high value-added BioBusiness opportunities (knowledge- and innovation-intensive "Summit" opportunities); and innovative ideas and solutions which are likely to make a great impact in the future but are still not yet commercially ready ("Cloud" opportunities)[4] (see also Figure 4.1, pg 48).

There already exist over 6,000 companies worldwide that classify themselves as "biotech" companies.[5] We currently have more than 150 biotech-derived drugs on the market, with some 400 more in various stages of clinical development. Over 70 varieties of biotech-derived crops have already been approved for cultivation in North America alone, and many more are being assessed for possible cultivation in countries around the world.[6]

The publication of genome maps of a growing range of organisms and the understanding this is helping to generate can be viewed as a watershed event in life science and biotech development. The preceding period can be described as the "pre-genomic" era, while the current period is often called the "post-genomic" era.[7]

With the explosion of new knowledge and insights arising from our growing ability to understand life processes at the fundamental genetic level,

---

[4] For more details on BioEnterprise Asia's landscape-based conceptual framework for understanding and capturing the value and potential of different BioBusiness-related opportunities, see Chapters 3 and 4 and Figure 4.1, pg 48.

[5] Source: BioEnterprise Asia, 2004. While over 1,500 "biotech" companies are based in the US and a further 1,800 or so are found in Europe, the Asia-Pacific region is home to a rapidly rising number of such companies – the regional figure grew substantially from about 1,200 in 2001 to over 2,500 by 2004 (see also Table 10.2, pg 150). This trend clearly reflects a growing level of interest in the Asia-Pacific region for BioBusiness innovation and the potential of biotechnology (see "Why Asia?" section).

[6] Source: BioIndustry Organization, 2003.

[7] Technically, it would be more accurate to describe the current period as the "genomic" rather than the "post-genomic" era since we now have the ability to gain insight from genomic analysis. This was simply not available to us in the "pre-genomic" era.

all BioBusiness sectors are expected to experience substantial transformation over the next several decades – with very real and high impact implications through the creation and exploitation of "Summit" opportunities in a wide variety of areas including the biomedical, agribiological, environmental, and industrial BioBusiness sectors.

Why Asia?

The full potential of life science and technology in the region can only be fostered through close cooperation and collaboration amongst scientists, institutions, national and international agencies, and the private sector.

Professor Kenichi Arai, Founding President of Asia-Pacific IMBN and former Director of the Institute of Medical Science, University of Tokyo

The Asia-Pacific region has around 30% of the world's land surface but is home to nearly 60% of the world's population (Figure 1.1). The region faces a myriad of challenges and opportunities (see also Box 1.2). These include:

- *Socio-demographic changes* – growing and rapidly aging populations as a result of the epidemiological transition; increasing urbanization; and growing demand for quality healthcare and health services
- *Rapidly evolving disease patterns* – resilient infectious diseases (including malaria, tuberculosis, dengue fever, hepatitis as well as the constant threat of new and emerging diseases including HIV, Nipah,

Figure 1.1   Estimated and Projected World Population by Major Regions

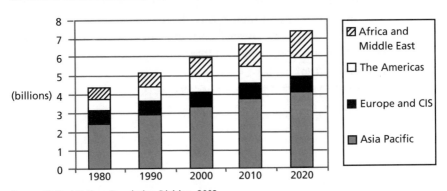

Source: United Nations Population Division, 2002.

Box 1.2   Some Life Science-related Challenges and Opportunities Confronting Asia

By 2001, Asia already held a population of over 3.6 billion people (out of a global population of about 6.5 billion), with regional population growth of about 1.5% annually. Life science-related challenges and needs with BioBusiness implications include:

Healthcare

- Resilient infectious diseases which are responsible for unacceptably high infant mortality rates in many parts of the region (these include largely vaccine preventable causes of acute respiratory infection as well as causes of diarrhoeal disease), and infectious diseases that were not eradicated in the previous decades (including tuberculosis, malaria, Hepatitis B and Hepatitis C)
- Emerging diseases, some of which may be particular to Asia (for example, HIV/AIDS, Nipah virus, Japanese encephalitis, and SARS)
- Diseases linked to rapid epidemiological transition as public health measures lead to reduced infant mortality and longer life expectancies – hence, growing incidence of chronic diseases such as cancers, diabetes, hypertension and heart disease with an increasing population of people aged over 65

Agriculture and food production

- Despite being home to nearly 65% of the world's population, Asia has only 35% of the world's arable land, of which some 38% is already estimated to have been degraded (for example, as much as 27% of agricultural soil in India has been affected by severe erosion and environmental concerns such as salinization)

Environmental challenges

- At least one in three Asians still have no access to safe drinking water and at least one in two have no access to sanitation
- About two-thirds of Asian wildlife habitats have already been lost with associated loss of biodiversity (for example, some one million hectares of Indonesia's national forests are destroyed annually; in 1996 alone, Mongolia lost more than three million hectares of forests due to massive forest fires)

Source: United Nations Development Programme, 2002 and Asian Development Bank, 2002.

and SARS); and growing incidence of chronic and degenerative conditions, as well as cancers, as the population starts to age

- ***Growing demand for agricultural produce*** in the face of on-going degradation of agricultural lands
- ***Increasing demand for fresh water*** for human consumption, agriculture and industrial use
- ***Growing waste management and pollution control concerns*** as a consequence of rapid urban population growth and poorly regulated waste disposal/treatment.
- ***Rapid and on-going destruction of natural habitats*** (including forests and marine habitats) with concomitant loss of endangered species and reduced biodiversity
- ***Increased energy and fuel consumption*** as countries in the region modernize and industrialize

In the Asia-Pacific region, and worldwide, the BioBusiness arena is in the midst of an exciting transformation as a consequence of a variety of factors of global moment including:

- Changing priorities and needs associated with demographic shifts as populations become increasingly urbanized, well-educated and wealthy – and demand access to better healthcare and services as well as to lifestyle and wellness products responsive to their needs
- New approaches to healthcare service delivery and financing
- Revolutionary breakthroughs and advances in information technology, and the life sciences and biotechnology
- Growing investment in life science research and development with implications across the BioBusiness arena

While the US and Europe have historically been at the forefront of innovation in the life sciences and biotechnology, Asia-Pacific economies are catching up fast. Advances in the life sciences and biotechnology can play a key role in providing solutions to the myriad challenges that the region faces in meeting healthcare, agricultural, environmental, and industrial needs while, at the same time, helping to boost Asia's economy through the generation of higher value-added BioBusiness-oriented opportunities and jobs.[8]

---

[8] Most leading international BioBusiness technology, product, and service companies have historically focused on the US, European, and Japan markets – tending to treat the rest of the world as relatively inconsequential. An increasing proportion of leading players now recognize the need for strong Asia-Pacific market and business development strategies if they are to compete effectively in the global marketplace (not least because the Asia-Pacific region often represents the fastest growing market for their products, services, and technologies).

In recognition of the potential of the life sciences and biotechnologies to contribute to economic and social development, many Asia-Pacific economies (notably Japan, Australia, New Zealand, Korea, Taiwan, Singapore, Hong Kong, China, and India, and more recently Malaysia, Thailand, Vietnam, Indonesia, and the Philippines) have invested heavily over the last several decades in building up research and development capabilities (see also Chapter 10).

Research and application of molecular biology and biotechnology are knowledge-intensive activities that are dependent on access to scientific infrastructure, modern research tools and capabilities, reliable telecommunications and information technology networks, highly skilled human resources, and financial investment and support.

A critical mass of competence and capability is being reached. Increasing emphasis is now shifting, in many Asia-Pacific countries, to creating value through innovation and commercialization of technology insights, and the application of new tools and technologies to transform and increase the value that can be derived from more traditional BioBusiness activities.

Asia's human genetic and ethnic diversity serve as excellent resources for data collection and analysis for clinical and molecular epidemiology, and for ethnopharmacology and pharmacogenomics. The region has a rich heritage of alternative, complementary, and herbal medical practices that are already making a significant and growing impact on mainstream healthcare and biomedical research and development efforts. In addition, many Asian countries are rich reservoirs of unique genetic resources including tropical and marine micro-organisms, fungi, flora and fauna. These promise to provide a strong base for bioprospecting for new and improved drugs, new agricultural products, novel industrial enzymes, and biomaterials.

Strong investment across the region in building up life science and biotechnology capabilities and resources, combined with a dramatic increase in entrepreneurial interest, are creating a growing pipeline of innovative products, services, technologies, and start-up companies with high growth potential.

On-going developments in the Asia-Pacific region offer those with the right approach and experience the opportunity to invest and participate in reaping the potential benefits that the BioBusiness arena offers at valuations that are very favorable. These investments are likely to give rise to significant capital uplift through trade sale, merger, flotation and the achievement of significant technology and product development milestones over the next several years. In addition, the BioBusiness sector promises to be a driver of new knowledge- and skill-intensive job creation as manufacturing and service opportunities in the life sciences and biotechnology expand over the coming decades.

There is danger, however, that Asian economies will waste resources and capabilities by duplicating efforts and attempting to compete with each other. Rather, they should seek opportunities to share expertise and resources to work synergistically together to solve common problems while building on complementary natural resources, strengths, and capabilities (see also Box 17.1, pg 268). The value and potential being created by the life science and biotechnology revolution will result in an expanding pie of opportunity and wealth for all who choose to participate in it. Asia stands to gain most when economies and enterprises overcome their natural tendencies to compete by choosing to work together to build value through strategic investment and cooperation in technology, market, and business development.

BioBusiness in Asia focuses attention on where things are likely to go in the BioBusiness arena over the next several decades, and seeks to provide useful insights into how key players can play a proactive role in helping Asia to capture the value that is already being created.

Key Points

1. BioBusiness is already BIG business. It currently accounts for more than 25% of global GDP (over US$9 trillion), and employs no less than 40% of the global work force.

2. Most BioBusiness activity today tends to be relatively commoditized and of low economic value. New insights in the life sciences, and new tools of biotechnology, promise to transform the BioBusiness landscape to create high value-added opportunities.

3. The Asia-Pacific region is well-placed to capture a very significant piece of the growing global BioBusiness pie.

BioBusiness: The Big Picture

Business more than any other occupation is a continual dealing with the future; it is a continual calculation, an instinctive exercise in foresight.

Henry R. Luce

Section A provides an overview of the fundamental issues, opportunities, and challenges in BioBusiness, and provides insight into how we can capture value and generate wealth through innovation.

Chapter 2 equips the reader with a survival level basic understanding of the life sciences and related technologies to appreciate the implications of on-going developments in the BioBusiness arena.

Chapter 3 considers the current impact and significance of BioBusiness from a global economic and social development perspective.

Chapter 4 builds on the concept of old (traditional), new (innovative, knowledge-based) and future-oriented BioBusiness-related activities, and differentiates between high value-added "Summit" opportunities, low value-added "Valley" opportunities, and pre-commercial "Cloud" opportunities.

Chapter 5 considers how value can be created as we make the transition from more traditional "Valley" BioBusiness activities to modern, technology- and innovation-intensive "Summit" BioBusiness activities – and begins to identify the fundamental needs and critical success factors to maximize value creation.

Chapter 2
Life Sciences and Biotechnology for BioBusiness 101

Biology is the science of life in all its manifestations and is the key to all our futures.

David Bellamy

Summary

This chapter is intended to equip the reader with a sufficient basic understanding and vocabulary to grasp the significance of life science-related insights and technology opportunities considered in subsequent chapters. It assumes no previous formal training in biology or biotechnology, and is not aimed at the working life scientist who will undoubtedly find the material presented somewhat simplistic. Readers interested in more detailed discussions of modern biology and biotechnology are referred to the many excellent books and articles on these subjects.

Background

Biology and the *life sciences*, broadly defined, refer to our understanding of life and its various processes. Modern or molecular biology refers to our understanding of life processes at the molecular level, as with our growing understanding of genomics and the processes of gene expression (including proteomics), and of the molecular basis of disease.

Biotechnology, broadly defined, is the application of insights from the life sciences (for example, reproductive biology, genetics, molecular biology, biochemistry, embryology, and cell biology) to economically and industrially productive processes. It is generally recognized to include any technique that uses living organisms, or parts of such organisms, to make or modify products, to improve plants or animals, or to develop micro-organisms for specific use. It ranges from traditional or classical biotechnology, as in yoghurt-, bread- and beer-making, to the most advanced modern – or molecular – biotechnology that builds on our growing understanding of molecular biology.

13

BioBusiness refers to the social, economic, and commercial application of our understanding of the life sciences and biotechnology. The BioBusiness arena (see Box 1.1, pg 2) encompasses a wide range of traditional as well as modern activities.

Historical Perspective

Industry pundits sometimes trace the roots of biotechnology to about 1976 with the founding of Genentech, the first modern biotech company.

The reality, though, is that biotechnology has been with us since humankind first learnt to apply our understanding of the life sciences for our social, commercial, and economic benefit. Classical techniques of biotechnology have been in use throughout recorded history (see Table 2.1) and include the making of yoghurt or wine, selective breeding of dogs and horses, and the development of new hybrid varieties of fruits and agricultural crops using classical non-molecular techniques.

While the term "biotechnology" was only coined in 1919 (Table 2.1), this does not take away the significance and value of the applications of classical biotechnology that were developed based on the relatively limited understanding of life processes that our forebears had at the time of their development.

Table 2.1   Some Milestones in the History of Biotechnology (and BioBusiness)

Date	Event	Implication(s)
circa 10,000 BC	Selective cultivation of crops begins	Birth of agriculture
8–9000 BC	Orchiectomy/castration of young bulls	Growth/behavior modification
5–9000 BC	Domestication of cattle, horses and other livestock	Birth of animal agriculture
circa 6000 BC	Yeast used to make beer by Sumerians and Babylonians	Birth of fermentation-based classical biotechnology
circa 4000 BC	The Egyptians discovered how to bake leavened bread using yeast. Other fermentation processes established in ancient times include making yoghurt from milk using lactic acid bacteria, using molds to produce cheese; making tofu, producing vinegar and wine by fermentation	

Table 2.1　(continued)

Date	Event	Implication(s)
circa 1400 BC	Artificial incubation of eggs	Birth of poultry "industry"
circa 400 BC	Hippocrates (460–377 BC) determined that the male contribution to a child's heredity is carried in the semen. By analogy, he thought there might be a similar fluid in women, since children clearly receive traits from each parent in approximately equal proportion	Early insights into reproductive biology
circa 300 BC	Embryo development systematized	Birth of embryology
100–300 AD	Indian philosophers first pondered the nature of reproduction and inheritance	Early insights into genetics
600–1700 AD	Selective breeding of horses, dogs, cats, and livestock species to produce animals with desired traits systematized	Selective breeding begins
1651	Circulation of blood (Harvey)	Modern physiological principles
1665	Plant compartments called "cells" (Hooke)	Concept of "cells" born
1674	Simple lenses used to study microscopic organisms (Leeuwenhoek)	Birth of microscopy
1780	Successful artificial insemination of dogs	Birth of "artificial insemination"
1856	Existence of microbes demonstrated (Pasteur)	Germ theory confirmed
1859	*On the Origin of Species* published (Darwin)	Theory of evolution
1865	Principles of transmission of genetic traits elucidated using pea plants (Mendel)	Birth of genetics
1891	First successful embryo transfer (Heape)	Birth of embryo manipulation technology
1900	Application of artificial insemination in food animal breeding (Ivanov)	Increased pace of genetic improvement for breeding
1919	Term "biotechnology" coined (Ereky)	"Biotechnology" in the lexicon
1935	First virus discovered	Vectors for genetic mutations

Table 2.1   (continued)

Date	Event	Implication(s)
1944	DNA identified as the genetic material	Molecular basis of heredity
1947	Elements of DNA found to be transposable (McKlintock)	Concept of natural genetic engineering
1949	Cryoprotectants used for cryopre-servation of sperm	Freezing/shipping of gametes and cells possible
1950s	Mammalian tissues/cells grown in laboratory	Tissue culture technology developed
1953	DNA described as "double-helix" of nucleotides (Watson and Crick)	Gene structure described — a key milestone in molecular biology and modern biotechnology, and the birth of genomics
1957	Liquid nitrogen cryopreservation	Long-term storage of cells/gametes
1961	Role of RNA and ribosomes in protein synthesis elucidated	Enabled subsequent controlled production of proteins
1966	Microinjection technology developed	Physical manipulation of genes
1972	DNA from one organism "recombined" with that of another	"Recombinant DNA" technology
1977	Human gene cloned (Itakura)	Genes can be copied
1978	Commercial estrous synchronization in cattle	Timed "artificial insemina-tion" and embryo transfer
1980–81	First transgenic mice (mice bearing foreign genes)	Mammalian genetic engineering
1981	Transfer of murine embryonic stem (ES) cells	Totipotent ES cells aid transgenics
1983	Polymerase chain reaction (PCR) described (Mullis)	Rapid amplification, detect-ion and cloning of genes
1985	First transgenic domestic animals produced (pig)	Genetic engineering of livestock
1987	Targeted gene disruption (gene "knockout")	Enabled studies and development of therapies for loss of gene function
1989	Targeted DNA integration and germ-line chimeras (mice)	Potential for tissue engineering and gametic transmission of transgenes

Table 2.1   (continued)

Date	Event	Implication(s)
1993	Recombinant growth hormone approved for dairy cows	Pharmacologically enhanced milk production
1993–95	Functional nucleic acid vaccines introduced	Potential for engineering medicines and for disease prevention
1996	Sheep cloned by somatic (body) cell transfer	True mammalian cloning possible
1998	Human embryonic stem cells derived	Multiple therapies for genetic and immunological disorders
1999	Draft of complete human genome sequence published	Watershed events marking our transition from the pre- to the post-genomic era
2001	Human genome mapped	

Exciting new developments in biology and our understanding of biological processes at the molecular level over the last several decades have led to a total rethink of the life sciences, and increasing awareness of the potential to translate these new insights into practical commercial and industrial application. We have experienced an exponential explosion in new information, data and knowledge generation accelerated by new genetic insights, the application of new techniques and biotechnologies, advances in information and engineering technology, and the development of new tools for knowledge management.

The unraveling of the human genome (and those of other organisms) has been dubbed the Holy Grail for the drug industry, although the implications of new knowledge and understanding in the genome sciences clearly extend well beyond the pharmaceutical sector alone. Our collective effort in deciphering the *Blueprint of Life* in our genomes through learning to understand and interpret the implications of genetic code differences amongst different organisms is paving the way for the next industrial revolution: the BioBusiness revolution.

We introduce some fundamental life science and related technology concepts in this chapter to enable the reader to appreciate why new developments and innovations are arousing so much interest and excitement.

Correlating Structure to Function

Where classical biology emphasized distinguishing life forms into the different biological kingdoms (bacteria, protists, fungi, plants, and animals) and classifying them in terms of families, genera, species, and so on, on the basis of externally observable morphology and biological processes, we have now entered a whole new era where we can determine the degree of interrelatedness or uniqueness of different species or genetic traits from understanding the molecular basis for observed differences in structure and function.

Box 2.1 outlines a very useful conceptual framework for analyzing biological problems and developing new solutions that is just as applicable for classical biology as it is for modern molecular biology: it emphasizes a focus on understanding how structure (of an organism, of a biological system, or even of a specific cellular component or genetic sequence) relates to function, and how applying our understanding of structure and function can lead to insights into biological problem-solving and the development of new products and technologies.

Box 2.1   Correlating Structure to Function to Application

One very useful approach to understanding and translating insights in the life sciences is to correlate structure to function, and then to apply this knowledge towards solving biological problems, developing products or creating new technologies:

- *Structure* – understanding the components of any system, and how they are organized at the molecular level and in relation to each other
- *Function* – understanding how the components of the system operate and interact with each other under normal circumstances as well as when things go wrong (for example, when genetic abnormalities cause components of the system to function abnormally)
- *Application* – using insights gained from understanding structure and function to develop interventions and find solutions to biological problems – for example, by taking advantage of unique structural and functional characteristics of each organism for diagnostic or therapeutic use, by reconstructing structures to make them function more normally, by adding components which may be missing, or even by altering the genetic makeup to enable diseased systems to function more normally (as in gene therapy)

By taking advantage of our understanding of structure and function by appreciating how the wing of a bird is structured and how structure correlates to function during flight, we have developed insights that have led to application of such knowledge to the development and refinement of airplanes. Similarly, by understanding how changes in gene structure in genetic mutations can lead to altered physiological function of the lungs in cystic fibrosis, we can apply this knowledge to develop patient management strategies that reduce the severity of disease, and can even develop gene therapy approaches in an attempt to correct or minimize the impact of the gene defects.

The Genome Sciences and the *Blueprint of Life*

The *genome sciences* refer to the integration of various disciplines (for example, genomics, proteomics, and bioinformatics) that are driven by the vision of being able to unravel and understand the genetic make-up of entire organisms with the aim of being able to utilize this knowledge for the benefit of humankind and the environment.

At the genetic and molecular level, all known forms of life are remarkably similar – whether one happens to be a human, a plant, or a bacterium, our bodies use fundamentally the same genetic language to communicate and coordinate our activities.

Imagine that each organism's genetic material (its genome) is organized as a comprehensive manual, its unique *Blueprint of Life*, which contains all the information on how to build the different components that make up that organism (in your case, you!), together with instructions on how the various parts should fit and interact with each other.

The genetic material, usually found in the nucleus of each cell, is organized as chromosomes. Each chromosome consists of DNA (deoxyribonucleic acid) and associated protein molecules.[1] Genes, which are the physical and functional units of inheritance that are passed from one generation to the next, occupy fixed positions (loci) on each chromosome and contain specific instructions coding for specific genetic products (usually proteins). Each chromosome can be considered as a complete chapter of the *Blueprint of Life* manual, while each gene can be considered as a section of that chapter.

The genetic material in each chromosome consists of a molecule of DNA organized in the form of two long thread-like strands wrapped around each other like a twisted ladder (the famous "double helix"), and essentially provides all the information for constructing a living, breathing, functioning organism – a full copy of the genome exists in almost every cell of the organism.[2]

---

[1] DNA constitutes the genetic material of all bacteria, protists, and multi-cellular organisms. Some viruses use RNA (ribonucleic acid) as their primary genetic material and do not contain DNA. Well-known examples of RNA viruses include the HIV/AIDS virus, the flaviviruses that cause diseases such as dengue fever and West Nile fever, and the coronaviruses that cause the common cold and SARS.

[2] Generally, reproductive or sex cells such as sperms and eggs contain only half of the genetic material found in somatic cells (see Box 2.2). Also, certain cells, such as red blood cells in our blood, lose their nuclei during their developmental process and hence, cease to contain a copy of the full genome.

Humans generally bear 23 pairs of chromosomes (or 46 chromosomes) holding genetic material in the nucleus of each cell in our bodies (see also Box 2.2). Other species have different numbers of chromosomes in their cells – our close relatives, the chimpanzee and the gorilla, have 24 pairs of chromosomes (or 48 chromosomes); while the fruit fly has eight chromosomes and some species of fern possess over 600 chromosomes in the nucleus of each cell.

The sequence of DNA that constitutes a gene (the so-called *exons*) would be the words that tell you exactly what goes into each specific component (usually proteins), while the DNA sequences which do not code for building components (the *introns*) make up the spaces and punctuations that help to organize each page of the manual.[3]

Box 2.2   Sex and Non-Sex (Autosomal) Chromosomes

The 23 pairs of chromosomes in the nucleus of every human cell consist of 23 chromosomes inherited from the mother through her egg, and 23 from the father through his sperm.

One pair of these chromosomes, the so-called *sex chromosomes*, determines whether you are male or female. The sex chromosomes come in two varieties – a larger X chromosome and a much smaller Y chromosome. Mothers pass on X chromosomes only (since they themselves possess a pair of X chromosomes), while fathers can pass on either an X or a Y chromosome (since they possess one X and one Y chromosome as their sex chromosome pair). If you end up with a pair of X chromosomes from your parents, you will be female. If you get an X chromosome from Mum and a Y chromosome from Dad, you end up being male.

The other 22 pairs of chromosomes that make up your genome are called *non-sex* or *autosomal chromosomes*.

Gene Expression

When genes are expressed, the genetic information coded in the DNA is generally *translated* through the synthesis of proteins coded for in the DNA – a process requiring another nucleic acid, RNA (ribonucleic acid). The gene code is first *transcribed* from the DNA in the nucleus of the cell onto so-

---

[3] The introns were previously called "junk DNA" or the "noncoding regions" because scientists could not, until recently, figure out their role since they clearly were not involved in providing structural information for each protein component. The introns are now increasingly recognized as playing useful regulatory roles – helping to provide instructions for how exactly to build and organize each protein component, how the various components should fit and interact with each other, and so on.

called *messenger RNA* (mRNA), which then carries the code to protein factories in the cytoplasm of the cell called *ribosomes* (which are cellular components composed of proteins and a class of RNA called *ribosomal RNA* or rRNA) (see Figure 2.1). Specialized *transfer RNAs* (tRNAs) then transport specific amino acids for attachment to the growing protein chain as the genetic code is translated by the ribosomes.

The Genetic Alphabet

The letters or nucleic acids that make up DNA on the chromosomes are the basis for understanding the nature and function of genes, and their control. What makes the genome instruction manual so interesting and complex is that it is written entirely in "code", a term computer programmers are quite familiar with.

It is only natural, then, that bioscientists involved in genome sequencing projects are working increasingly in coordination with computer experts to decipher the genetic code and its implications for structure and function. This increasingly important inter-disciplinary collaboration through Bio-IT and the fields of *bioinformatics* and *computational biology* is already beginning to yield exciting new insights and technology applications (see also Figure 2.5, pg 32).

The code to form words from the DNA letters was cracked by James Watson and Francis Crick in the 1950s (see Table 2.1, pg 16). Fundamentally, four different nucleic acids with the initials A (adenine), G (guanine), C (cytosine) and T (thymidine) constitute the letters of the genetic alphabet – A

Figure 2.1   Gene Expression: Transcription of DNA to RNA and Translation of RNA to Amino Acids and Proteins

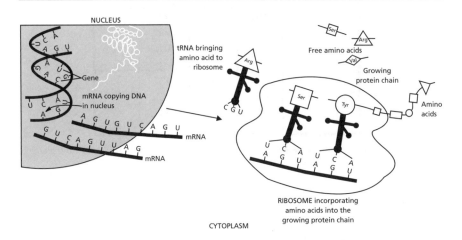

always binds with T, and C with G to form the steps of the spiral DNA double helix ladder (see Figure 2.1). Every sequence of three letters, the tricodon, forms a word coding for one amino acid, in turn, the building block of proteins.

RNA differs from DNA in that another nucleic acid, U (uracil) replaces T. Figure 2.2 shows how each three-letter code is decoded and translated from

Figure 2.2 Decoding the DNA/RNA Tricodon: How tRNA Works to Translate Nucleic Acid Code to Give the Amino Acid Sequences of Proteins in Gene Expression

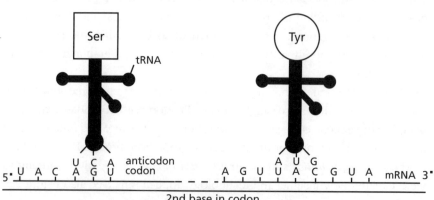

			2nd base in codon			
		U	C	A	G	
1st base in codon	U	Phe	Ser	Tyr	Cys	U
		Phe	Ser	Tyr	Cys	C
		Leu	Ser	STOP	STOP	A
		Leu	Ser	STOP	Trp	G
	C	Leu	Pro	His	Arg	U
		Leu	Pro	His	Arg	C
		Leu	Pro	Gin	Arg	A
		Leu	Pro	Gin	Arg	G
	A	Ile	Thr	Asn	Ser	U
		Ile	Thr	Asn	Ser	C
		Ile	Thr	Lys	Arg	A
		Met	Thr	Lys	Arg	G
	G	Val	Ala	Asn	Gly	U
		Val	Ala	Asn	Gly	C
		Val	Ala	Glu	Gly	A
		Val	Ala	Glu	Gly	G

Note: there are some 20 amino acids coded by each tricodon. In the figure, "Ser" refers to the amino acid serine, "Tyr" to tyrosine, "Val" to valine, and so on.

mRNA using transfer RNA (tRNA) to identify the specific amino acid to add to the protein chain at the ribosome.[4]

Genome Sequences

The first complete genome sequenced was the 5,386 nucleotide base (letters) genome of the phi 174 bacteriophage (a bacterial virus) in 1975, followed by the human mitochondrial genome of about 16.6 kilobases (about 16,600 bases) in 1981, and then the lambda phage genome of 49 kilobases (about 49,000 bases) in 1982 (see Table 2.2). In comparison, the full human genome consists of nearly three billion nucleotide base pairs (about three million kilobases). Interestingly, the human genome is not the largest genome, and there appears to be little correlation between the size of genome and evolutionary complexity (in other words, when it comes to the genome, size does not appear to matter – it's how you use it).

The genomes of many organisms in both the animal kingdom (for example, insects, crustaceans, and amphibians) and the plant kingdom (for example, algae and flowering plants) dwarf the size of the human genome. The distinction of possessing the largest genomes ever known (with as many as 500 to 1,000 chromosomes!) belongs to several protozoa (single-celled organisms belonging to the "protist" kingdom of living things). The largest genome is currently thought to belong to a species of amoeba, *Amoeba dubia* – the genome of this organism is some 200 times larger than the human genome (Table 2.2).

Table 2.2   Illustrative Sizes of the Genome in Various Organisms

Comparative genomic sizes	Nucleotide bases
phi 174 bacteriophage	5,386
Human mitochondrial genome	16,600
lambda phage	49,000
Yeast chromosome 3	350,000
Escherichia coli genome	4.6 million
Largest yeast chromosome	5.8 million
Entire yeast genome	15 million
Smallest human chromosome (Y)	50 million
Largest human chromosome (1)	250 million
Entire human genome	3 billion
Amoeba dubia genome	670 billion

---

[4] The tRNA for each amino acid bears a different "anticodon" which binds complementarily to its respective tricodon being "read" off the mRNA sequence in the ribosome to enable the placement of the amino acid in its correct position on the growing protein chain (see Figure 2.2).

Of Mice and Men

It used to be believed that there is substantial difference in genetic terms between humans and other species. It would certainly look this way on the surface, given the wide variety of shapes and sizes of different life forms and the variation in size of genomes.

Still, almost all life forms use the same building blocks, and operate in essentially the same way at the genetic and functional levels. Deciphering the genetic code has helped us to realize how interrelated we are, and how variations in just a few basic operations at the genome level can have a major impact on the structure and function of life as we know it.

It may be disconcerting for some to note that there is a very fine line separating mice and men (see Figure 2.3). Genetically, we share more than 80% of our genes with the mouse – we have only about 300 genes that mice do not. We share over 98% of our genes with the chimpanzee and the gorilla. We also happen to share some 50% of our genes with our distant relative, the banana.

Underlying Molecular Basis of Disease

Our susceptibility to most diseases (including infectious diseases) tends to be the consequence of a combination of genetic and environmental factors. Some,

Figure 2.3 Comparison Between Human Genome and Mouse Genome

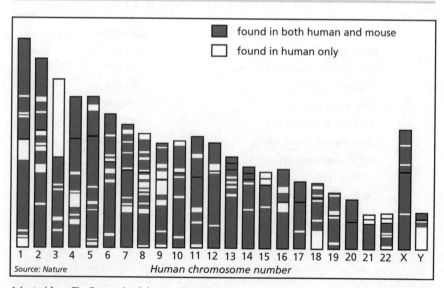

Source: Nature

Human chromosome number

Adapted from The Economist, February 17 to 23, 2001.

such as Down's syndrome,[5] arise from abnormalities at the chromosomal level. Others, such as sickle-cell anemia, arise from a single gene defect. Still others, such as diabetes mellitus or hypertension, arise from a combination of several genetic abnormalities as well as environmental risk factors. In seeking to effectively manage or treat any disease, it is critical to understand its underlying molecular basis.

Mutations

The critical importance of the DNA sequence and getting it right can be clearly seen, for example, in the case of a genetically transmitted disease called sickle-cell anemia – which is essentially caused by a single base-pair change in the mutated gene coding for hemoglobin, the key protein involved in oxygen transport in our bloodstream. This causes a single amino acid change, thereby altering the structure and, consequently, the function of the hemoglobin protein. Patients with this disease characteristically possess oxygen-carrying red blood cells that become sickle-shaped under certain circumstances as opposed to the normal disc-shaped cells, with resulting anemia due to accelerated breakdown of the misshapen red blood cells.

Sex-linked Diseases in Humans

As human chromosomes generally occur in pairs, each gene generally also has a counterpart in its corresponding chromosome.[6] An individual is described as *homozygous* if both chromosomes carry the same gene, and *heterozygous* if the genes are different. A genetic trait that expresses itself preferentially in heterozygous individuals is described as *dominant*, while the trait carried by the gene that does not express itself is *recessive*. At times, both genes in each chromosome of the pair will express themselves – in which case they are described as *co-dominant*.

The genes on X and Y chromosomes, by virtue of their sex chromosome link, have characteristic traits associated with their malfunction or mutation (see also Box 2.2, pg 20). Recessive X-linked traits are more easily identified than recessive autosomal-linked ones because males generally bear just one such gene on the X chromosome with no counterpart on the Y chromosome,

---

[5] Also called "trisomy 21", individuals with Down's syndrome have three copies of chromosome number 21 in each nucleus and not the usual two that would be expected in a chromosome pair. The condition typically arises as a result of defective cell division to form sperms or egg cells.

[6] This is generally true except in the case of the X and Y chromosomes in males where most genes on the larger X chromosome have no counterpart in the much smaller Y chromosome (see also Box 2.2, pg 20).

and will express the gene regardless of whether it is dominant or recessive. On the other hand, females have a pair of X chromosomes, and will express dominant and recessive genes in the same manner as they do autosomal-linked traits. Hence, people manifesting recessive X-linked traits or diseases are mostly males (males possess 46 chromosomes including XY, and females possess 46 including XX).

Examples of recessive X-linked traits or diseases include:

- *Haemophila* – an X-linked disease involving a blood clotting disorder (factor VIII)
- *Red-green color blindness*
- *Fragile X chromosome* – the tip of the long arm of the X chromosome shows a constriction to the point of breaking, resulting in various manifestations including mental retardation

Stem Cells: Cell Growth and Differentiation

Cells specialize, or differentiate, to serve different functions according to instructions received from other cells in their vicinity depending on where they are located in the organism. Hence, some cells are destined to be heart muscle cells, others to be liver cells or blood cells, and so on. In each case, they go back to the genomic instructions in the *Blueprint of Life* genome manual contained in the DNA in their nuclei to see which proteins to produce and how to regulate their respective activities in order to fulfill their functions.[7]

The more differentiated and specialized a cell is, the less it tends to be able to transform itself to serve new and different functions. Cells that remain relatively undifferentiated, the so-called *stem cells*, can transform to serve a variety of special functions. Stem cells can replicate almost indefinitely and can give rise to a wide and varied range of specialized cells like muscle or neural cells with the appropriate growth and differentiation signals. The least differentiated stem cells, called *pluripotent* stem cells, are found in the bone marrow (as well as in the brain, muscle, and other tissues) and are generally seen as having the greatest potential for transforming into specialized cells.

The art and science of taking stem cells and helping them to differentiate according to need is a growing area of life science technology called *tissue engineering*. The better we are able to control the transformation of cells through tissue engineering, the greater will be our ability to generate new organs to replace damaged ones (including skin, bone, livers, and even hearts).

---

[7] Genes typically express themselves through protein production. Proteomics is the study of the identities, quantities, and functions of proteins expressed in any system (organism, organ, cell, organelle, and so on) in health, disease, and different functional states.

Substantial controversy and ethical concerns have surrounded the use of embryos as a relatively abundant source of a type of stem cells called *totipotent* stem cells. These are stem cells that can essentially differentiate into practically any specialized cell, and are even less differentiated than the pluripotent stem cells found in adults. It is to be anticipated that with growing understanding of how to control differentiation of pluripotent stem cells that can be harvested from adult bone marrow, there will likely be reduced need to harvest stem cells from embryos in future, and therefore less controversy (see also Box 14.1, pg 227).

Apoptosis: Programming Cells to Die for Life to Progress

Apoptosis[8] (or programmed cell death) refers to the natural controlled way in which normal cells die after fulfilling their specific role. Thousands, if not millions, of cells (for example, epidermal skin cells and epithelial cells lining the stomach and intestines) undergo apoptosis and programmed cell death every day throughout the life of any individual.[9]

The process of apoptosis, common and conserved among all multi-cellular organisms, is an essential part of life. It is required to systematically eliminate superfluous cells in many basic biological processes such as development and homeostasis. The typical embryo undergoes apoptosis during each stage of development in order to develop into its final form at birth.

Consequently, when the apoptosis process malfunctions or fails, the results are usually disastrous – from autoimmunity to cancer, the paradoxical reality is that blockage of controlled death leads to fatal diseases. In HIV/AIDS, the apoptosis mechanism is prematurely turned on in healthy immune cells, destroying the immune system. Cancer, on the other hand, usually results from an uncontrolled increase in cells that escape the usual control mechanisms for growth and differentiation (see Box 2.3). Hence, it is crucial to unravel and understand the mechanisms that program for cell death at the genetic and molecular level, if we are to develop effective strategies for dealing with such diseases.

The biggest contribution to our understanding of apoptosis has come from studies of the worm, *Caenorhabditis elegans*. The regulatory mechanisms underlying apoptosis are highly conserved from worms to humans, a reality

---

[8] The term "apoptosis" is derived from the Greek word meaning "falling off," as leaves do in autumn.

[9] Apoptosis can be contrasted against the death of cells from damage or poisoning before their programmed time. Characteristically, damaged cells swell and burst, spilling their contents in their surroundings. This reactive and uncontrolled form of cell death is called *necrosis*, which tends to be messy.

that underlines the fundamental importance of the process in all multi-cellular organisms. The *caspases*, a group of enzymes that break down proteins, are known to be central to the apoptosis process – acting effectively as the final executioners in programmed cell death.

Box 2.3   Cell Differentiation and Cancer Biology

One area where knowledge and understanding of the differentiation of cells is critical is cancer biology where it appears that malignant cells escape from the normal control mechanisms that regulate cell growth and differentiation. Characteristically, they become less differentiated mavericks growing out of control (causing *tumors*), and often becoming capable of breaking away from the mother tumor and establishing tumor colonies in different locations in the body such as the lungs, the liver and bone marrow (*metastasis*).

There is growing interest in understanding what causes such cells to escape the usual control mechanisms, and to determine how to bring them back under control – which could potentially enable us to treat cancer by causing malignant cells to differentiate, for example.

Implications of New Insights from the Genome Sciences

Our growing understanding of the mechanisms of life that has been gained from the genome sciences and modern biotechnology (see also Table 2.2) is already having significant impact in a growing range of BioBusiness sectors, including:

- Prevention, diagnosis, and the development of tailored and effective treatments in molecular medicine
- Improved yields and nutritional value, breeding, livestock production, and bioprocessing in agriculture
- Bioremediation and biomining in environmental science
- Criminal investigation (forensics), product identification, and conservation of species

New insights promise to revolutionize the BioBusiness landscape and to bring substantial social and economic benefit to those who recognize its potential and take the lead to create innovative new products, services, and technology platforms that respond to opportunities and needs in the marketplace.

Table 2.2   Some Key Events That Have Shaped Our Understanding of the Genome Sciences and Modern Biotechnology

1869	"DNA" first described (Friedrich Miescher)
1900	Mendel's laws of genetics based on inheritance of traits in pea plants accepted (Gregor Mendel)
1910	Mendel's laws of genetics applied to the fruit fly to show that specific genes are located on specific chromosomes, and that genes on the same chromosome tend to be inherited together (Thomas Morgan)
1913	The first genetic map, based on physical relative locations of several known genes on the X chromosome of the fruit fly, was constructed (Alfred Sturtevant)
1928	Harmless bacteria transformed into disease-causing pathogens using bacterial cell extract (Frederick Griffith)
1944	Proven that the transformation extract used in Griffith's experiments was DNA (O. Avery)
1952	Radio-labeled viral DNA used to infect bacteria hence helping to establish DNA as the genetic material (Martha Chase and Alfred Hershey)
1953	DNA molecule recognized to be structured in the form of a double helix of paired bases or nucleotides (James Watson, Francis Crick, and others)
1956	The first enzyme that helps to make DNA, DNA polymerase, first isolated (Arthur Kornberg)
1961	The instructions for a protein shown to exist as a series of non-overlapping three-letter (base) code words, each triplet specifying one amino acid (Francis Crick *et al*)
1964	Radio-labeled RNA used to determine the specific triplet (codons) assigned to each amino acid (Marshall Nirenberg and Hargobind Khorana)
1964	mRNA shown to explain information transfer between the chromosomes (DNA) and ribosomes (protein) (Francois Jacob, Mathew Meselson and Sydney Brenner)
1973	Demonstrated that proteins take their specific shapes from the "directions" encoded in the amino acid sequence. This established translation of genetic information into functional differences through gene expression (Christian Anfinsen *et al*)
1973	The first genetically engineered organism created by moving rRNA genes from the African clawed toad (Xenopus) into bacterial cells (Stanley Cohen, Herbert Boyer and Paul Berg)
1975	First production of monoclonal antibodies (Georges Kohler and Cesar Milstein)
1977	Methods for sequencing DNA developed (Frederick Sanger and Walter Gilbert)
1979	The presence of protein coding and non-coding sequences demonstrated within eukaryotic genes (*exons* and *introns*, respectively) (Pierre Chambon, Philip Leder, and Bert O'Malley)
1983	PCR technology to make millions of copies of DNA sequences in a few hours established (Kary Mullis)

Table 2.2   (continued)

1996	"Shot-gun cloning" to quickly identify genes using Expressed Sequence Tags (ESTs) established (Craig Venter *et al*)
2000	Working draft of complete human genome presented (Francis Collins and Craig Venter)
2001	Noncoding DNA ("introns"), previously thought to be "junk" DNA, proposed to play a vital regulatory role in genome function (John Mattick)

Life Sciences, Biotechnology and BioBusiness

Biotechnology consists of a range of technologies, ranging from the long-established and widely used techniques of classical or traditional biotechnology, to novel and continuously evolving modern or molecular biotechnology applications. In fact, modern biotechnology can be seen as an integration of new techniques based on our growing understanding of life sciences at the molecular level with the well-established approaches of classical biotechnology such as plant and animal breeding, food production, fermentation processes, and the production of pharmaceuticals and fertilizers (see also Figure 2.4).

Over the past several decades the number of significant advances in modern life sciences and biotechnology for understanding, applying, and modifying the genetics of living organisms has increased dramatically. This has led to greatly increased interest and investment in biotechnology, and increasing concerns regarding the power of the new technologies and their potential

Figure 2.4   Growing Complexity in Biotechnology: Illustrative Examples

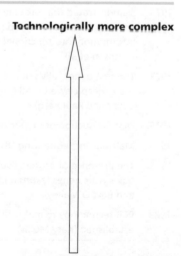

Technologically more complex

Modern (molecular) biotechnology

Tissue engineering

Cloning

Recombinant DNA technology

Polyclonal and monoclonal antibody production

Embryo transfer in animals

Plant tissue culture

Biological nitrogen fixation

Microbial fermentation

Selective breeding

Classical biotechnology

Technologically less complex

ethical and social consequences. Our capabilities and competence in applying such technologies are rapidly evolving and involve substantial research and development in their own right.

Figure 2.5 outlines a simple conceptual framework used by BioEnterprise Asia to show how modern knowledge-based BioBusiness builds on new insights and understanding being generated in the life sciences and biotechnologies. Capturing the value proposition of modern BioBusiness intrinsically requires strong competence and insights from a variety of scientific fields (*core competencies*) as well as the technological capabilities to translate scientific knowledge and understanding into practical products and solutions. Such technological capabilities include *enabling technologies* that are key to translating insights into products, services, and applications; and *supporting technologies* that are needed to facilitate production, testing, and the bringing of products and services to market. As shown in Figure 2.5, strong capabilities in Bio-IT (including *bioinformatics, computational biology* and, increasingly, capabilities for *knowledge management* and for *molecular modeling and simulations*) are central to modern life science and technology development endeavors.

Core Competencies

The core competencies for modern life sciences and modern BioBusiness include a growing range of areas including: gene mapping and sequencing; structural, functional, and applied genomics and proteomics; and a growing array of new areas of modern integrative biology (including systems biology) as well as the rapidly growing range of new "omics" (including, for example, cellomics, receptomics, metabolomics, phenomics, and so on).

Technologies

The rapidly advancing development and application of tools for both *enabling* and *supporting* biotechnologies will provide tremendous opportunities to utilize and capitalize on our growing knowledge and understanding of the modern life sciences to generate and bring products, services, and new technologies that promise to create substantial economic and social value to market.

Enabling Technologies

Enabling technologies for modern BioBusiness help to enable and facilitate translation of findings from research and the generation of products and services from the application of these technologies.

Figure 2.5   Some Modern Life Sciences and Biotechnologies for BioBusiness

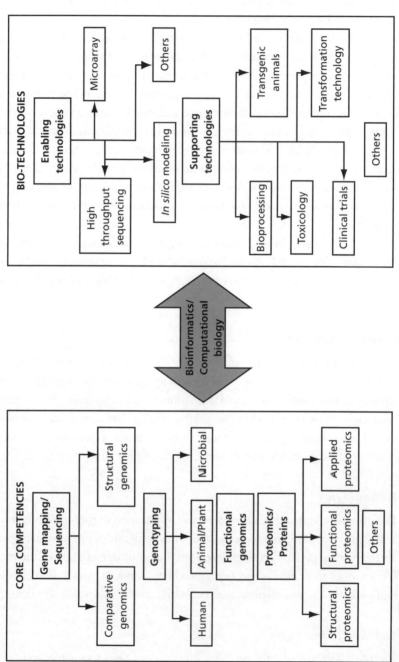

© *BioEnterprise Asia, 2001.*

During the 1970s and 1980s, scientists developed new methods for precise recombination of portions of DNA and for transferring portions of DNA from one organism to another. This set of enabling techniques is often referred to as *genetic engineering.*

Modern biotechnology incorporates the application of such biotechnologies as genetic engineering technology, technologies for generation of monoclonal and polyclonal antibodies, and new cell and tissue culture methods. Potential outputs from the application of these technologies to generate solutions to life science problems include the development of diagnostics and therapeutics; the production of biopharmaceuticals and vaccines; and the development of new and improved crop species that are more disease resistant or are capable of providing higher yields.

Additional examples of enabling technology tools that facilitate life science problem-solving and the generation of higher value-added BioBusiness products and services include:

- *High throughput sequencing and screening technologies* – to speed up the genetic analysis process and to facilitate rapid screening and identification of promising compounds for subsequent testing and development
- *Microarray technologies* – for example, DNA chip, protein chip, and related technologies
- *Nanotechnologies* – for example, application of microscopic "labs-on-chips," micromachines, incorporation of microfluidics and microphotonics for analysis and diagnosis, and so on

Supporting Technologies

Supporting technologies are technologies which may not necessarily be directly involved in solving life science-based problems or concerns but which are, nonetheless, important, especially in terms of translational biotechnology – helping to drive life science products, services, and technologies from concept toward commercial, social, and industrial application in the marketplace. Such technologies include:

- *Bioprocessing* technologies for optimized and cost-effective production of biopharmaceuticals, monoclonal antibodies, and other biologicals
- *Clinical trial* and *product development* technologies to help drive products through the various stages of clinical and field-testing, and toward registration and market entry

- *Plant transformation* and *tissue culture* technologies
- *Transgenic organism development* technologies

Bio-IT and the Life Science Revolution

As emphasized in Figure 2.5, our growing understanding and capabilities in both the core competence life science areas and the biotechnologies for modern BioBusiness build intrinsically on the power and potential of bioinformatics and computational biology (such technologies and capabilities can be collectively described as "Bio-IT").

Bio-IT involves the application of tools of information and communication technology to the understanding and analysis of biological phenomena, and the generation of new insights and applications from such analysis.

The life science revolution is intrinsically linked with the information and communication technology revolution. The development of increasingly more powerful computational power for data storage and management, for data mining and analysis, and for molecular and systems modeling and simulations, have gone hand-in-hand with new insights and understanding of the life sciences. The advances we have seen in the life and genome sciences in recent years would not have been possible without our growing ability to store, manage, and interpret biologically relevant data and information through advances in information and communications technology.

Current Trends and Future Directions

Current efforts in the genome and life sciences are still focused primarily on the generation of data and the building of a fundamental understanding of the "structural" aspects of genomics and proteomics (for example, high throughput genome sequencing and the determination of protein structure; see also Figure 2.6).

Already, we are beginning to develop an understanding of the "functional" significance of our findings (for example, through a growing understanding of functional genomics, functional proteomics, and systems biology).

The long-term goal of our efforts in the genome and life sciences is not just an understanding of the structure and function of biological systems, but the "application" of such understanding for the benefit of humankind and the environment. Exciting effort has already started in developing promising applications such as pharmacogenomic diagnosis and targeted (so-called "rational") design of effective therapeutics and vaccines.

Figure 2.6   Current Trends and Future Directions in Genome Science
                 Applications

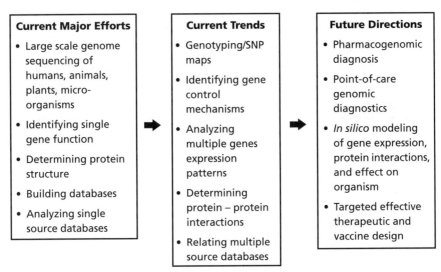

Current Major Efforts

- Large scale genome sequencing of humans, animals, plants, micro-organisms
- Identifying single gene function
- Determining protein structure
- Building databases
- Analyzing single source databases

Current Trends

- Genotyping/SNP maps
- Identifying gene control mechanisms
- Analyzing multiple genes expression patterns
- Determining protein – protein interactions
- Relating multiple source databases

Future Directions

- Pharmacogenomic diagnosis
- Point-of-care genomic diagnostics
- *In silico* modeling of gene expression, protein interactions, and effect on organism
- Targeted effective therapeutic and vaccine design

Source: Shahi et al, Singapore Ministry of Trade and Industry Ad-Hoc Working Group on Genome Science, 2000.

The power and effectiveness of our biotech translation and application development efforts will increase dramatically as our structural and functional understanding increases, and the tools of modern life sciences and biotechnology mature. Our growing ability to read, understand and even edit the *Blueprint of Life* manuals of a growing variety of different organisms promises to be a major driver of economic, social, and technological development for many decades to come.

Key Points

1. At the fundamental genome level, biological processes are essentially very similar whether we speak of animals (including humans), plants or microbes.
2. While new insights in biology have helped to greatly increase our knowledge and understanding, they also demonstrate how much more we need to understand. We are at the dawn of the era of translating new insights into practical application.
3. Application of our knowledge and understanding of biological processes and the development of new tools in modern life

sciences and biotechnology have substantial implications for increasing our success and efficiency in developing new products, services and technologies.

4. We stand to benefit greatly and to generate substantial wealth from innovation, entrepreneurship, and investment opportunities in BioBusiness through the development and provision of innovative life science and biotechnology-related products, services, and technologies.

Chapter 3

The Impact and Significance of BioBusiness

Progress lies not in enhancing what is, but in advancing towards what will be.

Kahlil Gibran

Summary

BioBusiness activities, especially agriculture, have always played a major role in employment and economic terms in human society. While this was particularly true in traditional agrarian societies where 80% or more of any population were typically engaged in BioBusiness activities, the role of BioBusiness tended to decline as societies industrialized. New understanding in the age of modern life sciences and biotechnology looks set to inevitably reverse historical trends, and to lead to the injection of innovative new technologies and approaches. They have the potential to cause a revolutionary reinvention of BioBusiness as a knowledge- and technology-intensive driver of economic and commercial growth and development. This chapter examines the impact, significance, and potential of BioBusiness activities today.

BioBusiness: The Big Picture

By any measure, BioBusiness is BIG business. BioBusiness-related activities are estimated to engage more than 40% of the global labor force,[1] and to account for over 25% of global wealth in gross domestic product (GDP) terms (see also Table 3.1 and Box 3.1). In Asia today, BioBusiness activities engage

---

[1] It should be noted that the bulk of those currently engaged in BioBusiness are low value-added subsistence farmers and low-wage workers in agriculture and food processing in developing countries. The global numbers are skewed by the reality that nearly 60% of workers in China, and nearly 70% of workers in India and other developing countries in Asia and Africa (collectively constituting as much as half of the world's labor force) are engaged in such work.

over 50% of the work force, on average, and contribute over 30% to regional GDP (Table 3.1).

BioEnterprise Asia estimates that 50% or more of the GDP of most countries today will be impacted by innovations in biotechnology and the life sciences – whether this be in the development of new tools for biomedical diagnosis or treatment: in new and improved crops; in the development of new biomaterials as substitutes for fossil fuels or plastics or textiles; in the development of more efficient industrial processes; or in the development of new approaches to protect our environment and replenish damaged land and marine resources.

Table 3.1   Relative Contribution of Various BioBusiness Sectors to Economic Activity (US$ billions and % of GDP), 2001

BioBusiness sector	Global US$ billions (% of global GDP)	South Asia US$ billions (% of regional GDP)	East Asia and Pacific Islands (excluding Japan) US$ billions (% of regional GDP)	USA US$ billions (% of US national GDP)
Agriculture, fisheries and forestry	2,611.4 (8.1%)	223.2 (28%)	362.1 (15%)	529.4 (5%)
Healthcare	2,933.8 (9.1%)	33.5 (4.2%)	108.6 (4.5%)	1,588.2 (15%)
Food sector (processing, manufacturing)	3,288.4 (10.2%)	100.5 (12.6%)	277.6 (11.5%)	1,016.5 (9.6%)
Biotechnology	40 (0.1%)	1.4 (0.18%)	4.1 (0.17%)	25 (0.24%)
BioBusiness-related R&D	257.9 (0.8%)	2.4 (0.35%)	12.1 (0.5%)	105.9 (1%)
Other BioBusiness	644.8 (2%)	15.9 (2%)	48.3 (2%)	211.8 (2%)
Total BioBusiness	9,776.3 (30.3%)	376.9 (47.3%)	812.8 (33.7%)	3,476.7 (32.8%)
Estimated GDP	32,239.0	797.3	2,414.2	10,588.0
GDP as % of global GDP	100%	2.5%	7.5%	32.8%

© BioEnterprise Asia, 2003.[2]

---

[2] Primary data sources for the analysis in Table 3.1 include United Nations Statistics Division (2002), Food and Agriculture Organization (2002) and World Bank (2002). See also Box 3.1.

Box 3.1   Challenges in Estimating the Economic Impact of BioBusiness

Most economies today classify economic activities in terms of three major categories: agriculture (including fisheries and forestry), manufacturing, and services.

Trying to figure out the contribution of BioBusiness activities (see Box 1.1, pg 2 and Table 3.1) in any economy is not easy given that data that can be used for comparison across countries and regions is generally available only in broad activity categories. Also, how one defines BioBusiness will clearly also impact on one's findings.

For the purpose of this analysis, we defined BioBusiness as economic activities that depend on application of insights from our knowledge of biology and the life sciences for commercial benefit. Clearly, all agricultural activities would be included in such a definition. In the manufacturing sectors, processing of food and natural products clearly falls into the BioBusiness arena, as do pharmaceuticals, biologicals, nutraceuticals, and industrial biotech manufacturing. In the service arena, healthcare and health services clearly fall into the BioBusiness category.

Other areas that might, with a more liberal definition, be defined as BioBusiness, were considered by our team to be in the "gray zone". Food supply chain management services (including, possibly, the operation of restaurants) could arguably be classified as being within the BioBusiness arena, for example. Should we treat the sex trade as a BioBusiness activity especially since it is an industry built upon responding to a very biological imperative? What about the cosmetics and beauty industries? What about ecotourism? What about energy sector activities based on fossil fuels like petroleum and coal, dependent as they are on biological processes millions of years ago? Rather than get ourselves bogged down with subjective definitions, we decided not to include these gray areas for the purpose of this analysis.

Also, we felt it was necessary to take due account of the reality that different accounting approaches used by different authorities to define and classify economic and social activities might well lead to the same activity being counted twice or more times (so-called "double counting"). This may happen, for example, when agricultural activity for food production is counted as agriculture by some authorities and as food sector inputs by other agencies or authorities. Also, inputs for the biotechnology sector might be counted as biopharmaceutical inputs, for example, or agricultural inputs or even R&D inputs depending on how different authorities choose to classify them.

We, therefore, chose to leave out any numbers for sectors that could not be readily obtained from internationally verifiable sources, and attempted to adjust our data for possible double counting wherever possible. Hence, the numbers obtained, while they clearly demonstrate the importance and value of BioBusiness in our various economies today, are almost certainly a gross underestimate of the actual size of the BioBusiness arena.

BioEnterprise Asia predicts that we will see substantial value creation in the BioBusiness arena over the next several decades. Our assessment is that growth in the arena is likely to exceed 8–10% annually, on average, for the next decade, which would be 2–3 times our expected annual rate of growth for the global economy as a whole during the same period.

A Historical Perspective

Without agriculture, the most important BioBusiness activity historically in both commercial and employment terms, none of us could survive much longer than a few weeks. Without medicine and public health, many of us would very likely have succumbed to infectious disease ailments in infancy; those that did not would be constantly under threat of dying from easily preventable and manageable ailments. And without a healthy environment we would constantly be at risk of exposure to hazardous and toxic agents that can impact on our health and well-being. Hence, BioBusiness activities tend to have a very direct impact on our lives, and our quality of life.

On the other hand, we could potentially live without cars, computers, and state-of-the-art telecommunications devices – at least longer than without food and medicine.

In more industrialized economies, industrial output and the manufacturing sector have historically been contributing relatively more and more to the economy than traditional BioBusiness sectors – largely because innovation in these sectors has allowed higher and higher value-added economic growth. In other words, such technologies have tended to generate substantially greater revenues per worker and have, therefore, allowed increasingly higher wages to be paid per employee than, say, traditional agriculture (see also Table 5.1, pg 61). Hence, it has not been surprising that the role of BioBusiness-related activities actually decreased substantially as countries developed during the industrial age – as economic interest shifted toward the manufacturing and service sectors, and away from agriculture.

Interestingly, though, the European industrial revolution in the 18th and 19th centuries started with the processing of agricultural commodities (in other words, higher value-added BioBusiness-based activities): the textile industry (depending, to begin with, on cotton, silk, and other natural products, for example) was one of the first industry sectors that developed in Great Britain. Later, tremendous productive power was applied to metal processing and other non-life science-related activities.

Large parts of Asia (and Latin America and Africa) were colonized by European powers, and forced to produce raw materials under extreme low-wage circumstances to fuel Europe's industrial advancements. In return, they served as captive markets for produce from the industries of the colonial powers. As a consequence, labor-intensive, low value-added production of food and agricultural commodities, as well as mineral resource mining industries, dominated economic activity in Asia (and Latin America and Africa) for centuries under colonial rule.

Industrialization started in Japan in the late 19th century, and it was only after achieving independence from colonial powers following World War II (post-1945) that most other Asian countries started on the faster track of industrial development, and away from being simply providers of low value-added agricultural and mineral raw materials. On the other hand, several Asian countries (such as Vietnam, Myanmar, and Afghanistan) found that the post-colonial era tended to be dominated by war or military rule, slowing and even reversing economic and social progress for decades.

As a result, Asia is today a continent full of contrasts. On the one hand, countries like Japan, Hong Kong, Singapore, and South Korea count among the most developed in the world, while Nepal, Laos, or Myanmar can still be described as largely agrarian societies.

BioBusiness in Asia

Despite progress, most of Asia's population still lives in countries that produce a substantial share of their economic output from traditional BioBusiness activities such as the production of basic foods and raw natural products from agriculture and forestry. As Figure 3.1 shows, the less developed the society, the more economically important traditional low-wage agriculture and related BioBusiness activities tend to be.

The picture is even more extreme when the focus shifts to sources of employment for the labor force. As productivity and economic value-added of traditional agricultural and related BioBusiness output is relatively low, the share of labor involved in these activities tends to be even larger (see Figure 3.2).

A large proportion of Asians earn their daily bread (or rice, in most cases) from BioBusiness-related activities. However, the bulk of these activities in Asia represent what BioEnterprise Asia calls "Valley" BioBusiness activities (see Chapter 4, Figure 4.1, pg 48) – commoditized, low value-added activities that are characterized by many competitors, low margins, and the law of diminishing returns.

Figure 3.1   Contribution of Agriculture and Healthcare to the Economy (in % GDP terms) in Selected Asia-Pacific Countries

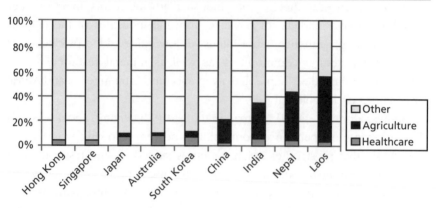

Source: World Bank, 2002.

Figure 3.2   Agriculture's Contribution to Economic Output (in % GDP terms) and to Employment in the Labor Force (% of Labor Force)

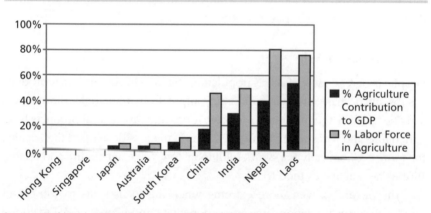

Sources: World Bank, 2002 and International Labour Organization, 2002.

Figure 3.3 shows the proportion of workers employed in two important BioBusiness sectors: agriculture and healthcare. While agriculture remains absolutely dominant in countries like Nepal, Laos, or Myanmar, the Asia-Pacific's more developed countries, such as Japan, Korea, Hong Kong, Singapore, and Australia, have seen a substantial decline in the contribution of agriculture to employment, and a concomitant increase in health sector employment.

The Impact and Significance of BioBusiness   **43**

Figure 3.3   Percentage Contribution of Selected BioBusiness Activities to Employment in Selected Asia-Pacific Countries and Regions

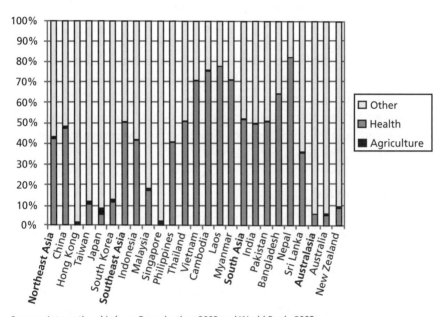

Sources: International Labour Organization, 2002 and World Bank, 2002.

It is also not surprising that there are huge gaps in productivity and income between these countries. Australia and Nepal have roughly the same number of inhabitants. Yet, in Nepal, 80% of the work force toil on mountain slopes to produce little more than US$200 each per year, while only 5% of Australia's work force cultivate the continent's vast land areas, each one generating more than US$20,000 annually on average (see also Table 5.1, pg 61).

The Importance of BioBusiness: From Traditional to Industrial to Post-industrial Societies

The mix of economic and social activities that contribute to development has shifted as societies have become more modern and technologically advanced. This shift can be considered in terms of three phases:

Traditional Agrarian Societies

Traditional societies are essentially agrarian with relatively low value-added "Valley"-type BioBusiness activities being a primary source of work and income for the population – agriculture focused on producing subsistence crops and related BioBusiness activities typically dominate all economic life. Such activities can constitute as much as 45% of all commercial activities in value terms in some of these societies (Figure 3.1), and employ 70% or more of the working population (Figure 3.2).

Because most of this work involves the cultivation and processing of relatively low value-added commoditized food and natural products, economic benefits from such activities tend to be low, and the population has no choice but to eke out a living at or near subsistence level (Table 5.1, pg 61). Importantly, as much as 40% or more of the meager household expenditure in these societies tends to go toward the procurement of food, with very little left over for purchasing other products or services.

Industrial Societies

As societies develop and become more industrialized, the mix of economic activities change as the role of higher value-added non-BioBusiness-related manufacturing and heavy industries, as well as non-BioBusiness services industries have tended to grow. Often, the early industrialization process has involved moving up the economic value-added scale in terms of BioBusiness-based manufacturing activities such as the processing of raw materials and the introduction of plantation-type agricultural production (as can be seen in such countries as Malaysia and Thailand).

Typically, BioBusiness activities have generally played a less and less important role in industrially more developed societies than in traditional societies as they moved toward heavy industrial manufacturing and the introduction of electronics and hi-tech industrial manufacturing, and grew their services sectors through developing their tourist industries, financial services sector, and so on.

Also, the mix of labor involvement in BioBusiness activities change as societies urbanize and undergo transition from agrarian to more industrialized societies – a substantially smaller proportion of the population is engaged in agriculture in more industrialized societies (typically about 15–25%), and total economic benefit from agriculture in GDP terms is typically less than 10% in industrialized societies.

One area of BioBusiness that has generally seen substantial increase with industrialization and concomitant urbanization is the proportion of expenditure on healthcare – it is typically less than 4% of GDP in poorer and more traditional societies, but rises to 8% and higher in wealthier and more industrialized societies.[3]

The proportion of the substantially larger household expenditure base spent on procuring food in more industrial societies falls to less than 8% (compared to 40% or more in the least developed societies), leaving a significantly higher proportion available for education, and the purchase of modern lifestyle products and services including electronic equipment, as well as information and communication tools.

Post-industrial Societies

Post-industrial societies have seen a resurgence in the importance and role of BioBusiness-related activities (especially healthcare) as populations age, and have been the first to begin seeing an even stronger role for BioBusiness as the new life sciences and technologies have begun playing a more central role as engines of innovation and growth. Scientific and technological advances in the life sciences and other disciplines, especially the genome sciences and information technology, are creating new opportunities to bring innovative and higher value-added products and services into the life science arena – and enable the establishment of entirely new BioBusiness industry sectors focused on "Summit"-orientated opportunities (see Chapter 4).

Conclusion: Opportunity to Redefine the Future of BioBusiness

Importantly, even though post-industrial societies have been the first to begin reaping the benefits of the new biology for BioBusiness, less developed economies (whether at the industrializing/industrial stage, or even the more traditional agrarian societies) can potentially benefit directly from new developments in life sciences and biotechnology, and use these developments to transform their BioBusiness sectors into higher value-added economic activities if they choose to.

Leapfrogging into the cutting edge of BioBusiness would be akin to what many developing countries have done in the information and communications arena by introducing wireless cellular phone networks, satellite television and state-of-the-art computer systems to escape the hopelessly inadequate and antiquated telecommunications infrastructure and traditional line-based

---

[3] While most industrial countries typically spend between 6–8% of GDP on healthcare, the US – the country which spends the most on healthcare on the planet – spends as much as 15% of its massive GDP on healthcare. As can be seen from Table 3.1, the US, with less than 5% of the world's population, accounted for more than 50% of global healthcare spending in 2001.

phone systems that many of these societies were stuck with as recently as the beginning of the 1990s.

Scientific advances in the life sciences and biotechnology have already begun to make a great impact on the lives of agricultural workers. The green revolution of the 1960s and 1970s, for example, made high-yield varieties of crops available so the same input of labor produced substantially higher crop output – enabling those agricultural regions that adopted more modern agricultural practices to become relatively more prosperous.

Even more recent scientific and technological advances in the life sciences and other disciplines, particularly the genome sciences and information technology, are beginning to create entirely new business opportunities and industry sectors that are beginning to impact greatly on BioBusiness in the region as we know it.

Key Points

1. The relative contribution of traditional BioBusiness activities (such as commodity agriculture and low value-added food processing) to economic growth and development has tended to decrease as societies have industrialized and become more urban and modern.
2. Asian economies are at different stages of development across the whole continuum – from traditional agricultural to modern industrial and even post-industrial. In general, agriculture remains a more significant contributor to the region's economy than in more developed parts of the world, but its relative importance has been diminishing with urbanization and economic growth from increasing industrialization.
3. Modern knowledge- and technology-intensive BioBusiness activities are beginning to transform the BioBusiness arena. These include growing contributions of new approaches to agriculture and agribiology, new developments in the healthcare and biomedical research sector, and new environmental and industrial applications.
4. The development of innovative life science and biotechnology-related products, services, and technologies will likely reverse the historical trend of declining importance of BioBusiness as societies modernize – both by fueling the development of new sectors as well as by transforming existing sectors.

Chapter 4

The BioBusiness Landscape:
The Importance of Innovation
and Value Creation

Life is pretty simple: You do some stuff. Most fails. Some works.
You do more of what works.
If it works big, others quickly copy it. Then you do something else.
The trick is the doing something else.

Thomas Peters

Summary

This chapter outlines BioEnterprise Asia's conceptual framework for describing the rugged and dynamic terrain of the BioBusiness landscape, and differentiates between commoditized low value-added "Valley" BioBusiness activities, modern knowledge- and technology-intensive "Summit" BioBusiness activities, and promising "Cloud" BioBusiness opportunities. It makes a strong case for why Asia-Pacific economies (and other developing economies) would benefit from establishing the knowledge and capability base to transform their respective BioBusiness landscapes by capturing the value proposition of "Summit" opportunities, while preparing themselves strategically to capture "Cloud" opportunities.

Introduction

The business of biology has been practiced since human prehistory. From the development of crop fields and animal farming, through selective breeding, genetic engineering and molecular biology, to the present era of DNA chips and computer-based molecular modeling, the BioBusiness landscape has been undergoing a gradual but rapidly accelerating metamorphosis.

The past decade has seen massive strides in the life sciences and biotechnologies, mainly through higher value-added, knowledge-based inputs as new insights and understanding have driven innovation. These developments can, at least in part, be attributed to the benefits of advances in data storage technology and communications through such media as the Internet and the development of new tools for biological data management and analysis that have allowed nearly real-time sharing of new insights and observations amongst academic and industrial scientists.

The BioBusiness Landscape: Identifying "Summit" Opportunities

BioEnterprise Asia uses the conceptual model of a very rugged and dynamic landscape to describe opportunities and challenges in BioBusiness (Figure 4.1). In looking across the various BioBusiness sectors, we see many "Valleys" (V), "Summits" (S), and dramatic "Clouds" (C) in each sector:

"Valley" opportunities: These are commoditized opportunities where there are many competitors, low barriers to entry, and low margins; "old" economy market principles apply (driven by the law of diminishing returns). This is the space occupied by most traditional BioBusiness activities (for example, subsistence agriculture, plantation cropping to produce raw materials, and traditional medicine). BioEnterprise Asia considers such opportunities as being of low perceived value in themselves, but very ripe for rethinking and injection of innovative and knowledge-intensive approaches that would help them rise up the slopes toward being transformed into much higher value-added "Summit" opportunities in response to market demand and need.

"Summit" opportunities: These are technology- and knowledge-intensive opportunities where there are few competitors, high barriers to entry,

Figure 4.1 The BioBusiness Landscape

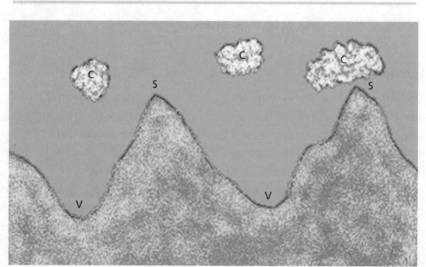

© BioEnterprise Asia, 2002.

high margins, and clear business case validation; "new" economy principles apply (driven by the law of increasing returns). BioEnterprise Asia considers such opportunities to be of very high interest. The problem, and the challenge, is that "Summit" opportunities very quickly find themselves under threat from competitors offering similar products or competing technology solutions because the potential returns are so high – such opportunities could very quickly find themselves sliding down the rugged BioBusiness terrain toward the "Valley" unless there is clear commitment and investment in on-going innovation and new knowledge creation to maintain the competitive edge.

"Cloud" opportunities: These are technology- and knowledge-intensive where there are few competitors, and high barriers to entry. They differ from "Summit" opportunities in that the business case for such opportunities is not well-developed or unproven in thay they are still experimental and pre-commercial ("future" economy principles apply). BioEnterprise Asia considers such opportunities to be of potential future interest in that they may well become very big in the future even though no one has quite figured out how to translate the idea into money. We recommend tracking and even proactively working to develop scientific and technological capabilities to allow for quick capitalization of the "Cloud" opportunity area when it does become economically viable. In other words, we treat such opportunities as "KIV"[1] opportunities.

Table 4.1 summarizes the key characteristics of "Valley," "Summit," and "Cloud" opportunities. Most economic activity can be classified somewhere in this continuum. "Valley" BioBusiness activities have become commoditized with low barriers to entry as the knowledge to capture the opportunity is generally available so no player can really establish an unfair competitive advantage.

For example, rice farming in Asia reflects substantial experience and knowledge accumulated over dozens of generations (just consider, for example, the knowledge and understanding required to regulate the water levels on countless terrace fields). Yet rice production knowledge is generally available and not kept proprietary – every individual farmer can learn the methods and use them, and there are many small-scale suppliers of rice. As a result, rice has become "commoditized." The market price reflects primarily the cost of the required inputs, such as land, labor, and capital. In that sense, there is very little "value-added" on top of these costs to enable higher income to farmers.

---

[1] "KIV"(Keep in View) – a commonly used expression in Asia when referring to issues that need to be borne in mind. People often maintain a "KIV" list, or keep a "KIV" file or box on their desks to keep track of how things evolve in relation to the issue, concern or opportunity.

Table 4.1   Comparing "Valley", Summit", and "Cloud" Opportunities

"Valley" opportunities	"Summit" opportunities	"Cloud" opportunities
Commoditized	Knowledge-based (innovative)	Knowledge-based (innovative)
Market fundamentals important (law of diminishing returns)	Market fundamentals important (law of increasing returns)	Market fundamentals untested (law of potential returns)
Generically available information and competencies	Specialized information and competencies	Specialized information and competencies
Technology well validated	Technology validated	Technology may not yet be validated
Business case validated	Business case validated	Business case not validated

© *BioEnterprise Asia, 2003.*

"Summit" opportunities are characterized by the "law of increasing returns" in that the returns from the use of new knowledge and insights tend to increase the more such knowledge and insights are applied. However, as the new knowledge and insights underlying the "Summit" opportunity become more generally available, the originators find that the premium they can command tends to keep shrinking. This happens as products and services from the application of the new technology become increasingly "commoditized" with new entrants and competing technologies entering the field. Prices go down, and the "Summit" opportunity inevitably gets eroded in time to become a "Valley" opportunity unless there is on-going innovation (and the injection of new knowledge and insight) to maintain a strategic advantage building on the use of the new technology.

Higher value-added can be obtained either from translating cutting-edge new technology- and knowledge-intensive "Cloud" opportunities into "Summit" opportunities, or from rethinking and transforming traditional "Valley" opportunities toward becoming "Summit" opportunities through strategic investment in innovation for new product, service, and technology development in response to market interest and demand.

"Summit" opportunities can and do exist in all sectors of BioBusiness – from crops which provide higher yields in agriculture; to the use of micro-organisms for food processing and environmental clean-ups; to novel approaches to drug development in the pharmaceutical industry. We are increasingly discovering newer and better technologies and approaches to defining, and then increasing, the value of our inputs so higher value outputs can be produced.

While traditional agricultural methods generally fall in the realm of "Valley" opportunities,[2] tissue culture-based propagation of high-yield varieties, or the development of transgenic (genetically modified) crops with higher yields and higher pest resistance can clearly represent potential "Summit" opportunities and capabilities, yielding substantially higher incomes and returns on investment – until the knowledge base and the production principles become widely available, supply starts to exceed demand, and players can no longer extract a premium in pricing or higher yields (in other words, the opportunity becomes "commoditized").

Recognizing and developing innovative products, services, and technologies to capture the potential of "Summit" opportunities is likely to boost BioBusiness in Asian economies (see Box 4.1), just as it has begun to make an impact in post-industrial societies around the world. Importantly, such innovation should always be focused on market interest or demand, responding to unfilled gaps and unmet needs in the marketplace. Finding better ways to make a generic commodity product simply does not add as much to income as producing products that are in high demand for which consumers are prepared to pay a premium.

Box 4.1   Asia and the BioBusiness Landscape

Most of Asia's BioBusiness activity today builds on so-called "Valley" opportunities such as rice farming or traditional food processing and packaging: The inputs are standardized, the outputs are commodities – resulting in low prices and low income for those who are involved in these activities. These industries are characterized by the "law of diminishing returns" where the price of a commodity tends toward reflecting only the cost of producing it, and does not allow for substantial mark-up or economic value-added (and hence can only support low wages). Also, given the highly competitive marketplace for such produce, there is constant downward pressure on pricing and margins.

The price of virtually every commodity exported by developing economies and imported by the industrially more developed economies has fallen from peaks around 1995–1997. The reasons: record world output of these commodities arising from both better technology and changes in government policies, combined with slumping demand.

---

[2] It should be noted that there is growing market interest in and demand for "organic" produce grown using traditional organic agricultural methods that do not involve chemicals or genetically modified crops. In this situation, changing market demand and interest have helped transform previously "Valley" opportunities into "Summit"-type opportunities for farmers.

Innovation and Value Creation in BioBusiness

The key to success and maintaining a premium is to constantly innovate and create products and services that allow "Summit"-oriented positioning and valuation. This comes from both adapting existing product and service offerings so they are transformed from "Valley"-type opportunities into higher-value offerings for which the market is prepared to pay a premium, as well as from finding ways to efficiently translate "Cloud" opportunities into "Summit" opportunities.

The time available to capture the value of any advantage that a player can gain from innovation and creating new "Summit" opportunities is rapidly decreasing (see also Box 4.2) – not unlike the halving of the cost of computer memory every 18 months or so, or the increasingly short interval that pharmaceutical players have to capitalize on innovative new products before competing technologies and products enter the marketplace.

It needs to be constantly borne in mind that today's "Summit" opportunity is tomorrow's "Valley" opportunity – hence the need for continual improvement, re-invention and innovation. Innovation and the spirit of entrepreneurship are fundamental to the new knowledge-based economy, and to long-term success and value creation in BioBusiness (see also Box 4.3).

Box 4.2   Information Technology and Value Creation in BioBusiness

Information and communication technology, and the Internet, play a double-edged role in fueling the new, knowledge-based economy. On the one hand, these technologies provide access to new insights and understanding that enable savvy players to quickly obtain an advantage in the marketplace and command a premium in pricing and value add for their new products, services, and technologies – hence allowing micro-"Summit" opportunities to be captured by those who have access to the relevant information and capabilities.

On the other hand, they facilitate rapid transmission of information regarding innovation to competitors, hence greatly reducing any knowledge advantage that one player might have as competing products and technologies come quickly to market – resulting in ever reducing timescales to capitalize on innovation before knowledge-based capabilities become commoditized. The almost inevitable consequence is that any advantage from newly developed "Summit" opportunities quickly becomes eroded and transforms in time toward becoming "Valley" opportunities.

Box 4.3   New (Knowledge) Economy Laws and BioBusiness

Some phenomena of the "new (knowledge) economy" cannot be explained by traditional economic principles. "Old economy" laws explain the efficient allocation of countable resources such as labor, capital, land or other natural resources. If knowledge and knowledge creation become key elements of economic activity, these laws break down.

The new economy is dominated by increasingly intensive focus on knowledge and innovation. Suppose you learn a new technology to produce twice the output with the same inputs. If you are the only farmer using this new production method, you are likely to become relatively well-off. Eventually, the technology will become public knowledge, old economy, as more of your competitors also learn to use the technology and the premium you can command will tend to fall. Hence, constant innovation and continuous change is a prerequisite for maintaining an "unfair advantage" in the marketplace.

The pharmaceutical industry is a good example of a sector that is dependent on constant renewal and the creation of new knowledge. Large pharmaceutical companies spend tremendous amounts of money to develop, test, and market new drugs. They are rewarded by a premium price that they can charge until patents expire or competing products enter the marketplace. When generic drug producers enter the marketplace, prices inevitably become more affordable, and margins for the innovator from sale of that product tend to be substantially reduced.

The new economy is constantly turning into the old: a system that constantly produces new solutions and cures, and eventually makes them affordable even to the less fortunate, creating long-term value and benefit for society while rewarding inventors and innovators.

Understanding the "Research–Development–Application" Translation Process

The fundamental challenge of successful life science industry development is to facilitate what BioEnterprise Asia calls the "Research–Development–Application" translation process (or the "R–D–A" translation process for short) so new knowledge and insight can be transformed to practical application in a manner that brings maximum likelihood of success while minimizing execution risk and failure in the translation process.

Figure 4.2 provides a useful conceptual framework for understanding how new insights and knowledge are translated into practical application. BioEnterprise Asia defines *Research* as the realm of new knowledge and insights, while *Application* refers to the use of products and services coming

Figure 4.2   The Research–Development–Application (R–D–A)
                  Translation Process

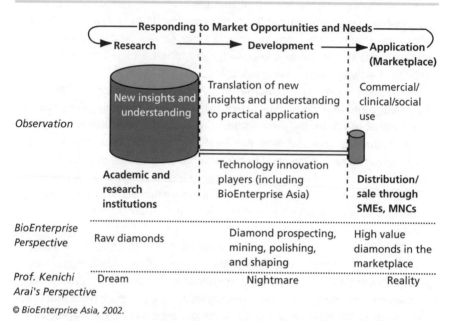

© BioEnterprise Asia, 2002.

out of the *Development* process for social or commercial use. *Development* is
defined as the process of translating knowledge and insight from the *Research*
effort into practical *Application*. As emphasized in this framework, the
generation of new knowledge and insights through *Research*, and the
translation process through strategic investment in driving the *Development*
process are central to technology innovation and value creation.

Note, in particular, the relative sizes of the *Research* and *Application*
tanks in Figure 4.2, and the narrow, inefficient and rather atherosclerotic
Development pipeline. The large (and rapidly expanding) *Research* tank is
intended to depict the reality that we are being bombarded with exponentially
increasing new information and findings from research activities. The very
small *Application* tank depicts actual practical application of our knowledge
base (in other words, we have, so far, been generally not very efficient or
successful in translating what we know into high value products, services,
and technologies). We would clearly be more successful in innovation if we
can increase the rate of translating new insights and understanding into practical
application by increasing the efficiency of the Developmental process.

Another analogy that BioEnterprise Asia often uses to facilitate appreciation
of the opportunities and challenges involved in the R–D–A process is to describe
it in terms of diamond mining (Figure 4.2). Using this analogy, new ideas and

creative concepts emerging from research efforts (for example, at academic and research institutions) can be considered to be raw diamonds; the development process as the process of diamond prospecting, mining, shaping, and polishing; and the application stage as the marketing and use of polished diamonds in the marketplace. It is crucial to differentiate raw diamonds from worthless gravel – hence, strong technology sensing and assessment capabilities are critical for maximizing the value that is subsequently created. Otherwise, a lot of effort and expense may be wasted trying to shape and polish gravel.

Unfortunately, there generally tends to be little understanding or appreciation of the challenges involved in the innovation and development process, or of what it requires to traverse the innovation development pipeline more successfully[3] (see also the next section and Figure 4.3). In fact, this lack of understanding of what it takes to translate insight into application more

Figure 4.3   Understanding the Value Creation Pipeline from Concept to Market Entry and Growth

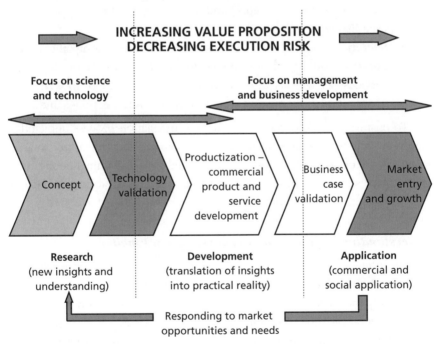

© BioEnterprise Asia, 2002.

---

[3] Professor Kenichi Arai, a leading Japanese molecular biologist and founding President of the Asia-Pacific Molecular Biology Network, indicates that Japanese scientists and technologists sometimes describe the challenge of traversing the developmental gap between concept (the "dream") and practical application ("reality") in terms of the "nightmare", given how treacherous and difficult the development process can potentially be (see also Figure 4.2).

successfully, and the concomitant lack of strategic investment in ensuring that sufficient resources and expert capabilities are made available to support the process, are, in BioEnterprise Asia's opinion, the most important bottlenecks to increasing efficient and successful innovation in most societies in Asia (and indeed around the world).

Potential beneficiaries and stakeholders in the effort to make the R–D–A translation process more efficient and successful include:

- ***Enlightened policy-makers*** who understand the opportunity and value that helping to provide appropriate infrastructure, trained human resources and a conducive policy environment can bring to facilitating successful innovation and the establishment of a viable and sustainable life science industrial base
- ***Technology innovators and entrepreneurs*** who take on the innovation challenge and seek to work to bring new products and services to market while establishing high growth enterprises
- ***Investors and other stakeholders*** who facilitate and support the technology innovation effort and stand to benefit from supporting the establishment and growth of successful enterprises
- ***Society*** as a whole, which stands to benefit from, among other things: improved quality of life and health from innovative products and services; as well as directly through the creation of jobs and the generation of income and wealth from revenues, royalties and taxes

To ensure maximum impact, the R–D–A translation process depicted in Figure 4.2 should not operate in isolation from existing social and market realities – the opportunity to respond to unfilled gaps and unmet needs in the marketplace should be the driver for innovation and new product, service, or new technology development.[4]

Understanding the Innovation Value Creation Pipeline

Understanding how the R–D–A translation process works and brings value is critical to being able to maximize returns on investment in innovation by successfully increasing the success and efficiency of translation through the developmental pipeline. Building on the R–D–A framework, the life science innovation and value creation pipeline can be considered in terms of five discrete phases (Figure 4.3):

---

[4] In other words, the innovation and technology development process should be market-driven rather than technology-driven. Always bearing market needs in mind increases the likelihood that a ready market will exist for new products, services, and technologies that are responsive to such needs.

- **Concept** – the creative ideas and insights that underlie innovation
- **Technology validation** – demonstrates that the concept is technically feasible and workable (also described as "proof of concept"). As shown in Figure 4.3, the technology validation process serves as the interface between research and development.
- **Productization** – the process of converting validated concepts or technologies into commercially ready products, services or technology platforms meeting the performance and quality standards that one would expect from any high-quality product or service available in the marketplace. The productization process is central to the development effort.
- **Business case validation** – demonstrates that a market exists for the product, service or technology, and that the proposed approach to bringing the product to market is feasible – for example, determining whether it is best to sell through distributors, to use a network marketing strategy, to sell only on the Internet or, perhaps, to use a combination of different channels and business models. The business case validation process operates at the interface between development and application.[5]
- **Market entry and growth** – bringing the product, service or technology to market.

Our experience working with fundamentally different life science product, service, and technology offerings across the BioBusiness landscape as well as in other technology areas clearly validates that no matter what sector or industry one operates in, the same fundamentals apply, and one needs essentially to progress through each of these same five phases in the developmental pipeline.

The length of time to progress from one phase of the innovation development pipeline to the next varies according to the sector and the product, technology, or service being developed. Hence, the productization phase might require as little as three to six months when one is developing a new software solution, say, but may take eight years or longer with new drug development, given the fact that the productization phase in this case would

---

[5] Several reviewers of the pre-publication manuscript for this book, including Professor Nancy Ip and Joseph Hoess, point out that consideration of the business case should start as early in the innovation development process as possible, and that it might be advantageous to depict Figure 4.3 with business case validation running in parallel with productization to emphasize this reality. Their view is entirely consistent with the author's perspective that innovation and productization should generally be responsive to market realities and need to ensure maximum impact and likelihood of success (and, hence, should be market-driven in the first place).

essentially encompass taking the product through the entire pre-clinical and clinical trial development process before it can be approved and made available in the market.

It is also important to note, as emphasized in Figure 4.3, that driving the innovation process from concept to market requires a very wide range of expertise and capabilities. A careful examination of the five discrete phases in the pipeline clearly demonstrates that the first half of the process – from concept through technology validation to productization – is heavily dependent on strong strategic science and technology development capabilities.

On the other hand, the second half of the process – from productization through business case validation to market entry and growth – requires strong management and market/business development skills.

Hence, a successful product, service or technology platform development effort (or an enterprise development effort, for that matter) depends on a combination of very different skill sets and capabilities – with each phase in the process requiring very different capabilities and resources. Clear milestones can be defined for each of the five discrete phases in the value creation pipeline, with successful completion of each phase generally increasing the value proposition and reducing the execution risk involved in bringing the initiative to fruition.

Conclusion

We are truly living in exciting times. Even though BioBusiness has always been a major activity for humans, much of this activity has traditionally been low value-added "Valley"-type opportunities that have become commoditized and bring relatively low returns economically, and therefore limit the wages that can be paid to workers engaged in these traditional activities.

Our growing understanding of the life sciences and the increasing maturity of the biotechnologies have begun to fundamentally transform the BioBusiness landscape. Not only do we have the opportunity and potential to establish totally new BioBusiness sectors (for example, nanobiotechnology), but we are beginning to re-invent and transform existing BioBusiness activities through the injection of innovative technology and business ideas in response to market interest and demand.

In effect, we have been presented with a historic opportunity to create new value and economic wealth for our societies through BioBusiness innovation (see also Box 4.4) – those who recognize the increasingly obvious potential, and proactively invest in capturing the proposition by working to strengthen capabilities and open up bottlenecks in the innovation development pipeline, will reap its benefits. Those who fail to grasp the opportunity will inevitably find themselves left behind.

Box 4.4 "Creative Destruction" and Critical Mass for Bioinnovation

The idea that innovation is destructive to the established economy, its players and its rules, is not new. Early in the 20th century, the economist Joseph Schumpeter called this process "creative destruction," the destruction of established rules in favor of something new, something more beneficial.

Since Schumpeter's time, there has been disagreement regarding whether innovation is essentially random, or whether it can be systematized through formalizing the process of improving the efficiency of translating inputs into valued outputs and products.

The role of knowledge in a society can be visualized as a nuclear chain reaction: the spontaneous fission of nuclei releases protons and neutrons. Most of them vanish in space. However, if a neutron hits another nucleus, it can cause it to undergo fission as well, releasing more protons and neutrons. Only if the chance of hitting another nucleus before leaving the system is high enough will there be a nuclear chain reaction, resulting in a nuclear explosion. In order to increase this likelihood, there needs to be a "critical mass" of nuclei.

This describes to a large extent how ideas have traditionally related to knowledge creation and innovation in society. Breakthrough ideas and concepts have initially been random. Yet, only if they hit another smart head will something greater be developed. In order to create value from superior knowledge, society needs a "critical mass" of skilled and educated people, sufficiently funded research, technology-oriented organizations, and entrepreneurs to translate exciting ideas into successful products in the marketplace (see Figures 4.2 and 4.3).

Experience demonstrates that the innovative concept is only the first step in the process of driving innovation, and that the process can and should be systematized and made far more efficient and effective through better understanding and management of the R–D–A translation process.

Societies need to build the "explosive critical mass of life science innovation" that will blast "creative destruction" and create sustainable value for local economies.

Key Points

1. Most BioBusiness activity currently operates in the realm of the "Valley" – old economy, focused on production of low value-added commodities, highly competitive, low barriers to entry, relatively low wages.
2. The process of transformation from "Cloud" to "Summit" to "Valley" BioBusiness activities is a continual one – yesterday's "Cloud" opportunity can be transformed into today's "Summit" opportunity but will likely be tomorrow's "Valley" opportunity unless constant innovation keeps it close to, or at, the "Summit".
3. There is real opportunity to raise the returns on investment in BioBusiness through investing in the development of knowledge- and technology-intensive inputs to raise value-added from agriculture, food processing, environmental protection, healthcare, and pharmaceuticals in response to gaps in the marketplace and unmet needs. This would effectively mean creating innovative "Summit"-oriented products, services, or technologies from previously "Valley" activities through the injection of knowledge and technology. Success in this exciting endeavor requires clear understanding of the R–D–A translation process and the innovation pipeline – as well as a clear appreciation of market opportunities and needs.
4. Those economies and enterprises that stand to be the winners in bioinnovation (and bioentrepreneurship) will be those that are most prepared to build the capabilities and make the smart and necessary investment to open up the innovation pipeline – thereby increasing the likelihood of successful innovation and value creation. Such investment will inevitably enhance efficiency and success in generating higher value-added products, services, and new technologies (and related intellectual property) through the R–D–A translation process.

Chapter 5

Opportunities and Challenges for Wealth Creation

Opportunities multiply as they are seized.

Sun Tzu

Summary

This chapter identifies the opportunities and challenges for capturing "Summit" opportunities for wealth creation in the BioBusiness arena. It examines the fundamental needs for success in life science and biotechnology innovation, and considers the critical success factors for viable life science industry development.

Background

Different sectors of the economy bring different returns for the people engaged in those activities. The same is true for the different BioBusiness sectors (Table 5.1).

Table 5.1 Estimated Annual Economic Contribution in Selected BioBusiness Sectors in Different Parts of the World, 2001 (US$ per worker)

	Agriculture	Food	Healthcare	R&D	Biotechnology
Global	2,331	7,340	11,459	20,149	20,833
East Asia	731	2,372	4,023	6,705	5,694
South Asia	410	1,046	1,674	1,993	1,944
US	35,293	49,825	110,291	147,055	173,611

Source: BioEnterprise Asia, 2003.[1]

---

[1] Primary data sources for the analysis in Table 5.1 include United Nations Statistics Division, 2002, Food and Agriculture Organization, 2002, and World Bank, 2002.

While people engaged in traditional agriculture tend to belong to the lower income segment in most Asia-Pacific economies, there is substantial difference in the income of farmers from the more developed countries such as Japan, Australia or the US (averaging US$25,000 per year or more), compared to those from India or Nepal (averaging US$400 per year).

The higher per capita income and value-added associated with agriculture in more developed economies come about as a result of a combination of innovations and economies of scale arising through improved farming methods, the use of higher yielding and more climate and disease resistant crops, larger land holdings per farmer, the use of modern mechanized farming technology, and the application of more capital intensive approaches (including the use of modern fertilizers, pesticides, and herbicides).

While these improvements have already made a substantial impact on modern agriculture as we know it, anticipated developments in agriculture technology promise to be even more exciting and rewarding as new tools and techniques in molecular biology and biotechnology can lead to accelerated development of even higher yielding crops, improved approaches for integrated pest management, more environmentally-friendly approaches to maintaining and increasing the fertility of soils, and so on.

Although somewhat simplistic, Figure 5.1 outlines how advances in the life sciences and biotechnology serve as know-how generators for major BioBusiness sectors, including agriculture and the food industry, healthcare and the biomedical sciences, as well as the industrial and environmental sciences and technologies.

Advances in the genome and other life sciences promise to tremendously increase our understanding of the mechanisms of life; spawn the development of entire new industries; impact all aspects of our lives; and necessarily raise provocative ethical and social issues that we will need to manage effectively and responsibly (see Chapter 12 and also Box 5.1).

Technological Advances

It is being increasingly recognized that advances in the life sciences and biotechnology are already having a major impact on healthcare, agriculture, food production, environmental protection, and biotechnology-based industrial processes. The potential economic and social benefits for humankind are enormous.

Figure 5.1 Biotechnology and Its Potential Impact on Selected BioBusiness Activities

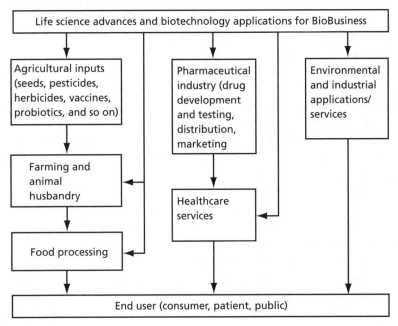

© BioEnterprise Asia, 2003.

Box 5.1 Can Biotechnology Solve the World's Hunger and Population Concerns?

Thomas Malthus published an article in 1798 claiming that population growth is exponential (meaning that population will double in a constant period of time), while food production tends to increase in direct proportion to land use. His conclusion was that no matter how much progress there is in expanding farming, eventually food shortage would be the only factor that could control population growth as population levels would inevitably outpace food production growth.

A lot has happened in the period of over 200 years since Malthus wrote his article. Among other things, the "green revolution" of the 20th century, driven largely by the introduction of new cultivars developed using modern genetics and selective breeding techniques, chemical fertilizers and new irrigation and farming techniques, exploded food production. While Malthus' England, with a population of only 7 million was "already" occasionally hit by famine, over 50 million now live the most comfortable life ever in the United Kingdom.

Nevertheless, world population is still growing rapidly with more than one England being added every year. Is it true that no matter how much progress there is in food production technology, global demand for food will eventually grow beyond our ability to supply it? Will advances in life sciences and biotechnology only "delay the painful solution of a worsening problem," as some fatalists see it?

Malthus has so far been proven wrong on several fronts. For one thing, injection of new technology and farming techniques have led to growth in food supply that has almost consistently outpaced population growth. For another, we have since learnt that population growth tends to slow down after the initial growth spurt with development as societies undergo transition from high birth rate, high death rate *traditional* societies (with relatively stable population size) through rapidly growing high birth rate, low death rate *transitional* societies (with consequent rapid population growth) arising from increased investment in public health, education, basic sanitation, and improved nutrition, to low birth rate, low death rate *modern* societies (with relatively stable population size).

This transition process, the so-called "demographic transition," has meant that global population growth, while being dramatic during the first half of the 20th century as developing countries started to benefit from improvements in healthcare and sanitation (with many Asian and African societies experiencing rates of growth in excess of 2–3% annually), has since slowed down as societies have begun to benefit from growing wealth and development.

World population is expected to stabilize around 2050 at between 9.5–10 billion – a far cry from the 15 billion or more predicted by doomsayers in the 1960s in the midst of the global population explosion, but substantially higher than the 250 million or so during Malthus' time at the start of the industrial revolution when Europe and then the US experienced mini-population explosions until population growth stabilized as the countries reached more developed modern society status.

Interestingly, contrary to the expectations of Malthus and other doomsayers, it has not been famine and disaster that have limited population growth, but rather increasing wealth and development from new innovation and the application of new technologies which, at the same time, have helped fuel rapid increases in agricultural and food productivity.

Development and all its attendant benefits – escaping the poverty trap, growing wealth, greater economic and social freedom (especially for women), and increased food and livelihood security – have proven to be the best contraceptive. The value and benefit that investing in the development of the still poor areas of Asia, Africa, and Latin America will bring are becoming increasingly clear.

Today, the growing body of knowledge available in various fields of biological research (for example, cell biology, genome sciences, biomedical sciences, agriculture, environmental science), together with the new tools and technologies we have in hand, have enabled, among other things:

- Directed/target-specific approaches for the development of novel drugs, vaccines, and biomaterials
- A gravitation toward gene-based approaches for disease treatment and diagnosis
- An increased reliance on automation and information technology for data generation, management and analysis for healthcare and the life sciences industry

As Asian countries such as Japan, Korea, Taiwan, and Singapore (and increasingly China, India, Malaysia, Thailand, Vietnam, and other countries that have embraced a commitment to modern, innovation-based technological development) move from being primarily "imitators" to being true "innovators" in life science and technology development, there is clear opportunity for the creation of substantial wealth for these societies through identifying and creating "Summit" BioBusiness activities.

If economies in the Asia-Pacific region are to obtain maximum benefit from the life science and biotechnology revolution, there is need for investment to create a conducive innovation environment for the life sciences and biotechnology in each economy (see Chapter 10). Encouragement of innovation and world-class entrepreneurship are central to such an effort (see also Chapter 11).

A public that is enabled to make objective, informed decisions is a prerequisite for ensuring a ready market for the products, services, and applications resulting from innovation in the life sciences and biotechnology. A truly effective life science innovation environment should, therefore, cater not only to academic or industrial priorities but also needs to be responsive to the concerns of the lay public (whether these be philosophical, religious, ethical, social or economic; see also Chapter 12).

To capture maximum economic benefit, there is also need for respect for intellectual property rights and established technology transfer and licensing management practices (see Chapter 13), together with clear recognition of the value that strategic alliances and partnerships can bring (see also Chapter 11).

Fundamental Needs for Life Science and Biotechnology Development

The fundamental needs for development of life sciences and biotechnology in any society can be broadly classified into five categories (see also Figure 10.2, pg 147 and Table 10.1, pg 148), namely:

- **Infrastructure development**
  - Development of physical infrastructure at various levels: institutional, national, regional, and international. These include the establishment and maintenance of transportation networks, existence of reliable power supplies, a modern telecommunications network, and the existence and access to powerful, widely accessible information resources
  - Scientific infrastructure, including the establishment and maintenance of institutions of excellence, access to incubation facilities and technology development resources, and research teams focusing on the generation of fundamental and applied knowledge and technologies
- **Conducive regulatory/cultural environment**
  - Development of a regulatory, cultural, and policy environment that encourages research and investment in the life sciences and biotechnologies (for example, intellectual property rights regulations)
  - Supportive local environment/attitudes toward research and development, entrepreneurship, and risk/failure
- **Policy framework**
  - Development of national policies and a regulatory framework for promoting modern biological research, properly balanced between basic and applied work
  - Institutional policies and guidelines promoting scientific excellence and translation of scientific discoveries through application (for example, assessment systems, career development programs, encouragement of scientific entrepreneurship)
- **Human resource development**
  - Promotion of science and technology education and professional training from the grade school level and beyond
  - Strengthening of the academic infrastructure for life science and biotechnology education (including the promotion of university education and research at the undergraduate and graduate levels)

- **Finance and resource mobilization**
  - Promotion of biological and biotechnological research through allocation of research funding via national, regional, international public and private sources
  - Encouragement of investment in biotechnology industry, with a particular emphasis on strengthening the link and partnership between government, academia and industry

When considering these needs, an integrative view is crucial. The impact of policies, regulations, and priorities should be considered at the institutional, national, regional, and global levels. Furthermore, given the applicability of molecular biology and biotechnology in a range of sectors, it is crucial that policies should not be developed only for the narrow promotion of any particular activity or sector.

Asia-Pacific countries have done reasonably well in relation to investing in these fundamental needs (see Figure 10.2, pg 147). How the region compares to other regions, and how specific countries have performed in building up such capabilities and resources are addressed in Chapter 10.

Critical Success Factors for BioBusiness Innovation

BioEnterprise Asia has conducted a careful analysis of the experience of key hotspots for life science and biotechnology innovation internationally (also called "bioclusters," see Chapter 11) – from Silicon Valley (US), to Boston (US), to Cambridge (UK), to Medicon Valley (Scandinavia), to Munich (Germany), to Tsukuba (Japan). We have also examined the experience to date with efforts to jumpstart successful BioBusiness sectors by governments in the Asia-Pacific region over the last several decades.

We have found a confluence of four critical success factors in the innovation hotspots we studied. It appears that these factors need to be operating in concert to enable the establishment of sufficient critical mass for innovation and value creation in any given environment:[2]

- ***Smart people***
- ***Smart ideas*** (read: the readiness to allow zany and "out-of-the-box" ideas to thrive and be tested)

---

[2] Assuming, of course, the fundamentals are in place, including physical and scientific infrastructure; a conducive regulatory/cultural environment; a policy framework incentivizing life science and biotechnology innovation; strong human resource development programs; and the availability of adequate public and private sector funding support. Don Francis, President of Vaxgen, points out that in addition to all these factors, there is also need for (calculated) risk taking – Don notes, "If one is smart but risk averse, nothing happens."

- **Smart money** – refers to the availability of early stage financial resources that allow smart people with zany "out-of-the-box" ideas to get these tested, validated, and developed for commercialization and beyond. It does not generally matter whether the source of the smart money is public or private[3]
- **Smart alliances and partnerships.** Successful players recognize that good science and technology know no boundaries, and are prepared to reach out to work with smart colleagues in academia, industry, government, the financial community, and other potential allies (both within national boundaries and beyond) to achieve common objectives.

Conclusion

Capturing the value proposition of life science and biotechnology opportunities means identifying and capturing the "Summit" opportunities that are of particular interest to your economy, to individual entrepreneurs and to prospective investors. It requires an appreciation of the BioBusiness landscape as it relates to areas of importance to your economy, and identifying opportunities that you are well-placed to capture given your natural resources, agricultural and industrial base, scientific and technological capabilities, human resources, and existing market realities (including meeting unmet needs; and filling product, service and technology gaps in the marketplace).

Key Points

1. Different BioBusiness sectors have traditionally provided very different returns, and therefore allowed very different levels of compensation for workers in each sector (Table 5.1).
2. New insights and technologies promise to transform the BioBusiness landscape to enable more successful capture of "Summit" BioBusiness opportunities.
3. Fundamental needs for national/local success in the life sciences and biotechnology include the need for:
   - Infrastructure development – both physical and scientific

---

[3] The US is frequently touted as a model for privately driven bioenterprise, while Germany, over the last decade, can be seen as a publicly driven smart money environment for life science innovation. This characterization is, of course, a gross oversimplification, as explained in Box 16.1, pg 246.

- Conducive regulatory/cultural environment
- Policy framework
- Human resource development
- Finance and resource mobilization

4. Critical success factors for sustainable innovation-based value creation in BioBusiness, assuming fundamental needs are in place, include:
   - Smart people
   - Smart ideas
   - Smart money
   - Smart alliances and partnerships

Section B

Opportunities in BioBusiness: Implications for Asia

When there is an original sound in the world, it makes a hundred echoes.

John Shedd

Section B provides an overview of exciting new developments in various BioBusiness sectors and their implications for the Asia-Pacific region.

Chapter 6 examines directions, trends, priorities, and opportunities in healthcare for the Asia-Pacific region.

Chapter 7 assesses the implications of "Summit" opportunities in the biomedical sciences for the Asia-Pacific region.

Chapter 8 explores the opportunities and possibilities in relation to agri-biology and agri-biotechnology for the Asia-Pacific region.

Chapter 9 discusses implications in relation to environmental and industrial life sciences and biotechnology for the Asia-Pacific region.

Chapter 10 concludes this section by providing a quick overview of the strengths and capabilities in BioBusiness of key economies in the Asia-Pacific region.

Chapter 6
Healthcare

A society grows great when old men plant trees whose shade they know they shall never sit in.

Greek Proverb

Summary

This chapter examines global healthcare trends, and growing opportunities for innovative healthcare-related products, services, and technology platforms. Given the harsh realities in many developing countries, this has meant that they lack even basic public health infrastructure and services – resulting in a large proportion of their populations facing bleak prospects for health and well-being. The application of modern approaches and technologies bring the potential to radically transform public health and healthcare for those who cannot now afford such care, while enabling unprecedented levels of care for those who can. We stand at the threshold of an exciting new era in healthcare. Innovators and entrepreneurs who come up with newer and better ways of providing care are likely to benefit substantially – and they stand to make a real and very substantial difference in the lives of millions.

Introduction

We are in the midst of a major transition that will inevitably lead to exciting new opportunities in healthcare and health services – globally and in Asia (see Boxes 6.1 and 6.2).

Major segments of Asia's population continue to deal with the consequences of underdevelopment with high birth rates, high death rates and low life expectancy arising from infectious diseases and squalid environmental conditions. At the same time, education, rising income, increasing urbanization[1] and the

---

[1] Growing urbanization and increasing concentration of people in urban centers create both opportunities and challenges. From the entrepreneurial perspective, this means greater concentration of patients, and more cost-effective delivery of services and care.

73

emergence of growing middle and upper socio-economic classes, have meant that more and more of Asia's population is in the midst of making the epidemiological and demographic transition to a pattern of low birth rates, low death rates, and longer life expectancies that are more commonly associated with more developed societies.

Box 6.1   Global Healthcare Trends: Implications for Creating Healthcare-related "Summit" Opportunities

Rethinking the Healthcare Paradigm
- Shift from disease management to wellness management (emphasizing health promotion, disease prevention, and a focus on quality of life)
- From hospital- and institution-based care to community-oriented care
- Growing acceptance of alternative/complementary medicine

Changing Demographics
- Increasing urbanization
- Graying of populations
- Increasingly educated and affluent populations

The Need to Manage Costs While Ensuring Best Possible Outcomes
- From fee-for-service based healthcare to integrated healthcare management
- Accelerating privatization and consolidation of healthcare services
- Growing emphasis on cost-effectiveness and quality of care

Technological Advances
Biomedical and Diagnostic Advances
- Growing understanding of the genetic basis of disease
- Advances in drug development
- Point of diagnosis is shifting from central laboratories and facilities to point of care

Information Technology
- Increasing access to patient management/diagnosis/therapeutic data
- Increased empowerment and access of the consumer to state-of-the-art information
- Advances in "back-office" systems (for example, procurement, logistics, distribution management)

Changing Role of Government in Healthcare
- From primary provider of healthcare to partner in the healthcare enterprise (information provider, regulator, safety net provider)

Source: Adapted from Gurinder Shahi, The Economist Intelligence Unit Healthcare Roundtable, November 1999, Singapore.

Box 6.2   Some New Healthcare and Life Science Product/Service/ Technology Opportunities

Products
- Pharmaceuticals
- Biotech products
- Nutraceuticals
- Alternative and complementary medicines (including TCM, herbals, ayurvedic medicine)
- Medical devices
- Diagnostic tools
- Health-IT software and systems

Services
- Increase cost-effectiveness
- Increase convenience
- New approaches/applications
- Outsourcing opportunities

Solutions
- New insights
- New technologies
- Better integration
- Better ways of doing old things

Hence, even as there is need to deal effectively with the "diseases of deprivation" in the region, there is burgeoning need to deal with a rising incidence of the "diseases of excess" such as obesity, diabetes, hypercholesterolemia, and heart disease as well as the diseases of the aged such as degenerative arthritis, cerebrovascular disease, and cancers.

Governments around the region are re-examining healthcare delivery and its provision, presenting the healthcare industry with opportunities for rapid growth. There is also growing market demand for products, services, technologies and/or supporting infrastructure in response to changing healthcare needs.

This trend is being accelerated by a growing realization that traditional Western approaches to healthcare and disease management have been limited and limiting – while these specialization-oriented approaches brought ever deeper understanding of health and disease, they also limited understanding and appreciation of inter-relationships across and between specialized fields of study. We are moving toward increasingly integrated and more holistic perspectives on health and disease where we focus more on wellness and disease management, and where we recognize that prevention and health promotion are not only more cost-effective, but are also more rational. In fact, it may already be too late when a patient develops symptoms and signs of disease – there is increasing focus, therefore, on working to ensure that the earliest manifestations are identified, and disease progression is halted and reversed before any long-term sequelae occur.

This chapter and the next are closely intertwined – dealing with healthcare and the biomedical sciences respectively. Together, they provide an overview of how new technology and new knowledge are shaping the healthcare and biomedical landscape in the Asia-Pacific region and beyond.

This chapter will briefly overview the following areas of healthcare-related interest:

- Understanding health systems and health service opportunities
- Responding to public health needs
  - Dealing with underdevelopment: Meeting the challenge of poverty
  - Infectious diseases
- The pharmaceutical industry
- Responding to the wellness opportunity
  - Alternative and complementary therapies: Responding to the wellness imperative
  - Nutraceuticals
- Medical informatics and the application of medical and bio-IT tools for healthcare (Health-IT)
  - Health-IT and telemedicine
  - Medical devices for remote consultation and disease management

The challenge, and the opportunity, is to cater to the specific and varying market opportunities and needs in relation to health systems and healthcare in the region. In-depth domain knowledge of healthcare systems and practices is needed for innovators and entrepreneurs to succeed in developing and capturing "Summit" opportunities in this market sector.

Understanding Health Systems and Health Service Opportunities

Health systems are generally organized as follows (see Figure 6.1):

- The *public health system* – focusing on ensuring the provision of key
- · public health infrastructure and services, including: water and sanitation; epidemiology and infectious disease control; environmental health; and occupational health and safety

Figure 6.1   Typical Organization of Health Systems in Asian Countries

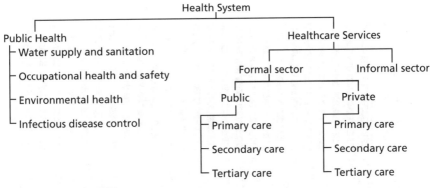

© BioEnterprise Asia, 2002.

- The *healthcare services system* – incorporating basic health services that are provided at the community level (*primary* care), general medical care available at referral centers (*secondary* care), and a range of specialist and inpatient care services available at "general hospital"-type facilities (*tertiary* care). Highly specialized and rehabilitative care may be available through such centers as cancer hospitals, cardiac centers, eye centers, and so on – these are increasingly being referred to as *quartenary* care facilities

Healthcare in most countries in the Asia-Pacific region has traditionally been primarily the purview of government and the public sector.[2] As societies have become more affluent, there has been a growing role for the private sector in healthcare service provision. In general, a snapshot in most Asian economies would show that primary and secondary healthcare services are largely provided by the private sector today, while tertiary and quaternary care is being provided largely through public sector and charitable facilities – even as there continues to be a dynamic transition toward a greater role for the private sector and a move toward closer public-private cooperation (see also Chapter 14 and Table 14.2, pg 233).

With growing wealth, the populations of Asia are increasingly expecting high quality healthcare. It is estimated that nearly 350 million or about 10% of

---

[2] Interestingly, while healthcare is generally publicly financed in the wealthier Asia-Pacific countries including Japan and Australia, responsibility for paying for healthcare has historically been largely with the private individual in many Asian countries such as the South Asian countries and Indonesia (see Figure 6.2).

Figure 6.2 Public vs Private Healthcare Spending in Selected Asia-
Pacific Countries

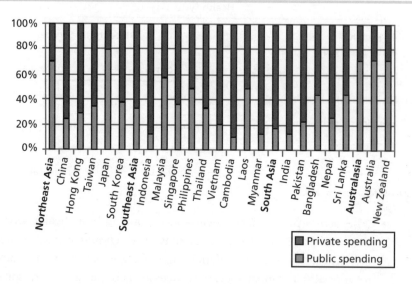

the region's population can already afford fully private healthcare services.[3]
Excluding Japan, the Asian market for healthcare was already projected to
exceed US$250 billion by 2001.[4]

Current trends in healthcare include:

- A move toward wellness management versus disease management
- A shift toward personal responsibility for maintaining health versus
  state responsibility
- Increasing shift toward point-of-care diagnosis versus traditional central
  laboratory testing (this has been partly enabled by advances in
  diagnostic technology)
- A move toward emphasizing economic viability and commercial
  discipline in the provision of healthcare services. In other words, a
  move away from subsidies for segments of the population who can
  afford to pay, and growing demand for autonomous operation and
  fiscal responsibility for services provided by both public and private
  sector healthcare providers.

---

[3] Calculations based on the urban population of Asian economies (UNDP Human Development Report, 2002)
adjusted for GDP per capita to reflect the population base able to afford private healthcare (BioEnterprise Asia,
2001). Clearly, the vast majority of people in the region who can afford to pay for costlier private services live
in major urban centers, and in the wealthier countries.

[4] "Healthcare Sector in Asia–A Growth Industry," *Asia-Pacific Biotech News,* 1 (5), 1997.

Health sector reform, which started in several countries as early as the 1980s, accelerated as a consequence of the 1997/98 regional economic crisis as government after government, saddled with rising costs, pushed for privatization and/or corporatization of public sector healthcare services and closer partnership between the public and private sectors (see also Chapter 14 and Table 14.2, pg 233).

Examples abound:

- In 2000 Hong Kong SAR announced a tender for the private sector to take over the operation of primary care public clinics and service provision for civil servant medical plans
- Since the 1980s, Singapore has launched a series of initiatives to rationalize public spending on healthcare. These include:
  - Corporatization of all public hospitals
  - Adapting an Australian-based Diagnosis Related Groups (DRG) system for determination of public subsidies for all public acute care hospitals and institutions in 1999 with the intent of applying the system to private sector healthcare within five years

Governments are increasingly recognizing that there is room for substantial partnership and collaboration with the private sector in provision of healthcare services. This has been accompanied by greater acceptance of a greater role for the private sector in the delivery of healthcare services, and a shift in the role of the government – from being a primary provider of services to: being a provider of information, having a key role in regulatory oversight, and in helping to provide a safety net for those who cannot otherwise afford to pay themselves.

Opportunities and Needs

The commercial potential of healthcare provision and management services is being increasingly recognized. Primary, specialist, and tertiary care providers are under pressure to provide high quality healthcare that is affordable to the consumer while still being able to generate profitability. All this has to be accomplished in a highly regulated healthcare environment.

Health tourism (combining holidays in exotic Asia with medical treatments at leading facilities around the region) is becoming big business that is increasingly attracting non-traditional private patients to countries like Singapore, Thailand, Malaysia, and increasingly, India.

Opportunities are also increasingly being recognized in the arena of clinical research as healthcare providers and research institutions begin to realize the direct and indirect economic benefits of generating revenues from, and the prestige of being involved in, regional and global clinical trials.

Responding to Public Health Needs

Healthcare systems are undergoing a profound change as we move from disease-oriented healthcare systems to wellness-oriented ones. With this transition has come growing emphasis on public health and preventative services – areas that were once treated as being less than exciting by medical practitioners, but that are now gaining increasing recognition and emphasis.

Dealing with Underdevelopment: Meeting the Challenge of Poverty

The public health picture in Asia is very mixed. While more advanced economies like Japan, Singapore and South Korea have achieved public health standards that are equal to the best in the world, there remains a desperate need to improve healthcare in many parts of Asia, especially the more rural and impoverished areas.

Approximately 1 in 10 babies born in Cambodia or Pakistan today will not survive past their first birthday (this compares with 1 in 250 in Singapore). In some rural areas in Asia, the chance of survival for the first year of life can be 1 in 2 or less. Such high infant mortality reflects the lack of access to safe drinking water and sanitation facilities in these areas, and the need for basic public health services including immunization and access to oral rehydration salts (ORS) to manage diarrhoeal disease.

Giving birth to babies in many Asian countries can not only lead to grief because of early demise of newborns, it can also be very hazardous to the life of the mother – more than 1 in every 200 women lose their lives as a consequence of pregnancy and child birth in Indonesia, Bangladesh, Cambodia, Laos, India, and Nepal – compared to less than 1 in 10,000 in Hong Kong, Singapore, and other more developed countries. High maternal mortality rates reflect lack of access to hospitals and specialized healthcare facilities or expertise, especially for women in remote rural areas.

Public health concerns tend to be substantially worse in rural areas than in urban areas – as of 2001, some 16 million urban Indonesians lacked access to safe drinking water and 20 million to sanitation compared to 58 million lacking safe drinking water, and 75 million lacking sanitation in rural areas.[5]

---

[5] Lack of access to safe water and sanitation exposes people to substantially increased risk of water-borne infectious and diarrhoeal diseases – a major killer of young children.

Similarly, while 1.2 million urban Thais lacked access to healthcare facilities, 4.7 million rural Thais lacked such access; while 0.5 million urban Pakistanis lacked access to healthcare facilities, over 60 million rural Pakistanis lacked such access; while nearly all urban Chinese and Indians had ready access to healthcare, 93 million rural Chinese and 140 million rural Indians still lacked such access.

As a consequence of unmet needs for sanitation, safe drinking water and basic social services and infrastructure (including healthcare), we find relatively low life expectancies in many countries in the Asia-Pacific region. Given current death rates and life expectancies, as many as 30% of Laotians and Cambodians alive today will probably not live to see their 40th birthday. This compares with some 20% of Indians, Bangladeshis and Nepalis; and about 10% of Filipinos, Thais and Indonesians. In contrast, just 2.3% of Singaporeans will not live to see 40.

Opportunities for Creative and Effective Solutions

Many of the healthcare problems and concerns in Asia associated with infectious disease and the lack of access to basic care, facilities, and resources are essentially preventable and manageable.

We are dealing with a situation where those who have the most need have the least access to (and least ability to pay for) capabilities and resources that can help them to help themselves. Innovative application of new developments in information and communication technology (including developments in telemedicine, and in remote consultation and patient monitoring technology) coupled with on-going advances in the biomedical sciences (including the development of new diagnostic and screening technologies) offer tremendous opportunity and potential for greatly enhancing the health and well-being of the poor and the underprivileged.

Strategic investment can also make a real difference in improving the supply chain for essential drugs and vaccines; improving nutrition and the quality of water supply and sanitation; and enabling sustainable livelihoods so individuals caught in the poverty trap can pull themselves and their families out of it. Best of all, such investment, through catalyzing economic and social development in rural and remote areas, would contribute to slowing population growth (see also Box 5.1, pg 63) while offering the poor and the underprivileged a real chance of making a meaningful economic and social contribution through increased health and improved productivity.

Key players who can potentially be encouraged to invest in such innovation, and to support the efforts of committed entrepreneurs and innovators to solve public health and poverty-related concerns, include: international organizations and financial institutions (including the World Bank and the Asian Development Bank); international foundations and other not-for-profit organizations; concerned national and state government ministries; and enlightened corporations that recognize the value and long-term benefit to society of such strategic investment.

Infectious Diseases

The SARS epidemic that hit the Asia-Pacific region in the first half of 2003 served as a major wake-up call to countries in the region on the need to focus on the fundamentals of preventative care, and to maintain high levels of disease monitoring and vigilance. It also underlined the critical importance of establishing a rapid response capability to contain and manage infectious disease outbreaks more effectively.

Despite substantial progress in developing new therapeutics and vaccines against infectious diseases, such diseases continue to be a very real threat to public health and well-being in Asia and, indeed, throughout the world. Infectious diseases that once seemed in decline have returned: tuberculosis (TB) has made a resurgence, malaria has come back with a vengeance. New and emerging diseases, including HIV, the various causes of Hepatitis, dengue, West Nile fever, SARS, and many other infectious diseases can, and do, bring substantial death and devastation to human populations.

When an epidemic hits critical mass, it spreads rapidly within a community with its own momentum and is no longer easily traceable as spread arising from known infected individuals bringing the disease into the community. It becomes a pandemic when it affects many communities simultaneously and spreads rapidly from community to community around the world.

The reality is that infectious diseases do not recognize or respect state or national boundaries. Any infection could spread rapidly around the world once it builds up critical mass as an epidemic or pandemic – and this spread can be accelerated by modern modes of travel. Such trans-border spread of infectious diseases has occurred throughout history, and will undoubtedly occur again and again in the future. In historical times, major outbreaks of smallpox, the plague and enteric diseases like cholera have had major impacts on human societies. In more recent times we have seen this with a range of diseases including pandemic influenza, HIV, Hepatitis B, Hepatitis C, dengue, West Nile fever, and most recently, with SARS.

Those of us who are concerned about such things have long feared the emergence of yet another global pandemic of influenza. Some 26 million people, mostly between 20 and 30 years of age, lost their lives in the Spanish Flu pandemic of 1918/19. We have since had smaller but still very significant pandemic outbreaks every 20 years or so, with the Asian Flu in the 1950s and Hong Kong Flu[6] in the late 1960s. Public health professionals generally believe that we are overdue for yet another influenza pandemic – which is why outbreaks of bird influenza, as has happened a few times in Hong Kong (in the late 1990s and early 2000s), in the Netherlands in 2003, and in several countries in Asia in early 2004, have been treated with great intensity and seriousness.

West Nile fever is thought to have spread from Israel to New York in 1999, probably through an infected patient carrying the virus across on a transatlantic flight. The disease appears to subsequently have been transmitted by mosquitos to birds and other animals that then spread it back to humans through mosquito bites – causing an epidemic that has spread throughout most of the US and has since returned each summer to leave a trail of disease and death in its wake.

In many ways, we were lucky with SARS in early 2003 in that spread of the disease was relatively slow, and that it depended on relatively close interaction before it passed from one person to the next. This slow spread and low infectivity enabled the use of fairly low-tech solutions – such as quarantine and barrier nursing – to contain the spread of the disease. We would not be so lucky if we were exposed to a fatal disease that spreads rapidly or is highly infectious like pandemic influenza. Even seasonal epidemic influenza can have a greater impact (see Box 6.3).

Box 6.3   Putting Things in Perspective: SARS Versus Seasonal Influenza

Estimated impact of seasonal influenza:
   Let us assume that about 10% of affected populations catch influenza each year, on average.[7]

---

[6] There is a reason why influenza outbreaks tend to start in Asia – the confluence of high concentrations of people, of birds like chickens and geese in South China and Indochina and of pigs and other farm animals, increase the chances for human viruses to cross from humans to birds and other species (and vice versa), and be genetically transformed in the process. Witness, for example, concerns surrounding bird influenza in Asia in late 2003 and early 2004.

[7] This is almost certainly a gross underestimate. Case infection rates with each seasonal influenza epidemic can vary from 10% to 80% or higher, and epidemics occur every two to three years. Most authorities estimate an average incidence of between 5% and 15% each year. For comparison, it has been estimated that the infection rate for the 1918/19 Spanish flu pandemic was about 30–40%, while the infection rate for the Asian flu pandemic appears to have exceeded 60%.

Fatality rates for seasonal influenza outbreaks generally vary from less than 2 per 100,000 cases in under 50-year-olds to about 20 per 100,000 cases in 50- to 75-year-olds, to over 200 per 100,000 cases in those over 75 years old.[8] The "age-adjusted mortality rate", taking age into account, is generally about 20 per 100,000 cases (but would, of course, certainly vary according to the age structure of each population).

Estimating Asia's population at 3.5 billion, this works out to an average of about 350 million cases of influenza a year in the region, causing an average of about 70,000 deaths each year (this compares to little more than 1,000 deaths from SARS globally in early 2003).

(Note: While this might initially sound like a rather large number, it really isn't. The US has a population of about 300 million. Every year, some 50,000 to 70,000 people are estimated to die in the US from influenza or pneumonia during each flu season. If Asia had the same death rate from influenza or pneumonia as the US, there would be over 700,000 deaths in the region each year. One reason why the region has a substantially lower mortality rate from influenza or pneumonia is that populations in Asia are generally much younger than in the US – fewer older people, hence lower mortality.)

We, therefore, have an average of about 350 million episodes of flu each year in Asia (epidemics tend to occur every two to three years so the actual number varies considerably each year) and about 70,000 deaths from influenza or pneumonia each year.

Looked at from this perspective, the number of deaths due to SARS in the first half of 2003 was relatively low. Still, SARS hit people in the prime of their lives rather than the old and the sick and the immuno-compromised. It is for this reason that SARS was so scary, and caused so much economic and social turmoil for those who lived through the experience.

Still, many lessons have been learnt from SARS, and both weaknesses and strengths in our public health capabilities were revealed in the course of the SARS outbreak, arguably the first pandemic of the 21st century. The fact is that global public health surveillance and rapid response capabilities have generally been woefully inadequate, and have not been given nearly the investment and infrastructure needed to deal with the public health concerns arising from infectious disease outbreaks. On the other hand, we saw, with the SARS outbreak, a coming together of scientists, policy-makers, and biotech enterprises from throughout the world to pool expertise and resources to quickly understand the disease, develop diagnostic tests, as well as develop preventative and

---

[8] Seasonal flu epidemics typically kill the very old, the very young, and the immuno-compromised, creating a typical U-shaped age-distribution curve.

therapeutic strategies.[9] It is to be hoped that these lessons will not be forgotten, and that we will proactively use the lessons learnt from this experience for the next big epidemic or pandemic that will inevitably impact us – sooner or later.

Responding to Outbreaks

Even with best practices and capabilities, it would take a minimum of two to four weeks to isolate and definitively identify the infectious agent causing a new outbreak of disease. It would take no less than six months to re-engineer vaccine production facilities and therapeutic capabilities to produce enough supplies of vaccines and therapeutics to respond adequately to a major flu pandemic (it would take substantially longer if the infection is caused by a new agent, such as the SARS virus). With modern international travel accelerating the process, there is real concern that a highly infectious pandemic could spread around the world and burn itself out within a matter of 12 to 16 weeks, potentially infecting and killing millions of susceptible individuals along the way.

In other words, while it may take six months or longer to prepare the vaccine, a very virulent pandemic would likely already have wreaked havoc long before therapeutics or vaccines are ready. Vaccine manufacturers simply do not have the bandwidth or the production capacity to be able to respond much faster to a real public health emergency. The disease would potentially have left a path of devastation before we would be able to even begin to mount a credible response.

Equity Concerns

One issue of very real concern is the question of equity of access to vaccines and other critically needed public health resources to fight against infectious disease outbreaks. In a pandemic situation involving a virus with high infectivity and high mortality, who should, for example, be the first to get access to the vaccines: healthcare professionals? the military? the politically connected? the wealthy who can afford to pay any price for the vaccine?

Several countries around the world have been very concerned about the need to be prepared in the event of just such an outbreak, and have established close working relationships with public health personnel, research institutions

---

[9] Working closely with the World Health Organization (WHO) and the US Centers for Disease Control (CDC), leading Asian institutions including the Genome Institute of Singapore (GIS) and key institutions in Hong Kong and other countries (including Canada) helped to play an important role in quickly elucidating the SARS viral genome. SARS now appears to be a zoonosis that spread to humans from civet cats.

as well as vaccine and drug manufacturers.[10] Few Asia-Pacific countries typically have such emergency support plans in place.

If a vaccine or therapeutics manufacturer is already working at full capacity trying to respond to the needs of countries and customers to whom they have already committed to supplying vaccines or therapeutics in an emergency situation, what chance is there that countries that have not even seriously contemplated the possibility of such an outbreak will be able to gain supplies of vaccines or needed therapeutics on short notice? With the inevitable limited production capability in the early stages of a pandemic when demand and need greatly exceed supply, what chance is there that the poor and the weak will get access to preventative resources early enough to prevent a major public health catastrophe?

The Need to Be Proactive

Most countries in the Asia-Pacific region have traditionally invested little in establishing public health surveillance and monitoring systems, and do not typically have the capacity or the infrastructure to track and try to stop epidemics in their tracks through such measures as providing protective clothing, establishing quarantine facilities for suspected cases, and developing and providing needed drugs, vaccines, and emergency medical supplies. When the SARS outbreak first emerged, for example, little thought had typically gone into planning for, and managing, such public health emergencies. Ill-prepared countries and societies are at particular risk of suffering the worst impacts of outbreaks.

People usually do not want to think about such concerns unless they absolutely have to (at which time it may already be too late), but many of our cities in the Asia-Pacific region are potential public health disasters waiting to happen. We live in overcrowded environments where we share each others' air and space (think of the number of times you find yourself sitting or standing within sniffing distance of a person with a cold or cough, sneezing or coughing aerosol droplets full of germs). Ventilation systems in buildings, in airplanes, in trains, if not well-planned or designed, tend to allow rapid spread of aerosol

---

[10] These tend to be the more developed countries in Europe, North America, and Australasia. Few countries in Asia, if any, had well-defined epidemic or pandemic response capabilities or vaccine procurement strategies in place prior to the SARS outbreak of 2003. Importantly, many countries in the region appear to have started taking influenza and other infectious diseases much more seriously in the wake of the SARS outbreak. It is to be hoped that this heightened state of awareness of the potential economic and social impact of infectious diseases will lead to sustainable change in the manner in which such disease outbreaks are planned for and managed in these countries.

transmitted infectious agents.[11] Usually, we find ourselves catching relatively mild diseases in such situations – for example, common colds or the seasonal flu – but what happens when we find ourselves being unwittingly exposed to highly pathogenic organisms such as legionnaire's disease or, as many in the Asia-Pacific region and countries like Canada found, SARS in early 2003?

SARS smouldered under cover for months in China before it spread to Vietnam and Hong Kong. Should China be blamed for not being more proactive in dealing with the disease when it first appeared? The fact is that we should all take collective responsibility. Rapid spread tends to occur in poorer countries without adequate resources to maintain state-of-the-art monitoring and surveillance systems – including regular screening and testing of organisms causing disease so genetic drift and sudden changes in the pattern of strains causing infection can be effectively monitored. The World Health Organization (WHO) is typically forced to depend largely on interest by individual member countries to set up and operate such systems – hence capability development tends to be patchy at best. SARS underlined the reality that we live in a truly global village – disease knows no borders. Somebody else's problem to begin with soon becomes our own.

Managing Infectious Diseases Effectively

Rather than expect the other countries and societies to put in place mechanisms to protect their own backyards, and then point disapproving fingers when their measures fail to control the situation, there is clear opportunity and need to establish a global coordinating and monitoring mechanism to respond proactively to future public health emergencies and crises. State-of-the-art equipment and resources – including Geographical Information Systems (GIS), tracking the spread and control of disease outbreaks, molecular epidemiological tracking of the genomic transformation of infectious agents, and so on – can and should play a much more substantial role in infectious disease monitoring and management. Emergency response systems need to be coordinated, and information freely and proactively shared, while new technologies and tools should be applied, when available, for monitoring and evaluation.

If we tie the need for strong surveillance and rapid response capabilities to managing local environments more effectively – keeping water supply

---

[11] Typically, we in Asia also share our living space with flies, mosquitos, cockroaches and rodents – all known culprits in the spread of infectious diseases.

clean and safe,[12] ensuring proactive outbreak management through a network of global tracking and monitoring centers, responding quickly and appropriately with disease containment and control capabilities – we can, and will, make a major impact in helping to reduce the burden imposed by infectious disease outbreaks around the world (see also Box 11.4, pg 175).

The Pharmaceutical Industry

The pharmaceutical industry was estimated to have generated over US$400 billion in revenues worldwide in 2001. While the US remains the largest market, the Asia-Pacific region is becoming increasingly important as economies have grown and wealth has increased. The Asia-Pacific market is among the fastest growing markets for pharmaceutical drugs in the world – it is estimated to be growing at a cumulative rate of at least 11% annually (in value terms) compared to the global average of about 8% annually.[13]

The pharmaceutical industry faces a variety of driving pressures in the Asia-Pacific region (Box 6.4). Some operational and market challenges faced by the industry will be addressed in this chapter, while the challenge to maintain and expand the pipeline of drugs through biomedical research and development is addressed in Chapter 7.

Box 6.4   Driving Pressures Affecting the Pharmaceutical Industry in Asia

Responding to the challenges of economic transition
- Changing buying power of consumers
- Government/Institutional market pressure to cut costs

Increased "management of care"
- Change of decision-maker in buying process from individuals to institutional/group purchasing
- Move from patented products to over-the-counter drugs (OTCs)/ generics even as lucrative proprietary products come off patent
- Increasing opportunity/need for pharmacoeconomic/cost-effectiveness studies to demonstrate affordability and economic benefit

---

[12] It is estimated that dirty and contaminated water is directly responsible for over 30% of infant deaths in developing countries, and is a contributory factor to at least another 30% of infectious disease-related mortality and morbidity.

[13] IMS World Review, 2003.

Maintaining shareholder value
- Maintaining pipeline of innovative new products
- Cutting overheads
- Maintaining operating margins
- Dealing effectively with declining effectiveness of field force

M&A (Merger and Acquisition) fever
- Challenges in integration and transition management of marketing and sales operations in the region

Pharmaceutical companies have been hard-pressed to maintain the double-digit levels of growth that their shareholders have become used to in recent decades. This has driven the tendency for these companies to enter into acquisition mode to increase their product and technology pipelines (see also Chapter 7). There is also greater interest in partnering with biotech players as well as other pharmaceutical players to bring innovative new products to market.

Another factor driving the industry is the world's rising elderly population. The population aged 65 and above is expected to exceed 700 million by 2025. This population segment typically consumes three times more drugs per capita than younger segments. About 150 products for age-related conditions were brought to market in the 1990s, and some 600 more are in development. Responding to the needs of the elderly is becoming a key factor raising demand for high quality and more affordable drugs in the US and internationally (see also Box 6.5).

It is to be anticipated that the Asia-Pacific region will become increasingly important for major international pharmaceutical players as regional economies continue to expand and demand for drugs continues to grow. Few players, if any, can afford not to have a well-defined integrated Asia-Pacific strategy, not just in relation to marketing and sales, but also in relation to manufacturing, the conduct of clinical trials, and the establishment of research and product development alliances with regional research institutions, biotech companies, contract research organizations (CROs) and other clinical trial centers,[14] and regional pharmaceutical manufacturers (see Box 6.5).

---

[14] There is growing capability for the conduct of world-class clinical trials in accordance with Good Clinical Practice (GCP) in several economies in the region including China, Hong Kong, India, Malaysia, Singapore, Taiwan and Thailand.

Box 6.5   Generic Players in Asia and Their Potential Future Impact

Asia, especially India, has long served as a manufacturing base for low cost active pharmaceutical ingredients (APIs) that are used by major pharmaceutical players in their proprietary formulations. Asia also serves as the home base for a large number of generic drug manufacturers in India, China, Indonesia, and Korea, for example.

While these players initially thrived on lax or non-existent enforcement of intellectual property rules to produce cheap versions of expensive proprietary drugs,[15] they have increasingly realized that there is much more to be gained by respecting and following international rules. Hence, players like Dr Reddy's and Ranbaxy have established lucrative markets in the US and other parts of the world by complying with US FDA requirements and responding to growing international demand for high quality generics at reasonable prices.

At the same time, they have discovered the value of developing and marketing their own proprietary products (some have even successfully licensed products to major pharmaceutical players). Given their low-cost base, the economies of scale they enjoy simply by virtue of supplying massive and rapidly growing home markets, their expertise in drug chemistry and manufacturing technology, and the growing quality of their output, it seems increasingly likely that pharmaceutical companies in India and other countries in Asia with a history and tradition of pharmaceutical manufacturing will be serious and important players on the global stage.

Major international pharmaceutical and technology players would do well to partner with leading Asia-Pacific players, and to find ways to cooperate in product and market development for mutual benefit.

Responding to the Wellness Opportunity

The overall market opportunity and need for effective wellness and disease management is huge, and growing rapidly in Asia and around the world as societies develop and become more urbanized. The global healthcare market is estimated to have reached about US$1.5 trillion annually by 2001. The wellness and disease management sector is a fast growing arena which overlaps substantially with the healthcare market and is projected to itself reach a global market potential of as much as US$1 trillion by 2010.[16]

A general rule of thumb that applies fairly well in many Asia-Pacific

---

[15] There were, for example, estimated to be at least three versions of Viagra available on the Indian market within 12 months of Pfizer's release of the drug in the US.

[16] Paul Zane Pilzer, *The Wellness Revolution*, John Wiley & Sons, 2002.

economies is the "1 +2 + 3" market size rule. Hence, for example, Malaysia's market for "ethical" or prescription pharmaceutical drugs is about US$1 billion a year; its market for traditional, alternative and herbal medicines is about US$2 billion; and its market for vitamins, nutraceuticals, health foods and other wellness-related products is about US$3 billion.[17]

Increasingly, as our populations age, older and better-off individuals become more prone to suffer from the "diseases of excess" – for example, nearly 10% of adults around the world have diabetes, more than 20% have hypertension, a similar number suffers from cholesterol and lipid abnormalities, and at least 25% of urban-dwelling adults are estimated to be overweight or suffering from the consequences of unhealthy lifestyles (including excessive stress, smoking, alcohol and inactivity).[18]

There is growing interest and demand for wellness-orientated products, services and technologies. Arguably "lifestyle" products and services, the market for nutraceuticals, cosmeceuticals, and technology solutions for disease monitoring and management (including electronic medical monitoring devices) is growing at a rate that is at least twice that of pharmaceuticals.

Additionally, health spas, massage therapy, beauty and "wellness" clinics (including those offering slimming services, plastic surgery, botox injections, and so on), and a host of new technology and service-based offerings operating on the fringes of the healthcare industry offer huge rewards for innovative entrepreneurs as baby boomers in Asia enter middle age and seek to extend their "shelf lives."

The next several sections focus on alternative and complementary medicines. The subject of wellness and disease management using medical devices and telemonitoring/teleconsultation technologies is discussed briefly in the section on IT in healthcare and medicine (Health-IT) below.

Alternative and Complementary Therapies: Responding to the Wellness Imperative

With the shift in paradigm from disease management to wellness management and disease prevention has come greater interest in alternative and complementary medicines/therapies by consumers not only in the Asia-Pacific region but globally.[19] The Asia-Pacific region is seeing annual growth rates for

---

[17] Datuk (Dr) M. Jegathesan, personal communication.

[18] Clearly, some individuals suffer from two or more of these conditions at the same time.

[19] Typically, the products offered are natural products, usually of herbal origin. They are described as "complementary" when they are used as adjuncts to conventional medicines, and as "alternatives" when they are recommended for use in lieu of conventional pharmaceutical products.

alternative and complementary products and services of at least 18–20%, compared to global average growth of 10–12% annually (and growth of the global pharmaceutical drug market at a rate of about 8% annually).

There is growing acceptance of alternative and complementary medicines/ therapies by consumers, healthcare providers, governments, and insurers. Even the World Health Organization, which has historically avoided involvement in traditional and alternative medicine, has made a substantial shift toward recognizing the importance and significance of such practices in the lives of people throughout the world by embracing these practices within its fold. Simultaneously, providers are recognizing the value of conducting scientific research to validate the safety and efficacy of their products and the number of clinical trials for such products is increasing rapidly.

Traditional medicine refers to alternative/complementary ways of protecting and restoring health that existed before the arrival of modern Western medicine.[20] Clearly, different traditional approaches to health evolved in different cultures and societies, and have been handed down from generation to generation.

China and India, for example, have developed very sophisticated systems such as acupuncture and traditional Chinese medicine and ayurvedic medicine, respectively. Similarly, other societies in Asia have established their own traditional medicines that incorporate elements from other practices while evolving their own unique elements – as is true, for example, of traditional Thai herbal medicines, traditional jamu practices in Indonesia, Korean traditional medicine, Japanese "kampo" medicine, and so on.

Many traditional medical approaches are based on the use of herbs and other medicinal products (typically of animal or mineral origin). Herbal medicine is also called herbology, phytomedicine, or botanical medicine. Herbs have been used for medicinal purposes in most cultures since ancient times, either as single entities, as complex mixtures of several herbs or as concoctions using herbs with other substances.

An increasingly important area of research and development focus in the Asia-Pacific region and internationally has been to look to traditionally used medicines and herbs as sources of active molecules for modern pharmaceutical drug development. As much as a quarter of pharmaceutical drugs in current

---

[20] The roots of Western medicine can be found in insights and practices arising from the Greek/Roman and Arabic traditions that were preserved and built upon by Middle Eastern practitioners and transferred to Europe following the Dark Ages during the period of the Renaissance. Leading Middle Eastern scholars who greatly influenced Western medical thinking, such as Avicenna (Ibn Sina), also incorporated many teachings and practices from traditional Indian, Chinese and African practices that found their way to the Middle East through ancient trade routes.

use are estimated to have been derived from traditionally used medicines and herbs.[21] The contribution of traditional medicines to modern medicine can be expected to grow rapidly over the coming decades as these products are systematically studied using modern scientific tools and biotechnologies.

Nutraceuticals

Nutraceuticals, functional foods, and pharmafoods are terms often used to describe food or products that demonstrate physiological or health benefits and which can help reduce the incidence or impact of chronic diseases. The use of the term "nutraceutical" varies quite considerably depending on geographical location and culture. In Europe, the term is generally reserved strictly for natural products of herbal origin only, as a result of strong consumer interest in homeopathic and herbal medicines. In the US and the Asia-Pacific region, where consumers tend to be more interested in physical fitness and effectiveness, nutraceutical ingredients do not necessarily have to be purely of herbal origin, and often include added vitamins and minerals aimed at increasing efficacy.

Nutraceuticals (and cosmeceuticals) have only recently been identified as a separate market segment within the natural health and food products industry. The nutraceuticals market is estimated to already be as large as US$250 billion globally, with strong and robust growth potential over the coming years.

The market for nutraceuticals in the Asia-Pacific region, and especially in East Asia, is particularly interesting – with strong consumer interest in products that combine traditional herbal products with demonstrable health benefits. Hence, the popularity of ginseng-, green tea-, and royal jelly-based products as well as products that demonstrate high anti-oxidant and other functional benefits (including increasing mental alertness, providing greater "vitality" – a common Asian code-word for sexual energy – and other benefits including improved skin complexion, and so on).

Medical Informatics and the Application of Medical and Bio-IT Tools for Healthcare (Health-IT)

Health-IT and Telemedicine

The deepening relationship between the electronics and life science sectors is responsible for creating a growing range of novel technologies such as gene and protein chips (with varied potential uses including rapid disease diagnosis

---

[21] World Health Organization, 2002.

and management, and "high-throughput" natural product screening), as well as cutting-edge medical devices for patient monitoring and management.

Telemedicine refers to the electronic transfer of patient-specific medical information from one location to another for the purpose of improving patient care. This broad definition encompasses any technology used for the delivery of healthcare services and medical education over a distance, including teleconsultation and remote monitoring of patient vital signs for disease management.[22]

Opportunities clearly exist for the development and implementation of integrated information and knowledge management systems for healthcare and health services. These include areas such as patient information management systems, electronic medical records, clinical data management systems, and archiving and analysis systems (including medical imaging).

Medical Devices for Remote Consultation and Disease Management

The opportunity and potential to apply new tools and technologies to facilitate non-invasive, ambulatory measurement and monitoring of biometric parameters for wellness and disease management is potentially enormous. This is especially true in relation to chronic conditions such as diabetes mellitus (affecting as many as 10% or more of most adult populations), hypertension (affecting about 25% or more) and lipid/cholesterol abnormalities (affecting 17% or more). Substantial work in developing innovative diagnostic tools and devices in these areas is currently underway in major centers throughout the world. In the Asia-Pacific region, there exists a notable concentration of cutting-edge technologies and companies in Singapore and Taiwan, in particular.[23]

Recent advances in bioengineering, and in information and communication technology, have enabled the development of a growing variety of biomeasurement and biomonitoring tools and devices that promise to revolutionize healthcare and wellness management. It is anticipated that the next decade will see facilitated translation of these new developments into

---

[22] Given Asia's expansive land area and the lack of skilled healthcare personnel in remote areas, there is substantial opportunity and potential to incorporate new tools and capabilities for telemedicine into the public health infrastructure of countries in the region – capitalizing perhaps on growing broadband capabilities in urban areas and satellite- and radio-communications in remote rural areas. Done right, such infrastructure can also play a critical role in disaster management and epidemic outbreak detection and control.

[23] Dr Ting Choon Meng, CEO of Healthstats, a promising Singapore-based start-up that has developed a proprietary ambulatory blood pressure monitoring watch-like device that promises to revolutionize hypertension and critical care management, notes, "We are going to see the emergence of new and unprecedented ways of tracking and managing these conditions – and of defining both normality and disease states. This is exciting."

practical and useful application, improving quality of life for individuals in the Asia-Pacific region and beyond.

One area of interest is real-time non-invasive blood glucose monitoring. In the US alone, the direct and indirect economic cost and impact of diabetes mellitus is estimated to be some US$100 billion each year. Diseases associated with lipid abnormalities and obesity are estimated to cost a similar amount, while cardiovascular diseases (including hypertension) cost society about twice as much.[24] Costs associated with such conditions escalate if patients are poorly controlled and their condition is allowed to deteriorate. A recent study in Germany, for example, showed that annual medical costs for a diabetic with no complications was about €2,000 (US$1,760) a year, but exceeded €5,000 when complications developed.[25]

The reality is that complications arising from deterioration of diseases such as diabetes and hypertension are essentially preventable, and patients can be maintained in good health with more effective control of disease. Such solutions can be expected to bring savings of 50% or more in direct and indirect healthcare costs, while maximizing patient well-being and improving patient-provider interaction and continuity of care.

There is clear opportunity and need for technology players to work in partnership with patients and their healthcare providers in Asia (and, indeed, throughout the world) to ensure affordable and effective wellness and disease management for each disease of priority concern. The potential market for such technologies in the Asia-Pacific region alone is already quite significant, and growing rapidly (see Table 6.1).

Technology players who will be most successful and effective will be those who work collaboratively with key stakeholders and meet their needs through ensuring that:

- Healthcare providers (physicians, nurse practitioners, and others) are incentivized to become partners in providing their patients with world-class wellness and disease management support
- Patients are motivated to be more proactive in their own care at an affordable price
- Employers save money and increase productivity by lowering absenteeism through improved worker health and well-being, and a lowered incidence of secondary sequelae or complications from disease

[24] US Centers for Disease Control, 2001.
[25] McKinsey Study on Disease Management, Germany, 2001.

Table 6.1 Estimated Size of Private Market for Wellness and Disease Management in Selected Asia-Pacific Metropolitan Areas (listed in alphabetical order)

Metropolitan area	Estimated total population (million)	Estimated target population base (million)	Diabetes	Hypertension	Heart disease	Geriatric care	Juvenile asthma
Bangkok	9.2	3.7	184,000	257,600	386,400	220,800	17,664
Beijing	12	2.4	120,000	163,200	244,800	144,000	12,480
Brisbane	1.54	1.2	61,600	81,312	121,968	160,160	20,698
Hong Kong	6.6	5.3	264,000	374,880	562,320	580,800	19,008
Jakarta	10.3	2.1	103,000	133,900	200,850	103,000	12,360
Kuala Lumpur (including Klang Valley)	3.75	1.5	112,500	137,250	205,875	90,000	15,750
Manila	10	2.0	100,000	118,000	177,000	80,000	14,800
Melbourne	3.32	2.7	132,800	175,296	262,944	345,280	44,621
Perth	1.31	1.1	52,400	69,168	103,752	136,240	17,606
Seoul	10	6.0	300,000	426,000	639,000	420,000	26,400
Shanghai	13	2.6	130,000	176,800	265,200	156,000	13,520
Singapore	3.9	3.1	156,000	224,640	336,960	218,400	13,104
Sydney	3.94	3.2	157,600	208,032	312,048	409,760	52,954
Taipei	2.6	1.6	78,000	109,200	163,800	124,800	6,864
Tokyo	12	9.6	480,000	652,800	1,440,000	1,632,000	28,800
Total			**2,431,900**	**3,308,078**	**5,422,917**	**4,821,240**	**316,628**

Source: BioEnterprise Asia, 2001.

- Insurance and managed care providers also benefit by saving on healthcare compensation payouts which could save them millions of dollars annually
- Public healthcare authorities benefit by providing the public with access to state-of-the-art wellness and disease management programs, and reduce the burden on society from having to deal with the long-term consequences and complications arising from these conditions

The opportunity and potential for future growth is exciting. We are still in the very early days of developing and implementing biomeasurement and biomonitoring tools and devices, and of translating research and development findings into practical application.

Conclusion

The healthcare arena offers tremendous value and opportunity as populations in Asia and other developing regions undergo demographic and epidemiological transitions and become increasingly educated, urbanized and wealthy, and demand higher quality care and services. At the same time, advances in information and communication technology, and in the life sciences and biotechnology, are enabling the provision of products, services, and technology solutions that would have been impossible only a decade ago.

These are indeed exciting times for those of us engaged in working to create value for health and well-being.

Key Points

1. There is substantial opportunity and potential to develop and apply innovative and entrepreneurial solutions in response to changing public health and healthcare service realities in the Asia-Pacific region.

2. New paradigms in healthcare and wellness have created new opportunities and growing interest in such areas as alternative and complementary medicine, nutraceuticals, and functional foods.

3. New developments in information and communication technology, and in medical devices for disease and wellness monitoring, create the opportunity to establish innovative service delivery approaches that are more cost-effective and can result in great improvements in health outcomes.

Chapter 7
Biomedical Science

There are only two ways to live your life.
One is as though nothing is a miracle.
The other is as though everything is a miracle.

Albert Einstein

Summary

It is generally thought that the biggest impact of the unraveling of the human genome will be in the biomedical sciences. The sequencing of genomes represents only the first step in translating the newly understood genetic data to practical application. The implications are far-reaching and will have a myriad of socio-economic effects ranging from better and faster disease diagnosis, to improved drugs, individually tailored medical treatments and more proactive disease prevention. The field of Bio-IT represents a marriage of cutting-edge information technology with frontier science to enable scientists to make better sense of the data and information glut arising from various fields of biomedical research, and will facilitate testing and evaluation of biotech products and their subsequent registration and marketing. We are truly living in exciting times – the next several decades promise a radical transformation of the biomedical sciences and, with this, the practice of medicine.

Background

This chapter will briefly survey the following opportunities and challenges in the biomedical science arena:

- Pharmaceuticals and drug development
- Diagnostics
- Biopharmaceuticals: recombinant proteins and immunotherapeutics
  - Vaccines
  - Opportunities for production of biologicals and vaccines

- Biomedical outsourcing opportunities
  - Contract research organizations
  - Contract manufacturing opportunities
- Bio-IT and computational biology

Pharmaceutical and Drug Development

> *Ever tried. Ever failed. No matter.*
> *Try again. Fail again. Fail better.*

> Samuel Beckett

Pharmaceutical drug development[1] has traditionally been perceived as a high risk, capital-intensive, scale-intensive, and highly regulated business. The process of taking a product from the laboratory to regulatory approval can be an expensive proposition – over US$800 million by some estimates.[2] Marketing and distribution costs are also high in this price- and performance-sensitive sector.

Drug companies did extremely well in the 1980s and 1990s, consistently earning double-digit growth in revenues and profitability. But maintaining such growth over the long term will be difficult as they are under pressure from a variety of factors including the need to maintain a pipeline of new drugs, the reality that blockbuster proprietary drugs are increasingly coming off patent, and growing consumer demands to keep costs down (see also Box 7.1). These pressures are also driving the trend toward industry consolidation, and related merger and acquisition activity – pooling R&D potential and building larger pipelines has been part of the logic behind major pharma mergers such as that between Glaxo Wellcome and SmithKline Beecham to establish Glaxo SmithKline.

Box 7.1 Some Drug Development Challenges Faced by the Pharmaceutical Industry

- Pressure to maintain 10–15% growth in sales revenue
- Many blockbusters are going off patent
  - 1999–2004 = US$43 billion

---

[1] Sometimes also described as "small molecule" drug development, as compared with large molecule biological pharmaceutical (biopharmaceutical) development – see later.

[2] Tufts University Center for the Study of Drug Development, 2001.

- Need more new drugs in development pipelines
  - 1999–2004: Need for at least 500 new chemical entities (NCEs) or new candidate drugs
- Increasing cost of drug discovery
  - Up to US$850 million/drug (pharma), US$500 million/drug (biotech)
- Need more novel drug targets
  - Pre-genomic era: Identified about 50 targets/annum
  - Post-genomic era: Need to identify some 200 new targets/annum
- Need to move away from non-strategic "high throughput" drug target discovery approaches – decreases success rates in pre-clinical phase, increases costs

Another strategy for building drug pipelines has been for big pharma players to enter into alliances with biotechnology companies. The pharmaceutical industry clearly recognizes the potential of biotechnology to greatly improve on available technologies and capabilities for drug discovery and development. Hence, pharmaceutical players are proactively seeking partnership and acquisition opportunities with biotech companies with promising technologies, while investing 20–25% of their R&D budget on outsourcing and collaborative relationships with academic institutions and biotech companies.

New tools and technologies in molecular biology and biotechnology have long captured the imagination of drug development visionaries as ways to cut through the inefficiency of traditional approaches for drug development, and to find and develop blockbuster drugs at relatively low cost. However, the promise of biotechnology did not initially translate into drug development success – there have been boom and bust cycles in the biotech sector, and regular periods of investor backlash when over-hype by biotech players led to unrealistic expectations of delivery of biotech blockbuster drugs within impossible timelines. The risks involved in drug development and the cash burn rates required to take a drug through the developmental pipeline are generally projected as being very high. The historical experience of biotech companies being able to deliver successful drugs to market (relative to failures) has been less than spectacular.

History, in this case, should be seen as a point of departure as new technologies and capabilities that were still embryonic just 5 or 10 years ago mature and come to fruition.

Many biotech players today generally tend to seek to respond to the need of big pharma for promising products in their drug development pipelines rather than attempt to control the entire drug development value chain themselves (see also Figure 7.1). Many involved in drug development therefore look to out-licence their products or to partner with big pharma to take their products to market. Others focus on providing specific technologies or information resources for increasing the efficiency and productivity of different elements of the drug development process.

Such approaches are less capital-intensive, less risky and more attractive to investors in biotech due to prospects of near-term revenue generation from big pharma partners through upfront licensing fees and milestone-based payments.

Biotech drugs still constitute only a small proportion of the global pharmaceutical market which itself is estimated to have reached over US$450 billion in 2003. So far, about 200 biotech drugs have made it to market, and they collectively still account for less than 10% of the revenue of the pharmaceutical industry. But the reality is that biotech, and modern biotech-related approaches, are already capturing a growing proportion of new drug approvals in the US (see Table 7.1), and investment in biotech approaches are beginning to pay off handsomely as biotechnologies mature.

Figure 7.1 The Traditional "Pre-Genomic" Drug Development Process

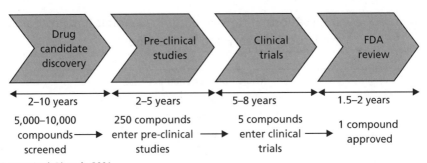

Source: Lynk Biotech, 2001.

Table 7.1 Biotech-related Drug Approvals in the US (1990–2001)

	Biotech drug approvals	Estimated % of total drugs approved
1990–1995	5	16.7
1997	11	22.5
1999	12	30
2001	24	66.7

Sources: The Coming Biotech Age, 2002; US Food and Drug Administration (FDA), 2002.

The reasons for big pharma's interest in biotech, and for the growing contribution of biotech approaches to drug development, are not difficult to understand. While estimates based on recent insights from mapping the human genome suggest that there may be as many as 10,000 potential drug targets in humans, currently available drugs developed in the "pre-genomic" era target only about 500 or so of these targets. This leaves some 95% of potential drug targets still untapped (see Figure 7.2). Pharmaceutical companies recognize that new tools and techniques for drug target identification and drug development pioneered by biotech players can greatly increase their success in developing drugs against these previously untapped targets.

The traditional approach to drug discovery and development, including taking a drug candidate through pre-clinical testing and then the clinical trial and regulatory approval process, has been an inefficient and long-drawn out process that could take as much as 10 to 15 years or longer (see Figure 7.1), and cost as much as US$800 million or more.

Pre-clinical studies involve a range of *in vitro* and animal studies, as well as ADMETox studies.[3]

The clinical trial process consists essentially of four phases: three phases before drug registration and approval for marketing, and the last phase conducted after marketing.

Figure 7.2   **Implications of New Findings in Genomic and Proteomics for Drug Discovery and Development**

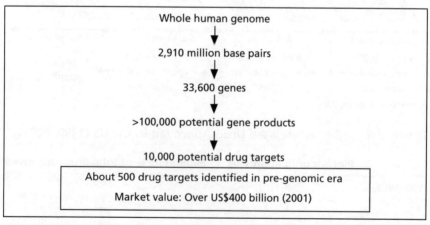

Source: Lynk Biotech, 2001.

---

[3] As the name implies, ADMETox studies involve absorption (A), distribution (D), metabolism (M), excretion (E), and toxicology (Tox) studies.

- Phase I studies involve first use of a new drug in humans, often described as "first in man" studies. The primary objective is to test for safety and side effects. Phase I studies are also used to determine appropriate dosing. Usually, only a small number of people are enrolled.
- Phase II studies involve a larger number of people and are designed to see if the drug is effective. Phase II trials also seek to further evaluate drug safety and to fine-tune dosing.
- Phase III studies involve giving the drug to large groups of people to confirm its effectiveness in comparison to commonly used treatments, to monitor side effects, and to collect information that will allow the drug or treatment to be used safely.
- Phase IV studies are "post-marketing" studies – in other words, they are conducted after the drug has been released into the market to gather information on the drug's effects in different populations, and to determine any side effects associated with long-term use.

BioEnterprise Asia's assessment is that the pharmaceutical drug development process has been limited by often non-standardized, unsystematic, highly inefficient, and even random, screening and validation practices. This reality, coupled with a highly regulated review and approval process, greatly increases the cost and time involved in attempting to take any new drug through the development process.

It is generally estimated that only 1 in 10,000 drug candidates makes it through the developmental process to enter the market. Even when a drug gets to clinical trials, only 1 in 5 have historically made it to market. History, in this case, should be treated as a point of departure toward a newer, better way of managing the process – and should not, in our opinion, serve as a reference for likely future trends.

The high failure rate for drug candidates, the long-drawn out process, and the expense involved in taking even a single drug to approval through the developmental process are completely unacceptable – and long overdue for a total rethink.

While some would seek to blame the US Food and Drug Administration (FDA) and other regulatory authorities for over-regulating the process and making it slow and expensive, BioEnterprise Asia sees pharma and biotech players as having been more than partly responsible for the low success rates and the rising costs.

The fact is that drug candidates with limited efficacy and unacceptable side effect profiles have all too often been brought to clinical trial when an objective assessment by the company would, and should, have resulted in their elimination long before they entered the clinic. Undoubtedly, the pressure to maintain stock prices, raise additional cash, and keep shareholders and analysts excited about a company's prospective future earnings pipeline (with x number of drugs for specific indications at each stage of clinical trials, for example) has contributed substantially to this loss of objectivity on the part of companies eager to push their products through at all costs – and has forced regulatory authorities to increase their levels of vigilance to ensure safety and efficacy of products that eventually do make it to market.

All the steps involved in drug development can be substantially and systematically telescoped into much quicker development cycles through less inefficient and random approaches: use of smarter drug development and screening technologies (as a result of biotech innovation as well as the use of *in silico* technologies), streamlining of trials as well as the regulatory review and approval process, and so on. The increasing availability and use of software-based systems for clinical trial monitoring, for data management and integration, and for submission of clinical trial findings to regulatory authorities are clearly helping to expedite the review and approval process.

Advances in biotechnology are not only opening up new product opportunities but are also trimming the time and expense of development – they have the potential to help make the process more rational by eliminating potential failures long before they enter clinical trials.

As shown in Box 7.2, there are three fundamental ways to identify and develop new drugs that are in use today.

The first approach outlined in Box 7.2 is to screen large numbers of natural and synthetic compounds to determine if they have any effect on a specific target of interest. New technologies have been applied to increase the rate and number of molecules that can be screened for any specific activity (so-called "high-throughput screening") – but such "brute force" laboratory-based approaches are expensive (and drive up the cost of drug development).

Also, because millions of molecules are often randomly screened, such approaches often simply result in increasing the failure rate of the screening process – where maybe 10,000 to 20,000 compounds used to be assayed for their activity against a specific target in the wet laboratory (wet lab), it is now increasingly common to assay as many as two to five million compounds because the "high throughput screening" technology to do this quickly now exists. This process is highly expensive and inefficient, and seldom results in the identification of any drug candidate "hits" of significance.

Box 7.2   Basic Approaches to Drug Discovery and Development
- **Identification of bioactive compounds (natural and synthetic) through screening for biological activity** – traditional approach that has recently been enhanced by the development of high-throughput screening capabilities. This approach is still highly random and inefficient, with substantial risk of failure of identified compounds due to toxicity or lack of clinically significant activity.
- **Modification of known bioactive compounds to optimize desired activity and eliminate side-effects** – classical approach to drug development. Exciting recent advances include molecular evolution and new insights into drug-receptor interaction
- **Rational drug design based on structure-function relationships between drug and receptor site** – this approach has attracted increasing interest – growing potential and success arising from breakthroughs in genomics, proteomics, receptomics, bioinformatics, and *in silico* drug design capabilities

Source: Lynk Biotechnologies, 2002.

It is far more efficient and cost-effective to conduct the bulk of such screening *in silico*[4] (in other words, through computer-based simulations and prediction of efficacy and potential side effects), and only move to wet laboratory-based testing to validate and confirm the most promising candidates identified through lower cost, and increasingly more predictive, computer-based methodologies.

The second approach is to start with compounds already known to have some biological activity, and to modify these compounds to optimize their effects. This is the classical approach to drug development, and has certainly had its fair share of success. It is clearly a smarter and less expensive process than high-throughput, wet laboratory-based screening.

The third approach has always been seen by leading practitioners in the drug design and development field as the biggest opportunity and challenge for drug development. Rather than randomly screen molecules, this approach takes advantage of our knowledge and understanding of structure and function to design molecules that would likely have the desired effect *in silico,* and then validate the predicted effect through wet lab studies. There is growing appreciation of the power and potential of such approaches to greatly reduce the time and cost of drug development.

---

[4] BioEnterprise Asia and our colleagues at Lynk Biotechnologies describe this approach as "dry" screening – as opposed to the substantially more expensive and inefficient "wet" screening in the laboratory.

There are already some companies (including a BioEnterprise Asia associated start-up, Lynk Biotechnologies) that have developed new and innovative ways to "short-circuit" drug discovery and development using smart laboratory science and the best that bio-IT has to offer for computer-based analysis and molecular simulation. Our experience has shown that it is entirely feasible to telescope the process of going from identification of a drug target to the generation of optimized candidate drugs in three to six months rather than the three to five years it has traditionally taken (see Figure 7.1).

As new technologies and capabilities for drug target identification and drug candidate development have become increasingly validated, we are already beginning to see a shift from too few drug candidates to too many. Our growing awareness and understanding of more and more potential drug targets, high-throughput screening technology, and new approaches to designing and developing new drugs are beginning to lead to an almost bewildering array of drug targets and drug candidates.

It is increasingly likely that molecular modeling and simulations of interaction of drug candidates with targets of interest; computer-based studies of metabolic and excretion pathways, cell, whole organ and even whole organism effects; and other *in silico* approaches to studying drugs will enable systematic and far more cost-effective assessment of drug candidates of interest than has been hitherto possible. Such developments should hopefully lead to greater selectiveness and discretion in deciding which specific drug candidates to bring into the clinical trial process, and to an increase in success rates for drugs traversing the clinical development pipeline.

At the same time, as advances in drug development and streamlining of the clinical trial process are leading to prospects of greater efficiency and lower cost for drug development, there is increasing realization of the need to customize treatment in response to individual variations in genetic make-up. Advances in pharmacogenomics and increasing understanding of how genetic variations can contribute to varying drug efficacy or the risk of adverse reactions are pushing us increasingly toward personalized medicine. While a move in this direction will undoubtedly benefit individual patients, it may spell, in time, a move away from "one-size-fits-all" mass manufactured blockbuster drugs to having small batches of customized drugs made to order at friendly neighborhood pharmacies or laboratories. Such dynamics will inevitably alter the face of the pharmaceutical industry internationally and in the Asia-Pacific region over the coming decades.

Diagnostics

The global market for *in vitro* diagnostics was estimated to be about US$24 billion in 2003. The market is growing at a rate of about 3–4% annually in the US, Europe, and Japan, and about 8% annually in the rest of the world.

While the focus remains in areas such as immunoassays (about US$8 billion), clinical chemistry (about US$5 billion), and blood glucose (nearly US$4 billion), molecular diagnostics (including nucleic acid probes) are a fast growing segment with sales in 2001 exceeding US$1.5 billion. Key drivers of growth in the diagnostics sector in the future are expected to include molecular diagnostics, point-of-care diagnostics (primarily immuno-based), and diabetes testing.

New developments in genomics and proteomics have fueled rapid growth and interest in the development and marketing of molecular diagnostic tools and technologies for research and future clinical application – for gene-based diagnostics, pharmacogenomic screening and diagnostics, and in high-throughput drug screening and discovery. Hence, microarray-based diagnostic tools and DNA sequencers have witnessed growth in excess of 20% annually in recent years, while DNA synthesizers and nucleic acid amplification technologies have experienced growth exceeding 10%.

Estimated total sales for these products already exceed US$4 billion, and they are expected to experience double-digit growth of at least 15% annually for at least the next five to ten years as they become increasingly accepted and validated, first as research tools, and possibly even as adjuncts for clinical use. Asia is expected to be a primary driver of growth in this sector with substantial research and development interest focused on developing diagnostic tools in genomics and proteomics, and on drug screening and development.

Point-of-care diagnostics accounted for some US$360 million in sales in 2001, and is another segment of the diagnostics market that is expected to grow substantially in line with growing demand and interest for improved diagnosis in healthcare settings (see also Box 6.1, pg 74). Primary interest in Asia is expected to focus on rapid infectious disease diagnostics, drug testing, as well as cancer and chronic disease screening.

The Asia-Pacific region promises to be a major growth market for diagnostics over the next several decades. A growing base of world-class diagnostic companies in the region (especially in Korea, Malaysia, Singapore, and Taiwan) is working to develop innovative and promising new diagnostic products and technologies.

Biopharmaceuticals: Recombinant Proteins and Immunotherapeutics

The global market for therapeutic proteins was estimated to be about US$27 billion in 2001, and is expected to reach US$50 billion by 2010. The market is growing at a pace exceeding 15% annually. Market growth has been driven primarily by erythropoeitin (EPO) and insulin, but therapeutic monoclonal antibodies[5] (also called immunotherapeutics) and vaccines are playing an increasingly important role in the market. The market for monoclonals is expected to exceed that for erythropoeitin by 2010.

Besides erythropoetin, there is growing interest in a range of other biologicals and recombinant proteins – including the various interferons (alpha, beta and gamma) as well as important cytokines such as the interleukins, CSF, G-CSF, EGF, and human growth hormone.

The immunotherapeutics market is currently bustling with interest. Over 300 companies worldwide are working today to develop monoclonal antibodies for use in human therapeutics or diagnostics. As many as 1,000 antibodies are currently under development – about 30% of which are directed against cancer targets, while the rest are directed against infectious diseases and autoimmune diseases, and for the prevention of transplant rejection.

Vaccines

The global vaccine market is estimated to be about US$10 billion, and is growing at a rate of about 12% annually. Higher priced proprietary vaccines targeted for use in more developed countries have driven market growth over the last decade or so. Sale of vaccines in high income private markets now account for over 80% of revenue for the vaccine industry, but only account for about 12% of total volume of vaccines sold worldwide (see also Box 7.3).

There is growing acceptance and recognition of the value of vaccines, and a growing willingness of consumers to pay for such prevention. This was clearly demonstrated in Asia during the SARS outbreak when private sector vaccine supplies against influenza and other infectious diseases ran out in several economies in the region. Stakeholders are increasingly accepting that new and improved vaccines cannot be made available as cheaply as the traditional vaccines, but will necessarily cost a premium. The use of cost-effectiveness and cost-benefit analysis can clearly help demonstrate the value of immunization against specific diseases, and increase acceptance of the opportunity and need for immunization.

---

[5] Antibodies are proteins that are produced by our immune systems to attack foreign antigens.

Box 7.3   Public Health Concerns and the EPI Vaccines

The vaccine market has traditionally been dominated by the public sector in response to public health concerns and needs – given that the people who need vaccines the most are characteristically the ones who can least afford them. International agencies, including the World Health Organization and the UN Fund for Children (UNICEF), have played a critical role in raising awareness and understanding of the key preventative and protective role that vaccines can play in treating and managing infectious diseases – and have recommended core vaccines for routine use in the so-called "Expanded Programme on Immunization" (EPI).

EPI vaccines dominate vaccine production and sales in volume terms – accounting for over 80% of the vaccine market by volume, they represent a low margin, high volume segment. The economics of vaccine production are driven by economies of scale – in general, the greater the volume of sale, the higher the returns for each dose sold. Tiered pricing, with differential pricing according to ability to pay, has been a useful mechanism to enhance availability of EPI vaccines – to ensure affordability and broad access. Multi-dose packaging and low-cost base suppliers enhance affordability of traditional EPI vaccines.

Major centers for vaccine production exist in Asia and account for the bulk of traditional vaccines produced worldwide (in volume terms). These include both traditional vaccine manufacturers and biotechnology players in India, China, Indonesia, Korea, and Japan. The number of WHO-prequalified vaccine producers from Asia, including Korea and India, has increased in recent years. These suppliers have a substantial cost advantage over developed country producers but typically lack facilities and resources for R&D and for process development. Their production tends to be limited to older vaccines, although they are generally keen to cooperate and collaborate with leading vaccine and platform technology players from around the world to transfer technology and improve their production capabilities.

In recent years, the Bill and Melinda Gates Foundation and other players such as the Global Alliance for Vaccines and Immunization (GAVI), the International AIDS Vaccine Initiative (IAVI), and the International Vaccine Institute (IVI) have been playing an increasingly important role in supporting research and development efforts for new and improved vaccines against diseases of the poor which are typically of little interest to commercial vaccine manufacturers (among other diseases, these include tuberculosis, dengue, and diarrhoeal diseases).

There has been growing interest in the development and use of vaccines for new and emerging diseases. The availability of newer vaccines has, in turn, increased revenue and profitability for major vaccine manufacturers. This has stimulated an increase in R&D for new vaccine development and production, not just by the leading pharmaceutical players involved in vaccines, but also by biotech players around the world. The major vaccine players alone spent over US$700 million for vaccine-related R&D in 2001.

Heightened interest in vaccines has also been fueled by the development of new tools and insights in vaccinology from genomics, proteomics, the application of DNA-based vaccine technologies, new adjuvants under development, and the development of new approaches to enhancing mucosal immunity, as well as by growing understanding of antigenic epitopes for enhancing both T- and B-cell immunity. This has resulted in the entry of a variety of new biotech players with a growing array of new tools and approaches to vaccine development (see Box 7.4).

Exciting progress has also been made in expressing efficacious vaccines in plant systems (including the potato and the tomato) – raising the possibility of "biopharming" (see also Chapter 9) as a potentially affordable and low maintenance production system compared to the relatively high cost, high maintenance, good manufacturing practice (GMP) production facilities that are currently needed.[6]

In addition, there is growing use of vaccine-based technology against diseases that have not been traditionally targeted by vaccines. These include growing interest in, and availability of, cancer vaccines and vaccines against autoimmune diseases.

Box 7.4   Major Approaches to Vaccine Development

The repertoire of strategies for vaccine development available to vaccine players today include:

- Live attenuated vaccines
- Inactivated (killed) vaccines
- Vector-borne vaccines
- Sub-unit vaccines
- DNA vaccines
- Mixed formulation vaccines using combinations of the above approaches

---

[6] Professor Charles Arntzen, Arizona Biodesign Institute, US, 2003.

The vaccinology arena is experiencing a renaissance internationally and in the Asia-Pacific region. In addition to long-standing capabilities in countries like China, India, Korea, and Indonesia, new entrants like Malaysia, Singapore, Taiwan, and Thailand are likely to play an increasingly important role in both public and private sector driven investment, product development, and manufacturing. The sector clearly has a bright future and is likely to see substantial growth in new product development and value creation in the coming decades.

Opportunities for Production of Biologicals and Vaccines

There has been growing international interest in the development of new vaccines and biologicals. This has led to increasing concern regarding potential lack of sufficient production capacity for such biopharmaceuticals – and has fueled a perceived opportunity for establishing contract manufacturing facilities for recombinant proteins, for monoclonal antibodies, and for vaccines. At the same time, several major pharma and biotech companies with products in the pipeline are also in the process of building new manufacturing plants.

There are currently over 300 biological drugs and vaccines at various stages of development.

In general, the quantities of recombinant proteins needed to meet global demand are relatively small – between three and ten kilograms would generally be sufficient to meet annual world demand for many recombinant proteins (including erythropoetin, currently the biggest biopharmaceutical seller with global sales exceeding US$7.5 billion in 2002). It is anticipated that substantially larger quantums of monoclonal antibodies and vaccines will be needed (in volume terms), and growing emphasis is being placed on such products.

There is general consensus among leading authorities today that there is currently a dearth of quality monoclonal production facilities in the US and Europe, as well as in Asia. Additionally, there is a clear need for production facilities to support the production of vaccines requiring special containment facilities or those that may be needed in emergency situations – for example, pandemic influenza vaccines, and facilities for manufacturing vaccines against future outbreaks of new and emerging diseases of concern, such as SARS.

Many biological products are expected to come off patent in the near future – a reality that looks set to create substantial value and opportunities for Asia's biogeneric manufacturers with low-cost bases and high economies of scale (especially those in China and India). There is, therefore, growing interest among leading manufacturers in developed countries and players with core platform technologies to identify strategic alliance and joint venture possibilities with Asian vaccine players. There is also strong interest among prospective investors in setting up vaccine and biologicals production capabilities and facilities in the region.

Care must be taken to avoid foibles akin to real estate market cycles in relation to biologicals manufacturing – careful attention must be placed on tracking needs and responding to them without over-building in response to perceived demand. Otherwise, manufacturers risk finding themselves in a situation of over-capacity when demand either does not meet projections, or when regulatory failure or delays in testing and approval of candidate products result in a need to consider other uses for purpose-built facilities.

BioEnterprise Asia's assessment is that we may already be heading into an over-capacity situation in Asia, and globally, for the manufacture of biogenerics (and recombinant proteins that are expected to come off patent in the near future) fairly recently. A price war, as happened – given the number of facilities being established, each planning to manufacture essentially the same product range in India when Shantha Biotechnics and Bharat Biotech competed with each other to drive down the price of Hepatitis B vaccine, seems inevitable. While this will clearly benefit the consumer by making these biopharmaceuticals very affordable, manufacturers may find themselves struggling to achieve financial sustainability.

Biomedical Outsourcing Opportunities

There is an increasing trend among pharmaceutical and biotech players to outsource non-core aspects of their operations (see also Box 7.5) so that they can focus on building their core value proposition – especially in relation to product development, IP generation and management, and building brand equity. The ultimate expression of this move toward outsourcing is the "virtually integrated life science company".

Box 7.5   Commonly Outsourced BioBusiness Activities
- R&D/clinical trials (for example, CROs)
- Manufacturing (CMOs)
- Marketing and distribution (CSOs)
- Packaging
- Patenting
- Reimbursement
- Human resources
- Continuing employee education
- Internet services

The outsource market is dominated by the big pharma players as its biggest spenders and customers – spending some $35 billion on outsourced R&D alone in 2001. Worldwide, biotech R&D currently accounts for about 40% of total R&D spending on drug design and development, and is growing about 14% annually, compared with about 10% annually for traditional pharmaceutical R&D. The top 10 clients are estimated to account for nearly 50% of the outsourcing market, and the top 40 clients for about 80%.

Contract Research Organizations

Contract research organizations (CROs) offer services in product development and related activities to make the drug development process more efficient as they are often able to perform specialized services faster and cheaper than their client. Their core business is typically the design, monitoring, and management of clinical trials conducted on behalf of pharmaceutical and biotechnology clients. Some two-thirds of the pharmaceutical industry's R&D spending currently goes toward clinical trials, with CROs accounting for some 30% of outsourced clinical trial research. Other players involved in conducting and managing clinical trials include academic and research institutions, hospitals, and clinical diagnostic laboratories.

The CRO sector is expected to continue to grow as companies involved in drug design and development focus on efficiency and reducing fixed costs. Revenues in the sector have been increasing at about 20% annually, and are anticipated to grow at similar levels for the next five to ten years, especially in Asia, with increasing globalization of research and clinical trials.

The CRO sector is highly fragmented. It varies from small, specialized, local service providers to several large fully integrated players with global operations and the ability to manage complex clinical trials simultaneously in several countries. The industry has been experiencing consolidation recently with the acquisition of smaller firms by larger full-service companies. CROs are also increasingly interested in forming alliances – with firms offering similar services in different parts of the world to expand their geographical reach, as well as with client biotech and pharma companies.

Contract Manufacturing Organizations (CMOs)

Most biotech companies have the facilities and in-house expertise to produce small amounts (usually milligrams or grams) of biopharmaceuticals for pre-clinical research. As product development proceeds to clinical trials and commercial production, they typically need to produce larger quantities (kilograms or more) under good manufacturing practice (GMP) conditions.

The cost of building GMP facilities can be US$25 to $50 million or higher. Many biotech companies, faced with the prospect that new products might not obtain market approval,[7] choose not to finance their own purpose-built facility, but prefer to outsource production to contract manufacturer partners (see also Box 7.6).

Box 7.6   Some Driving Forces for Outsource Manufacturing of Pharmaceutical and Biotech Products

These include:
- Need for flexibility in innovation versus full in-house integration
- Experienced alternatives to in-house manufacturing are available at CMOs
- Favorable regulatory environment for out-sourcing
- Company chooses to focus on core competencies
- Access to world-class capabilities in out-source partners
- Enables acceleration of time to market (no need to build new infrastructure)
- Allows freeing of resources for other purposes
- Reduces operating costs for company by reducing overheads for production team

---

The contract manufacturing industry can be divided into several segments including R&D, fermentation or culturing of cells, cell banking, product isolation and purification, stabilization, analytical testing, and packaging/filling. Process development and regulatory assistance services are also often provided by out-source partners.

CMOs are increasingly offering more flexible multi-product and multi-user facilities. There is a growing trend toward equipment being standardized and designed as modular units. Also, advances in computer software are enabling higher efficiency in production automation.

Asian players are likely to play an increasingly important role in the CMO sector. Korea, Singapore, and Taiwan have strong plans to establish and offer specialty CMO capabilities. It is anticipated, given their very low cost base, access to large markets, and growing recognition and respect for intellectual property rights, that leading players in China and India will play increasingly

---

[7] Success rates for biopharmaceuticals are typically higher than those for small molecule drugs – there has historically been about a 1 in 3 or higher chance that any biopharmaceutical product will make it through the clinical trial process to market (this compares with about a 1 in 5 chance for small molecule drugs).

important contract manufacturing roles – especially for both small molecule and biological generic products.

Bio-IT and Computational Biology

Bio-IT and computational biology enable business and scientific advances in the BioBusiness arena. Bio-IT provides the necessary and essential tools to create, organize, analyze, store, retrieve, and share genomic, proteomic, chemical, and clinical data in the life sciences.

The continued development of IT systems will undoubtedly benefit the life science industry – which in turn creates software, hardware, services, and network development opportunities for IT companies. It is estimated that by 2006, storage will represent the single largest element of bio-IT spending. There will clearly also be substantial demand for high performance computing systems providing for better knowledge and database management; integrated data analysis; the application of virtual reality tools for molecular modeling and simulations; software and capabilities for systems biology; and computational algorithms, data-mining capabilities, and analysis tools for integrating genomic research with clinical data.

Given cost advantages, Asia-Pacific companies and institutions are expected to play an increasingly important role in helping international partners meet custom bio-IT software and tools development as well as out-source service support needs for leading edge technology players in the region and internationally. Building on relationships and capabilities established during the information technology and dot.com boom, players in India (especially in Bangalore and Hyderabad) have already begun to support the needs of partners and clients throughout the world. At the same time, there is growing bio-IT competence and capabilities in China, Korea, Singapore, and Taiwan – and burgeoning interest in building such capabilities in Malaysia and Thailand.

Conclusion

Growing expertise and capabilities promise to place Asia at the forefront of regional and international research and development efforts in the biomedical sciences (including drug development, diagnostics, and the development of new tools for Bio-IT), process technology development, and clinical testing efforts.

Players in Asia are also gearing up to provide contract manufacturing and related outsourcing facilities, services, and capabilities. Asia is likely to play an increasingly important role as a manufacturing base for both small molecule drugs as well as biopharmaceuticals, and as a contract research base for the conduct of world-class clinical trials at an affordable price.

Key Points

1. Advances in biotech-based drug design and development technology in the post-genome era promise to lead to increased success and efficiency, as well as lower development cost, for new drugs. The increasing availability of novel technologies developed by biotech players is helping to drive collaboration and strategic alliances between big pharma and biotech players internationally and in the region.
2. The Asia-Pacific region promises to be a major growth market for diagnostics over the next several decades. Also, a growing base of world-class diagnostic companies in the region is working to develop innovative and promising new diagnostic products and technologies.
3. The biopharmaceuticals sector is generating growing interest in the development, testing, and manufacturing of vaccines, recombinant protein drugs, and monoclonal antibodies.
4. New opportunities are also being created in the outsourcing sector – especially in relation to contract research and contract manufacturing services. Asia-Pacific players stand to capture a significant piece of the out-sourcing pie.

Chapter 8
Agribiology

Discovery is seeing what everybody else has seen, and thinking what nobody else has thought.

Albert Szent-Gyorgi

Summary

Asia is still largely agricultural in economy and employment. Unfortunately, the bulk of agricultural BioBusiness in the region tends to be commodity-based and low value-added. The application of new tools and biotechnologies promises to transform relatively low value-added "Valley" opportunities in agriculture to "Summit" opportunities. The agribiology and agribiotechnology sector is expected to see substantial growth and exciting new developments in response to the need for increased food supply, as well as growing market interest and demand for quality, premium agricultural products. There also exists substantial scope and potential for plant- and animal-based production of highly valued and premium molecules of biological origin that could entirely revolutionize agriculture and the value and benefit that farmers[1] can generate over the coming decades – including vaccines, recombinant biopharmaceuticals, antibiotics, biofuels, biofibers and other new biomaterials.

Asia-Pacific economies would do well to invest in agribiological innovation and providing farmers with the knowledge and skills base to derive maximum value from new opportunities and developments. At the same time, there is clear need to put in place the necessary safeguards to maximize public safety and minimize the potential for environmental damage that could potentially arise from increased availability and use of innovative new developments and applications in agribiotechnology (including genetically modified organisms).

---

[1] Reviewer Chew Hong suggests that it may be more appropriate to describe the educated farmers of the future envisioned here, with specialized knowledge and skills across a wide range of disciplinary areas, as "farmists."

117

Background

The world's population today exceeds 6.5 billion people, and it continues to grow at about 1.5% annually, on average. It is anticipated that global population will stabilize at just under 10 billion people by 2050. Despite an expected population growth exceeding 50% over the next 50 years, we are fast reaching saturation in terms of arable land that can be used for cultivation. In fact, we are faced with the prospect of shrinking land for agriculture because of degradation of existing croplands due to soil erosion and reduced soil fertility arising from growing salinity (see also Box 8.1). We will, therefore, need to be able to feed more people on less land. We will undoubtedly need to invest in technology and innovation to increase yields and productivity in order to respond to growing population pressure on arable land.

Box 8.1 Facts About Agriculture and the Unmet Need for Food (Especially in Asia)

- An estimated 800 million people in the world today do not have enough to eat.
- In 1960, the world still had 0.44 hectares of arable land per person; today the figure is about 0.22 hectares per person, and by 2050 it is expected to drop to 0.15 hectares.
- As much as 90% or more of the world's grain tends to be consumed in the country where it is produced – the rest is exported for trade.
- Developing countries, especially in Asia, produce and consume more than 95% of global rice output. The demand for rice in these countries is expected to rise from about 350 million tons in 2000 to double that amount by 2025.
- Vitamin A deficiency is the cause of health problems for more than 100 million children. Transgenes could provide provitamin A with the rice diet.
- Insects cause a loss of at least 26 million tons of rice per year. The genetic transfer of proteins with insecticidal properties could mean environmentally friendly insect control without the need to resort to chemical insecticides that are hazardous to the farmer as well as to other plants and animals in the environment.
- Viral diseases devastate 10 million tons of rice per year. Transgenes derived from the *Tungro* virus genome allow the plant to develop defence systems. Bacterial diseases cause comparable losses – transgenes with antibacterial properties are the basis for in-built resistance.

- Fungal diseases destroy 50 million metric tons of rice per year. Varieties resistant to fungi could potentially be developed through the genetic transfer of proteins with anti-fungal properties.
- Iron deficiency in the diet is a health problem for more than one billion women and children; transgenes can potentially supply sufficient iron in the diet.
- By 2002, some 145 million acres around the world had already been planted with transgenic crops. For the first time in 2002, more than 50% of the world's population lived in countries where transgenic crops have been approved and grown.

Source: Food and Agriculture Organization, 2002 and ISAAA, 2003.

New developments in technology arising from our growing understanding of biology and its implications for increasing crop yields, and a focus on growing our food supply more economically and efficiently, have kept Malthusian predictions of doom at bay for over 200 years (see also Box 5.1, pg 63).

Asia did find itself in particularly challenging circumstances during the 1950s and 1960s when the region experienced rapid population growth that was not initially matched by increases in agricultural productivity – raising the specter of global overcrowding and mass famine (often described as the "population explosion"), and worries that the Malthusian predictions of doom would likely be fulfilled.

Investment in new technologies for rice and other staple crop cultivation through strategic investment in technology development by international players like the Ford and the Rockefeller Foundations helped to establish major new international resources such as the International Rice Research Institute (IRRI) in Los Banõs, the Philippines. Work at such institutions, operating in collaboration with scientists in countries throughout Asia and internationally, led to the development of new strains of rice and other crops that increased yields and were better adapted to different farming conditions, allowing new areas to be brought under cultivation.

The introduction of specially bred rice and other species of crop and commercially important plants helped fuel the so-called Green Revolution that enabled food production to keep ahead of growing food needs, prevented catastrophic famines and food shortages, and brought increased wealth and economic well-being in those regions that had introduced new agricultural technologies early.[2]

---

[2] Several international initiatives including the Consultative Group on International Agricultural Research (CGIAR) and the International Service for the Acquisition of Agri-biotech Applications (ISAAA) have made substantial contributions to agri-technology and agribiotechnology development in Asia and internationally.

This chapter will briefly review the following areas:

- Agriculture in Asia: The challenge
- The promise of agribiology and agribiotechnology
  - Potential biotech benefits
  - Potential biotech risks
  - The need for responsible and proactive action
- Capturing the value and potential of innovative agribiology and agribiotechnology
  - Enabling developing countries to benefit from new technologies and capabilities
  - Preparing farmers for the future
  - Organic foods: Back to basics
  - Biopharming and other innovations

Agriculture in Asia: The Challenge

The majority of countries in the Asia-Pacific region are still primarily agricultural – with Indonesia, the Philippines, Thailand, and all other emerging Asian countries, as well as China and India, each having 40% or more of their workers operating primarily in agriculture (see Figure 3.3, pg 43). Because farmers have traditionally been confronted with ever-shrinking land as landholdings are divided amongst surviving children with each successive generation, agricultural work in most of Asia has not provided sufficient income for farm workers to escape from the poverty trap. The region is rapidly urbanizing with more and more of the region's workers finding work in the manufacturing or service industries (either permanently, or as seasonal migrant workers).[3]

At the same time, there is substantial under-employment among the poor in many developing countries in that there are insufficient jobs to meet the needs of burgeoning populations. Unemployment rates of 40% or higher are not uncommon in some communities.

Individuals, families, and small and medium enterprises (SMEs) engaged in agriculture and the manufacture of processed foods and industrial products often have substantial difficulty getting their products to market. At the same time, families living in poverty often try to supplement their incomes through

---

[3] 2002/2003 marks an important milestone in the dynamics of rural/urban migration – for the first time in the history of humankind, 50% or more of the world's population now lives in urban environments. While Asia is still predominantly rural, the trend is clearly for people to move from rural to urban environments. It is estimated that Asia will have 50% of its population living in urban environments by 2007/2008.

making handicrafts. However, a situation often arises that buyers cannot be found locally for their handicrafts or that everyone makes the same handicraft product – with consequent drastic reduction in the ability of individuals to earn a living.

The Promise of Agribiology and Agribiotechnology

The application of new tools and technologies, and the identification of high value-added agricultural produce in response to market interest and demand, promise to transform agriculture in the region and internationally over the next several decades (see Table 8.1).

There were already about 100 million acres of genetically modified and transgenic crops grown globally by 1999 representing a jump of almost 50% from 1998 figures (the number had risen to over 145 million by 2002, see Box 8.1). The market in genetically modified crops reached $3 billion by 1999 and is projected to exceed $25 billion by 2010.

Over 70 varieties of biotech-derived crops have been approved for cultivation in North America alone, and many more are being assessed for possible cultivation in countries around the world. As noted in Box 8.1, 2002 marked a threshold year in that biotech crops were approved and grown in countries holding more than 50% of the world's population.[4] The most common genetically modified crops currently grown are canola, cotton, soybean, corn, sugar beet, and papaya. The most common traits introduced into genetically modified crops so far are pest resistance and herbicide tolerance. At the same time, selective breeding tends to focus on drought-resistant, faster growing and higher yielding crops. Combining classical with modern biotechnology has the potential to contribute to substantial value creation in terms of crops that will yield substantially greater output for less input; are environmentally more friendly (requiring reduced or no pesticides or tillage); and are more beneficial to consumers in terms of being more nutritious and having a longer shelf-life.

While the Green Revolution of the 1960s and 1970s was fueled by classical rather than molecular techniques in biotechnology, recent advances in biotechnology offer powerful tools for the sustainable development of agriculture, fisheries, and forestry, as well as the food BioBusiness industry

---

[4] It is estimated that nearly 6 million farmers in 16 countries grew genetically modified crops in 2002. Countries in the Asia-Pacific where genetically modified crops were grown in 2002 include Australia (since 1996), China (since 1997), Indonesia (since 2001), and India (since 2002). In all, it is estimated that some 27% of genetically modified crops worldwide were grown in developing countries. Source: ISAAA, 2002.

sectors (Table 8.1). When appropriately integrated with advances in engineering and other agriculture-related technologies, biotechnology can be of significant assistance in helping us meet the agricultural and food needs of an expanding and increasingly urbanized population in the face of limited, and shrinking, agricultural land resources.

Table 8.1   Some Applications of Modern Biotechnology in Agriculture and Fisheries

Subsector	Applications
Crop production	*Diagnostics.* To diagnose plant pests and pathogens, contaminants, and quality traits *Micropropagation techniques or tissue culture.* To multiply disease-free planting materials on a large-scale *Development of transgenic crops.* To develop commercially new genetically modified crop varieties *Modern plant breeding.* To develop superior plant varieties rapidly and more precisely *Marker-assisted selection.* To use genetic markers, maps, and genomic information in breeding for high yielding, disease- and pest-resistant varieties *Biodiversity characterizing.* Conserving and using biodiversity
Forestry	*Gene-mapping.* To accelerate tree breeding *Macropropagation.* Rapid vegetative propagation by means of cuttings from large plantation of pines and other trees *Micropropagation by tissue culture.* Large-scale multiplication of genetically superior plantlets *DNA fingerprinting.* To differentiate species, strains, and cultivars accurately *Wood security.* The selection of genetically superior trees for breeding purposes
Livestock production	*Livestock improvement.* To speed up the reproduction process in animals, allowing more generations to be produced *Transgenic livestock.* Development of transgenic lines in poultry and other animals which are faster growing or provide leaner, healthier meat *Livestock health.* Application of diagnostics for the control of major diseases of livestock *Vaccine development.* Development of vaccines for the control of epidemic viral diseases of livestock
Fisheries	*Transgenic fish.* Being explored for possible commercial use *Use of molecular markers in biodiversity.* Research, genome mapping, and trait selection in fish and other aquatic organisms

Source: ADB Paper on "Agricultural Biotechnology, Poverty Reduction and Food Security", 2002.

Potential Biotech Benefits

New tools and approaches in agribiology and agribiotechnology have the potential to help increase production and productivity in agriculture, forestry, and fisheries (Table 8.1). They could lead to higher yields on marginal lands in countries that today cannot grow enough food to feed their people. Rice, for example, has been genetically engineered to contain pro-vitamin A (beta carotene) and iron, which could improve the health of many low-income communities (see also Box 8.1).

Other biotechnological advances have the potential to improve food quality and consistency. Tissue culture-related propagation techniques have produced plants that are increasing crop yields by providing farmers with mass produced and healthier planting material. Biomarker-assisted selection and DNA fingerprinting allow faster and better targeted development of improved genotypes than was hitherto possible. These approaches also provide new research methods that can assist in the conservation and characterization of biodiversity. The new techniques are expected to contribute substantially to enabling scientists to increase the efficiency of selective breeding for such traits as the need for greater drought resistance and improved root systems for crops, or leaner meats in animals.

At the same time, application of biotechnology and selective breeding techniques to produce crops that are more disease resistant means reduced dependency and need for chemical insecticides and herbicides that can be toxic and hazardous to farmers, their children, their animals, and to the environment – especially when used in excessive amounts or not properly applied.

Potential Biotech Risks

While there is little controversy regarding many aspects of biotechnology and its application, genetically modified organisms have become the target of a very intense and often emotionally charged debate, especially in Europe (see also Box 12.3, pg 193, and Table 12.1, pg 196).

The idea of manipulating the genes of the food we eat continues to meet resistance by consumers, especially in Europe, who tend to shy away from genetically modified food (sometimes unflatteringly described as "Frankenfoods") – even though the reality is that modern approaches to biotechnology are little different from traditional approaches for selective breeding and cross-breeding of species that have been used for hundreds of years.

Even leading players who put together ambitious plans to operate as fully integrated life science companies with interests across the life science arena (from pharmaceuticals to agriculture to biomaterials, for example) have been forced to distance themselves from genetically modified foods in the face of a massive emotive onslaught by some environmental and consumer groups in the late 1990s and early 2000s. For example, Novartis and AstraZeneca had to spin off their agrichemicals units (as Syngenta) when they merged so that the new company could be seen to focus on drugs. Similarly, Pharmacia felt the need to give up its majority stake in Monsanto in late 2002 before being acquired by Pfizer in 2003.

Potential risks and concerns with genetically modified organisms generally fall into two basic categories: possible effects on human and animal health, and potential environmental consequences.

There is clearly a need for caution to reduce or eliminate any likelihood of mistakenly transferring toxins or carcinogenic factors from one life form to another; of creating new toxins; or of transferring allergenic components, for example, from one species to another which could result in unexpected allergic reactions. Potential risks to the environment include the possibility of "out-crossing," which could lead, for example, to the development of more aggressive weeds or wild relatives with increased resistance to diseases or environmental stresses – hence, upsetting the ecosystem balance. There is also concern that biodiversity might possibly be lost as a result of the displacement of traditional crop varieties by a small number of genetically modified crop varieties.

The Need for Responsible and Proactive Action

There is need for a cautious case-by-case approach to addressing legitimate concerns for the biosafety of each novel crop or animal species, product, or process prior to its release into local ecosystems in each economy.[5] The possible effects of introducing new varieties of plants and animals on biodiversity, the environment, and food safety need to be evaluated. The extent to which the benefits of any new species, product, or process outweigh its risks should be

---

[5] Despite sometimes alarmist perspectives expressed by eco-activists regarding modern biotechnology, the fact is that humankind has historically (without any help from biotechnology) wrought massive ecological disasters, damage to the environment, and loss of biodiversity through mindless destruction of habitats (see also Chapter 9). Responsible use of new techniques and biotech-based approaches can potentially do much to reverse the damage that our forebears have unsustainably caused, while providing developing country farmers with the prospect of earning sustainable livelihoods, and benefiting consumers through the production of more nutritious produce.

properly assessed. The evaluation process should also take into consideration the experience gained by other national regulatory authorities in relation to clearing and monitoring of the safety and environmental implications of such products, if any. Careful monitoring of the post-release effects of genetically modified organisms and products containing such organisms is also essential to ensure the continued safety and protection of human beings, animals, plants, and the environment.

Capturing the Value and Potential of Innovative Agribiology and Agribiotechnology

Enabling Developing Countries to Benefit from New Technologies and Capabilities

Current investment in biotech research tends to be concentrated in the private sector and oriented toward agriculture in higher-income countries where there is purchasing power for its products. Recognizing the potential contribution of biotechnologies for increasing food supply and overcoming food insecurity and vulnerability, there is growing consensus that efforts should be made to ensure that developing countries, in general, and resource-poor farmers, in particular, benefit more from biotechnological research while continuing to have access to a diversity of sources of genetic material (see also Table 8.1).

International agencies, such as the Food and Agriculture Organization (FAO), are working to address this need through encouraging increased public funding and promoting dialog between the public and private sectors. Working collectively, countries are developing a "Code of Conduct on Biotechnology" aimed at maximizing the benefits of modern biotechnologies and minimizing the risks (see also Table 12.3, pg 207). The proposed code is likely to be based on scientific considerations and to take into account the environmental, socio-economic and ethical implications of biotechnology.

The Codex Alimentarius Commission was created in 1963 by FAO and the World Health Organization (WHO) to develop food standards, guidelines and related texts such as codes of practice under the Joint FAO/WHO Food Standards Programme. Among other activities, the Codex Alimentarius Commission has established an ad hoc inter-governmental "Task Force on Foods Derived from Biotechnologies," which works through government-designated experts to develop standards, guidelines or recommendations, as appropriate, for foods derived from biotechnologies or traits introduced into foods by biotechnological methods. The Codex Alimentarius Commission is also considering the labeling of foods derived from biotechnologies to allow the consumer to make an informed choice.

Preparing Farmers for the Future

While the methods of selective breeding used before the advent of molecular biology and modern biotechnology were primitive compared to the tools and approaches available to us today, they were nevertheless effective. New developments in agribiology and agri-veterinary science promise to be even more effective and to bring wealth and benefit to those who invest in making things happen.

In addition to increasing agricultural yields and growing disease-resistant crops, there is real value to be obtained from identifying niche opportunities to provide the markets and consumers with produce that are in high market demand. Cultivating popular, traditionally hard-to-obtain products (such as mushrooms, specialty herbs, and nutraceuticals) can also be a real value driver. Other high potential opportunities include breeding highly desirable livestock, fish (including ornamental fish), prawns, and other produce in response to market demand.

It is important to remember, though, that trends and market demand will change with time, so farmers need to be innovative and responsive to changing market interest, and to develop new products and applications while holding on to popular, high-income products. There is also value to changing farming practices, especially in developing economies where generations of population growth have left farmers with smallholdings of agricultural land that are simply too small to be viable individually. By increasing the size of farm holdings, through agriculture and land reform and the establishment of farming cooperatives, for example, economies of scale can be built up, and mechanization and new technologies can be introduced that would be unfeasible and uneconomical on smallholdings.

A true win-win can be created by farmer cooperatives partnering directly with end-customers for herbs, nutraceuticals and other products of interest, and supplying these directly to the customer according to the quality and standards sought by the buyer. This helps to create long-term working relationships that could only be beneficial.

Yet another strategy for increasing value is to focus on moving up the value chain by processing agricultural output in response to customer and market demand and interest. Hence, if the consumer is interested in packaged dry fruit, for example, farmers might find it beneficial to set up a drying and packaging facility cooperatively and sell finished produce rather than raw materials. Similarly, there may be value in setting up juicing, bottling, and packaging facilities.

Additionally, establishing cooperative markets and supermarkets can also keep suppliers advised of market trends, and ensure that supplies of high value crops, vegetables, meats, and other produce of interest is made as efficiently as possible.

Farmers need guidance and assistance in raising the value and benefit of their produce. This means, among other things, access to technology, market and pricing intelligence. Real value can also be derived from establishing nurseries to mass produce high-yield varieties and making these available to farmers. Seed collection, technology investment in producing hardier and more disease-resistant organisms, research in plant genomics, maintaining seed and biodiversity banks, and so on, can all contribute to greater value and opportunity. Substantial value can also be derived in ensuring improved access to information and communication technology; education, training and skills enhancement; and improving time to market to reduce spoilage from insects and pests, as well as from disease.

A close working relationship with agricultural development authorities and research institutes can help ensure that farmers quickly gain access to improved seed and new technologies to build maximum value for their customer base. Proactive collaboration between farming communities, public sector agricultural officers, non-governmental organizations, and companies selling seed and farming supplies can make a substantial difference in helping agricultural communities to extract better returns and value from their output.

Organic Foods: Back to Basics

Even as we work to develop newer and better ways to increase agricultural yields based on innovative new technology inputs, farmers are finding growing market interest and demand from consumers for crops that are grown organically – these can command premiums of 50% or more.[6] Hence, changing consumer perceptions and preferences can lead to changing market opportunities for the astute entrepreneur and innovator.

Biopharming and Other Innovations

Biopharming refers to efforts to grow pharmaceuticals by using genetically modified plants and animals – with genetically modified maize or potatoes containing vaccines, for example, or cows and goats producing milk containing human proteins that can then be separated from the milk and used for therapeutic purposes.

---

[6] That farmers can now command premiums from moving back to traditional farming techniques by avoiding the use of chemicals or genetically-modified crops is an interesting example of a situation where previously "Valley" opportunities have now moved up the slopes toward becoming "Summit"-oriented opportunities because of changing consumer interest and demand (see also Figure 4.1, pg 48).

Some proponents of biopharming note that it is faster and less expensive to use plants than animals to serve as biological factories. Also, some argue that drugs made from mammalian cells and animal milk might potentially carry viruses that could pose risks to humans while plant viruses generally pose no known risk to people.

Nevertheless, growing interest in using plant and animal systems to express vaccines, biopharmaceuticals, and antibiotics, while still largely experimental, brings the prospect for substantially higher income for farmers. Similarly, the development and use of sustainable agriculture-based approaches for new sources of bioenergy and biofuel production (see Chapter 9) and the development and production of innovative new bioplastics and other biomaterials (see also Chapter 9) mean new and potentially more lucrative opportunities for farmers to grow and supply these highly valued resources.

Conclusion

New advances in agribiology and agribiotechnology are beginning to create substantial value and benefit to farmers and consumers in the form of higher agricultural yields, expansion of the range of environments in which crops and animals can be productively grown, reduced use of environmentally damaging pesticides and herbicides, more nutritious foods, and agricultural products having properties that are more responsive to modern industrial and consumer preferences and interests.

While it is entirely legitimate to be cautious in introducing genetically modified organisms into the environment and genetically modified foods into our food chain, there is clear need to balance such caution with recognizing that the potential impact of genetic modification and technological innovation in food and agriculture introduced by scientists often pales in comparison to nature's own experiments in evolution and genetic manipulation.

There is nothing fundamentally different between modern biotechnology approaches and classical approaches based, for example, on selective breeding or hybridization – other than the reality that modern approaches often allow more focused and pinpoint development of traits of interest in response to market opportunities and needs. Nevertheless, there is a need for vigilance to ensure that scientists and innovators work according to the highest ethical standards, and that societies throughout the world (through their appropriate regulatory authorities and concerned non-governmental organizations) work to ensure safety and environmental integrity before allowing the general release and use of genetically modified organisms and foods.

Future prospects for transforming the BioBusiness landscape in agriculture look very bright. Managed appropriately, there is every reason to believe that we will see tremendous progress over the next several decades in moving farmers up the slopes from the "Valley"-based survival-level subsistence farming approaches which are all too prevalent in the Asia-Pacific region today where farmers barely eke out a living (see also Figure 4.1, pg 48 and Table 3.1, pg 38). There is need for strategic investment in training and education of farmers so that they can themselves take the lead to introduce promising new technologies and capabilities, to push themselves up the value chain by investing in downstream processing capabilities, and thus have the ability to produce and market finished products in response to consumer interest and demand.

The Asia-Pacific region promises to be a major beneficiary of new advances in agribiology and agribiotechnology. Farmers throughout the region could see a substantial increase in economic returns from the responsible introduction and use of new technologies, and the provision of higher value products and services in response to changing market realities.

Key Points

1. Agribiotech promises to greatly accelerate economic growth and wealth generation for farming communities and societies that see its potential and choose to apply it wisely.

2. New developments in agribiology and agribiotech promise the potential of newer and better ways to feed the world's population, and to provide farmers with the knowledge and skills they need to substantially increase the value of agricultural output. This will only have its maximum impact through enlightened efforts by governments to achieve agricultural sector reform, and to ensure greater productivity while enabling the creation of newer and more viable options for farmers and farming communities.

3. The application of new technologies and approaches to agriculture will enable innovators and entrepreneurs to identify and create new product and service opportunities, as well as find newer and better ways to reach their markets.

4. Even as we work to introduce and expand the role of innovations and new technologies in agriculture to create products in response to market demand, we need to be ever vigilant about the need to protect the safety of consumers and safeguard the environment.

Chapter 9
Environmental and Industrial Life Sciences

Some see things that are, and ask why.
I dream of things that never were and ask why not.

Robert F. Kennedy

Summary

This chapter focuses on life science-based technologies to conserve and sustain the environment, as well as the application of new tools and approaches for biotech-based contributions to industrial development.

Significant progress has been made in the last decade in confronting environmental challenges in both developing and industrial nations. There has been marked progress in several countries in the form of reduced environmental pollution and improved resource conservation. Still, on the whole, the environment has continued to degrade during the past several decades, and significant environmental concerns and problems need to be addressed and resolved. This has sparked growing interest in finding alternative means of waste disposal and novel technologies to decontaminate polluted resources.

At the same time, new approaches to mining and innovative opportunities to develop and use new products and technologies, such as industrial enzymes and biomaterials, promise a true revolution in industrial application of biotechnology in its own right.

Environmental Life Sciences and BioBusiness

Sustainable development means different things to different people, but the most frequently quoted definition is from the report *Our Common Future* (also known as the Brundtland Report):

> *"Sustainable development is development that meets the needs of the present without compromising the ability of future generations to meet their own needs."*

Sustainable development focuses on improving the quality of life for all who share this biosphere without increasing the use of natural resources beyond the capacity of the environment to supply them indefinitely.

Many of our current processes and consumption patterns are fundamentally unsustainable – they consume excessive amounts of non-renewable energy resources, and often result in environmental contamination and even destruction. We have denatured soils, destroyed and polluted waterways, and depleted our fisheries. We are losing some 3,000 square meters of forest and 1,000 metric tons of topsoil every second; numerous species of flora and fauna are being wiped out (some estimates suggest as many as 25% of known species are at risk of being made extinct within the next several decades). Available arable lands shrink by an average of 20,000 hectares each year. Erosion alone has so far made nearly a billion hectares of soil unusable for agriculture. At the same time, we have played a key role in destroying natural habitats for other species as we cut or burnt down forests and replaced them with crops or plantations, and unthinkingly worked to destroy biodiversity.

Working to achieve sustainability requires appreciation that inaction and failure to act to change current practices have their consequences. We must find innovative ways to influence individual, institutional, and societal behavior, and to introduce new technologies and practices that are more sustainable and substantially less destructive.

Progress on developing the concepts of sustainable development has been rapid since the 1980s. In 1992, leaders at the Earth Summit in Rio built upon the framework of the Brundtland Report to create agreements and conventions on critical issues such as climate change, desertification, and deforestation. They also drafted a broad action strategy – Agenda 21 – as the workplan for dealing effectively with environment and development concerns for the coming decades.

Regional and sectoral sustainability plans were developed during the rest of the 1990s. A wide variety of groups – ranging from businesses to non-governmental organizations to municipal governments to international organizations such as the World Bank and the United Nations Industrial Development Organization (UNIDO) – have adopted the concept and given it their own particular interpretations. These initiatives have increased our understanding of what sustainable development means within many different contexts. Still, progress on implementing sustainable development plans has been slow.

Environmental Impact Assessment

Since the early 1980s, many countries, internationally as well as in the Asia-Pacific region, have required the conduct of environmental impact assessments (EIAs) for large-scale agricultural and industrial development projects.

An EIA is an analysis of the likely environmental consequences of a proposed human activity earliest possible stage in the development of the project, program, or policy. More than 70 developing countries have EIA legislation of some form, while others are in the process of planning or drafting new EIA legislations. EIAs have become regular tools for the initiation, implementation, and evaluation of major development and investment projects in many countries around the world.

This chapter will overview a range of areas of interest in relation to environmental and industrial BioBusiness. These include:

- Environmental BioBusiness
  - Waste management and environmental clean-up technology
  - Biofilms
  - Bioremediation
  - Plants and heavy metal tolerance: Phytoextraction
  - Biomass and biofuels
- Industrial life sciences and BioBusiness
  - Bioplastics and biomaterials
  - Biosurfactants
  - Industrial enzymes and biocatalysis
  - Biotech in mining

Environmental BioBusiness

Environmental biotechnology is the use of living organisms for a wide variety of environment-related applications.

Waste Management and Environmental Clean-up Technology

Hazardous waste treatment and pollution control are areas of growing importance and opportunity in BioBusiness, especially in the context of the Asia-Pacific region.[1]

Among other applications, naturally occurring microbes are being used to degrade hazardous wastes, such as polychlorobiphenyls (PCBs) to harmless

---

[1] Witness, for example, the heavily polluted *klongs* of Bangkok or the many polluted and smelly streams in Jakarta.

compounds. At the same time, new technologies are being developed that can be usefully applied for cleaning up polluted waterways, and for eliminating odor, decaying biological matter, and other harmful substances from such waterways.

Biofilms

Biofilms are composed of mixed microbial communities attached to an environmental surface. The micro-organisms in biofilms usually encase themselves in an extracellular polysaccharide or slime matrix. They may be found on any surface where sufficient moisture and nutrients are present.

Biofilms are also commonly associated with living organisms – tissue surfaces, such as teeth (plaque) and intestinal mucosa, rapidly develop a complex aggregation of micro-organisms enveloped in an extracellular polysaccharide matrix. Biofilms attached to the roots of some crops help cycle nutrients and can raise agricultural productivity.

Biofilms can also cause substantial industrial losses amounting to as much as US$500 billion annually – causing pipe-plugging, corrosion, and water contamination; being responsible for contamination and fouling of water-based industrial processes including water treatment, pulp, and paper production; and impacting the operation of cooling towers and air-conditioners – being associated, for example, with Legionnaires' disease.

Biofilms can be dangerous to our health – as in bacterial endocarditis. Similarly, they can cause problems with in-dwelling cathethers, medical implants and other medical devices.

Applications of biofilms include use in reactors to promote biofilm growth for biofiltration for treating environmental wastes including sewage, industrial waste, and contaminated groundwater. Biofilms can also be used to produce biochemicals for medicines, food additives, or chemical additives for cleaning products.

There is growing interest in studying the biology of biofilms, and to determine how to both encourage biofilm development in conditions where this proves beneficial as well as to inhibit biofilm development where this would be clinically or industrially damaging.

Bioremediation

Bioremediation refers to the process whereby biofilms or other living systems biotransform organic contaminants into less harmful forms.

In the US alone, the US Environmental Protection Agency (EPA) has estimated that the clean-up of toxic waste-covered lands could cost as much as US$1.7 trillion using conventional technologies such as toxic waste removal and incineration. The cost of environmental clean-up could be substantially reduced using bioremediation strategies.

Microbial remediation has been practiced routinely for decades by avid gardeners in the form of composting – allowing bacteria and fungi to break down kitchen and garden refuse into natural fertilizers. Now, microbes are being used to perform more compelling remediation tasks – for example, in helping to clean up toxic chemical spills.

Selected and specially grown microbes can help break down toxic chemicals and clean up contaminated areas. Studies have shown that chemotactic bacteria – those that can detect and respond to chemicals or pollutants in soil or groundwater – are naturally better at degrading toxic chemical mixtures than non-chemotactic species. Also, certain species of algae can be genetically modified to remove heavy metal including mercury, cadmium, and zinc from waterways, rivers, and lakes.

Phytoremediation is an innovative technology that utilizes the natural properties of plants in engineered systems to remediate hazardous waste sites. This exciting and rapidly developing technology uses green plants and associated life forms to remove, destroy, or detoxify environmental contaminants.

Depending on the contaminant environmental and the plant systems involved, the plant could take up the environmental contaminant and its enzymes metabolize it into harmless products, or it could just absorb the contaminant into its tissues which could then be collected. The plant's roots or associated microbes could also enzymatically degrade the contaminants into benign products. By sequestering the contaminants in the plants, phytostabilization enables less bio-availability of the contaminants to the environment and therefore less risk to health and well-being.

Bioremediation is an area of interest and focus that is likely to see substantial investment over the coming decades as we enlist plants and microbial systems to help us clean up contaminated environments and soils, and even return degraded lands to high levels of fertility and suitability for agriculture.

Plants and Heavy Metal Tolerance: Phytoextraction

The main idea of phytoextraction is to exploit the natural ability of some plants to accumulate elements of interest from the soil and to concentrate them in their tissues. Phytoextraction is especially useful in the context of specific metals – for example nickel, copper, cobalt, manganese, lead, zinc, and selenium.

Plants that can take up high amounts of metals such as zinc and nickel (the so-called "metal hyperaccumulators") have been studied at the molecular and genetic level. These plants are able to take up heavy metals from contaminated soils. Utilizing such plants as "mines" to extract the metals from the metal contaminant-laden soils is an exciting commercial prospect.

However, more often than not, metal hyperaccumulators are relatively slow growing and small plants. Consequently, the process of mining the metal from them remains a costly, inefficient process. The amount of biomass available for extraction tends to be too small to justify the cost and effort involved.

With the growing availability of successful plant biotechnology methods, one possible solution might be to engineer plants that combine the qualities of the hyperaccumulators with fast growth and high biomass. This entails a comprehensive understanding of the mechanisms and processes of heavy metal tolerance in plants, an increasingly promising area of research and development effort.

Biomass and Biofuels

The figures speak for themselves. Currently, some 15% of the world's population living in the more developed countries are estimated to consume close to 70% of the world's energy resources – while the remaining 85% have to make do with about 30%. On a per capita basis, this works out to every man, woman and child in the wealthier nations using nearly ten times more energy than people living in the poorer parts of the world. Modern economic development, industrial activities and lifestyles are highly energy-intensive – it is inevitable that poorer societies will need to consume more energy as they develop.

Asia's need for energy is growing at a faster pace today than that of any other region in the world. Energy consumption in developing parts of Asia is expected to grow at an annual rate of about 5% between 1995 and 2020. Already, the global environment is straining from the burning of fossil fuels, with related emissions of carbon dioxide (CO_2) into the atmosphere being generally thought to be a major factor contributing to global warming. The rise of Asian economies stands to increase the strain on global life support systems even further.

Biomass fuels can potentially help reduce environmental strain by reducing the depletion of fossil fuels while helping to lower atmospheric CO_2 levels when CO_2 is converted into biomass as it grows.

Biogas is generated when bacteria degrade biological material in the absence of oxygen (anaerobic digestion) to produce methane. Historical anecdotal evidence suggests that biogas was first used for heating bathwater in Assyria in the 10th century BC India has used biogas reactors in rural areas since the 1800s, and has a growing range of reactors using biological wastes and biomass for energy. The application of such technology and approaches has many benefits: biological waste can be used in the bioreactors – hence preventing pollution, enabling the generation of sustainable energy, and providing compost for agricultural lands and facilitating nutrient recovery.

Ethanol (ethyl alcohol) can be produced from grain, molasses, potatoes, biological wastes, or any material containing starch or other polysaccharides such as cellulose. Brazil was a pioneer in the use of ethanol as a fuel. Starting its National Alcohol Program in 1975, Brazil today consumes over 12 billion liters of alcohol for fuel. Brazil has been using hydrated alcohol (95% alcohol, 5% water) as a fuel for automobiles and other vehicles. The shift to hydrated alcohol has reduced the need to import expensive foreign petroleum by Brazil by about US$8 billion a year, and has rejuvenated the country's sugar cane industry and related bioreactor activities. Among other things, this has helped fuel job creation in rural areas of the country.

Gasohol (90% gasoline, 10% alcohol) is a partial biofuel that can be used in standard automobile engines, as can diesohol (15% alcohol, 85% diesel). E85 (85% ethanol, 15% gasoline) can be used in specially designed "flexible-fuel" vehicles. In an effort to promote sustainable energy consumption in the US, all cars manufactured since 1998 have been adapted to use E85 as a fuel.

Research and development efforts targeted at applying new life science insights and biotechnology tools for establishing newer and more efficient systems for renewable energy generation are clearly areas that offer tremendous promise. Such areas include: increasing sustainable biomass growth, improving fermentation and anaerobic respiration efficiency through identifying and developing more energy efficient organisms, and developing totally new systems for catalyzing these biological processes.

It is not inconceivable that we may one day develop efficient home bioreactors for converting household biological wastes into energy for powering our household appliances.

Industrial Life Sciences and BioBusiness

Industrial biotechnology is being applied in a variety of industrial contexts (see Box 9.1) to reduce the environmental impact of manufacturing, and to make the manufacturing process more efficient and cost-effective in such industries as textiles, paper and pulp, and specialty chemicals. Biotechnology looks set to play a major role in helping to enable industrial sustainability,

Box 9.1   Some Industries that Stand to Benefit from Biotechnology-based Tools

Chemical industry. Using biocatalysts to produce novel compounds, reduce waste byproducts, and improve chemical purity

Plastics industry. To decrease dependency on petroleum for plastic production by making bioplastics from corn, soy bean, and other sources

Paper industry. To improve manufacturing processes including the use of enzymes to lower toxic byproducts from pulp processes

Textiles industry. To lessen toxic byproducts of fabric dying and finishing processes. Fabric detergents are becoming more effective with the addition of enzymes to their active ingredients

Food industry. For improving baking processes, fermentation-derived preservatives and analysis of techniques for food safety

Waste management industry. To clean up biological wastes and reduce pollution of waterways

Energy industry. To generate biogas and other biofuels from anaerobic respiration of biomass

Mining industry. For bioleaching and extraction of precious metals from ore

Adapted from BIO, 2002.

employing processes that require less material and energy inputs, maximize renewable resources and biodegradable substances as inputs, minimize the generation of pollutants and harmful waste during product manufacture and use, and produce recyclable and biodegradable products.

Manufacturing processes using biotechnology-based biocatalysts, solvents, and surfactants are less polluting and can be carried out at substantially lower temperatures than comparable chemical processes, hence reducing energy dependency.

Microbes and enzymes can be used to convert biomass waste products into feedstock, biodegradable plastics, industrial solvents, and specialty lubricants. Specialty products – such as industrial enzymes, fragrances and flavors – are increasingly being used based on biotechnology processes. Biotechnological innovation can contribute to helping remove sulphur from fossil fuels – hence reducing their environmental impact as a result of sulphur emission.

There is growing interest in bio-based products that combine expertise and technology from agriculture, forestry, the chemicals industry, genomics, fermentation technology, and biotechnology chemical and bioprocessing, and to create plastics, and composite materials from renewable resources.

The US Department of Energy, through its "Industries of the Future" initiative, is helping to fuel development of industrial biotechnology through the award of strategic grants and the development of a "roadmap for bioenergy." Asia-Pacific countries would do well to adopt similar strategies.

Bioplastics and Biomaterials

Biotechnology offers the potential of replacing petroleum-derived polymers with biological polymers from grain or agricultural biomass. Instead of conventional production processes using non-renewable petroleum, plastics can be made from biologically-derived polysaccharides (corn starch, cellulose, chitin) or whey from cheese-making, soy protein polyesters, triglycerides, collagen (gelatin), casein, keratin (silk, wool) – any material, in fact, that can be used to form resins and biopolymers. Most biologically derived plastics are essentially biodegradable. A variety of synthetic resins are also biodegradable – including polyvinyl esters, polylactic acid, polyalkylene esters, and polyanhydrides.

Cargill Dow opened a biorefinery in Nebraska in 2001 to convert sugars from corn into polylactic acid – a compostable biopolymer that can be used for packaging materials, clothing, and bedding materials. Industrial scientists have genetically modified plants and microbes to produce polyhydroxybutyrate, a feedstock for biodegradable plastics.

Nature also provides abundant biopolymers that could find new uses. For example, the genes for making spider silk have been incorporated into goats, making possible the manufacture of strong ropes and the weaving of new biofabrics – using spider silk protein extracted from goat's milk.

Biosurfactants

Surfactants are surface-active compounds capable of reducing surface tension at the interface between liquids – allowing oil-based liquids, for example, to mix or disperse readily as emulsions in water. Hence, surfactants are active components in many detergents and emulsifiers – finding use in a variety of household products, including soaps, shampoos, cosmetic products, and detergents; in industrial and environmental cleaning products; and in more specialized applications in research and the pharmaceutical industry. With such a wide range of applications, the surfactant industry was already a US$15 billion market by 2000.

Many of the surfactants currently on the market are either synthetic petroleum-based chemical surfactants, or are made from a mix of petroleum and vegetable oil-based components. The vast majority of available surfactants may be damaging to the environment, being essentially responsible for the scum that is often found in polluted waterways, and are typically non-biodegradable. This limits their applicability considerably.

Biosurfactants are ampiphilic molecules made from common carbohydrates and vegetable oil-based fatty acids. They have advantages over their chemical counterparts in biodegradability, effectiveness at extreme temperatures or pH, and in having lower toxicity. Biosurfactants are increasingly being considered as optimal food additives, a base for pharmaceutical and cosmetic formulations, or environmentally friendly cleaning agents. The demand for biosurfactants greatly exceeds existing supply capabilities – increased availability of such biosurfactants will inevitably lead to substantial expansion of the surfactant market with potential applications in agriculture, cosmetics, pharmaceuticals, detergents, personal care products, food processing, textile manufacturing, laundry supplies, metal treatment and processing, oil, paint, pulp and paper processing, and the environmental waste management and remediation industries, among others.

However, there have been limitations with existing production processes, prohibiting commercial success on a large scale. One concern is that traditional production processes for biosurfactants typically rely on the use of toxic solvents, residues of which reduce the possible application of these surfactants for human consumption, unless extensively purified. Purification, however, can make the end product prohibitively expensive for many applications.

An alternative approach is to use microbial fermentation or enzymatically catalyzed synthesis of biosurfactants. These are difficult to scale up to industrial quantities, hence, the end product again tends to be too expensive for many applications.

BioEnterprise Asia is working with technology partners who are developing new proprietary processes for using plants-based carbohydrates and oils (including palm oils, coconut oils, and other oils commonly produced by agriculturally focused Asia-Pacific countries) to custom-produce biosurfactants that are environmentally friendly and non-toxic, and can be readily produced to pharmaceutical grades of purity. These biosurfactants can be adapted for a range of applications, for which both surfactants and biosurfactants have traditionally been used, as well as for totally novel applications in the biomedical and environmental areas.

The future for biosurfactants, and the potential for Asia-Pacific players to tap into this exciting new technology area to transform commodity agricultural products to become "Summit" opportunities is very strong. Smart application of such technology will enable the development of high value-added biosurfactants and secondary finished products, services, and applications based on biosurfactants.

Industrial Enzymes and Biocatalysis

Enzymes are proteins that all living things produce to catalyze biologically important processes (including the digestion of food, the generation of energy, and reproduction). Biocatalysis is based on the development and use of enzymes to catalyze commercially important processes (see also Box 9.2). The market for industrial enzymes and biocatalysis is estimated to be about US$2 billion.

Microbes have adapted to live and thrive in every conceivable environment since life began. Life in unusual habitats is often associated with very specialized adaptation of microbes (sometimes called extremophiles), with the development of unique proteins and enzymes that can potentially be adapted to the relatively harsh conditions of temperature, pressure, and other parameters often found in industrial application.

It is estimated that less than 1% of micro-organisms in the world have been cultured and characterized. Through bioprospecting, scientists are discovering novel enzymes that function optimally at extreme acidity, salinity, temperature, or pressure conditions found in some manufacturing processes. Biotechnology tools, including protein engineering and directed protein evolution, are being used to modify the specificity of enzymes, improve catalytic

---

Box 9.2   Some Examples of Biocatalysts Used in Industrial and Commercial Processes

Carbohydrases (family of enzymes that break down carbohydrates) – used in detergents, industrial cleaners, pulp and paper, and ethanol fermentation
Cellulase (specialty carbohydrase that breaks down cellulose to component carbohydrates) – used in the production of animal feeds, and in bioenergy production
Chloroperoxidase – used in steroid synthesis
Nariniginase – used to debitter citrus peel
Lactase – used to eliminate lactose from dairy foods
Lysozyme – used for antibacterial and germicidal applications
Pepsin – used for cheese production
Peroxidase – used in laundry and wood pulp bleaches
Proteases – used in a variety of applications including protein processing, brewing, lens cleaners, leather and fur, and laundry and dishwashing detergents
Adapted from BIO, 2002.

properties, broaden conditions under which enzyme systems will function, and mass produce quantities of these important proteins for commercial application.

Biotechnology in Mining

The mining industry uses acid producing bacteria such as *Thiobacillus* species for solubilization of pyrite ores for recovery of metals – such processes are used in Australia and South Africa, for example, for gold recovery – replacing the traditional approach of ore roasting (and thus helping to reduce sulphur dioxide and greenhouse gas emission). The process, sometimes described as bioleaching, can also be applied to nickel and copper mining, and is part of a growing field of study based on applying molecular biology to solve mining challenges called *biohydrometallurgy*.

Conclusion

We have only just begun to seriously explore opportunities and challenges in environmental and industrial BioBusiness. The application of new tools of genomics, proteomics, and the tools of molecular biology and biotechnology are already beginning to make a significant impact in a variety of areas.

Asia has been in the midst of a massive growth and development spurt that has produced more than its fair share of environmental contamination and pollution from industrial processes. The application of new tools to solve environmental and industrial challenges in the Asia-Pacific region promises to bring substantial benefits and opportunities, and to fuel the development of new BioBusiness sectors.

Key Points

1. Investment in environmental and industrial biotechnology and BioBusiness is likely to bring very substantial returns on investment. Such investment can potentially contribute in large measure to converting garbage into valuable resources; cleaning up the environment; and identifying new species for wealth generation.
2. Substantial opportunities exist for the industrial application of life science and biotechnology products and technologies for use as industrial enzymes, biofuels, biomaterials, and in a range of industrial processes including mining.

3. We have only begun to start capturing the opportunity and potential of "Summit" environmental and industrial BioBusiness opportunities. This area of focus offers tremendous scope to fuel the growth and development of entirely new technologies, entrepreneurial opportunities, and even new industry sectors.

Chapter 10

A Quick Survey of Life Sciences in Asia: How Ready is Asia for the Revolution?

You will never stub your toe standing still.
The faster you go, the more chance there is of stubbing your toe,
but the more chance you have of getting somewhere.

Charles Kettering

Summary

Recognizing the potential of the life sciences and their likely future socio-economic impact, governments throughout Asia have invested heavily over the past few decades in life science education as well as in the development of R&D capabilities and infrastructure. A critical mass is now being reached with increasing emphasis being placed on strategies and opportunities for commercialization and the development of indigenous life science industries.

Introduction

BioBusiness and biotechnology are increasingly seeing interest and investment from angel investors, venture capitalists, and corporate investors in Asia and around the world. This interest has spilled over into scientists and technologists and a growing number of entrepreneurs and innovators seeking to start up life science ventures in the region. The life science and biotechnology arena is one where domain expertise and in-depth market knowledge and insight are prerequisites for success.

The global biotechnology industry has been characterized by periods of hype and over-promise when speculators have driven up share prices of listed stock beyond any basis in reality, only to be brought back down to earth when the promised cures for cancer or HIV fail to materialize in the short attention span windows that speculators tend to see through. This is not a sector or industry for speculators – true value is being created in biotechnology over the medium- to long-term. Short-term boom and bust cycles in the sector are typically the result of media and investor hype than of any fundamental change in technology or product prospects or value propositions.

The opportunity and potential for biotechnology to revolutionize the BioBusiness landscape is clear, but this will not happen overnight. In BioEnterprise-speak, many new ideas and approaches at the cutting edge of biotechnology research and development are still "Cloud" opportunities; the successful translation of some of these to become "Summit" opportunities will require several years, if not decades (see also Figure 4.1, pg 48). Some cutting-edge technologies, including several outlined in this book, have already come of age and are already legitimate "Summit" opportunities.

On the other hand, as outlined in Chapter 4, far too much of what we do today in BioBusiness, especially in developing countries in Asia (and Africa and Latin America) is at or near the "Valley" base as far as value-add is concerned – tremendous opportunity exists to apply cutting-edge knowledge and technologies to transform these into more "Summit"-oriented opportunities, and this can happen far more quickly than many realize (*the caveat being that one needs to know what to do and why, as well as how to do it!*). But again, this will not happen overnight.

The challenge and the opportunity is to use the right tools to solve the right problems, and thereby to create value-added solutions in response to real needs and market demand in our societies. From the Asia-Pacific perspective, it is crucial to examine how we can begin to apply and capitalize on recent developments in biotechnology to understand and solve problems of particular concern to the region (including, for example, biological waste management, and the cleaning up of polluted waterways – common concerns in many Asia-Pacific economies), and reap rich benefits in the realms of biomedical, agricultural, environmental, and industrial BioBusiness.

The Asia-Pacific International Molecular Biology Network (Asia-Pacific IMBN) (see Box 10.1) was established to promote molecular biology and biotechnology development in the region, and to facilitate the efforts of Asia-Pacific economies to capture the value proposition of new tool and technology development.

Asia-Pacific IMBN initiated an effort to survey the state-of-the-art in life sciences and biotechnology development in 2000, and to lay out a strategic roadmap to help countries in the region and beyond capture the value and

Box 10.1   About Asia-Pacific IMBN

Asia-Pacific IMBN was established in 1997 by the coming together of leading scientists and institutions in the Asia-Pacific region. The organization was founded in the belief that molecular biology and biotechnology can contribute greatly to the benefit of humankind, and that such benefit will accrue through close cooperation and collaboration amongst scientists and scientific institutions, supported by national and international agencies, and industry.

The Network provides a forum and mechanisms for such interaction through a range of activities including promoting collaborative research, the provision of training and skills enhancement opportunities, and the dissemination of information.

Asia-Pacific IMBN counts over 260 leading scientists from 15 participating economies among its members, and is supported by nine leading institutions including the Biotechnology Research Institute, Hong Kong University of Science and Technology (Hong Kong), Institute of Biochemistry, Academy Sinica (Chinese Taipei), Institute of Molecular Biology and Genetics (Korea), Institute of Molecular and Cell Biology (Singapore), Institute of Molecular Biosciences (Australia), Institute of Medical Science, University of Tokyo (Japan), Shanghai Institute of Biochemistry (China), Walter and Eliza Hall Institute (Australia), and the Weizmann Institute (Israel).

benefit that new developments bring. The author served to coordinate this effort on behalf of Asia-Pacific IMBN.

In general, we found that Asia-Pacific economies have invested well in life science knowledge and infrastructure development, and have the potential to be key players in the on-going life science and biotechnology revolution.

Many Asia-Pacific economies – including China, Taiwan, Hong Kong, Japan, Korea, Malaysia, Singapore, and Thailand – have identified the life sciences as a priority growth sector, and have invested substantially in life science education, research, and capability development since about 1980. Their efforts have paid off handsomely in terms of the establishment of a strong science and technology base as represented by a growing number of world-class scientists and centers of excellence. However, the intellectual property and know-how developed by these scientists and institutions have, thus far, had limited translation into commercially and socially relevant applications.

Asia-Pacific economies will need to be more proactive in strategically strengthening R&D capabilities (see also Figure 17.1, pg 262), facilitating innovative product and technology development (see also Figures 4.2, pg 54 and 4.3, pg 55), and encouraging more life science entrepreneurship, if they are to capture maximum value (see also Figure 10.1).

Fundamental Needs for Life Science and Biotechnology Development

As outlined in Chapter 5, there are five fundamental parameters that are central to successful and sustainable life science and biotechnology research and development. These include:

- Physical and scientific infrastructure
- A conducive regulatory/cultural environment
- A policy framework incentivizing life science and biotechnology research, innovation and entrepreneurship
- Strong human resource development programs
- The availability of adequate public and private sector funding support

Figure 10.1 The Asia-Pacific Market: Opportunities and Needs for BioBusiness

Environment
- ✓ Heavy regional investment in the life sciences
- ✓ Growing scientific base
- ✓ Expanding portfolio of intellectual property

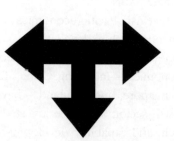

Hurdles/Challenges
- ✓ Limited translation of academic research and technology development into commercial application
- ✓ Lack of strategic and business management expertise in life sciences
- ✓ Lack of "smart money" funding for technology validation, productization, and business case validation

Opportunities and Needs
- ✓ Identifying and nurturing development of high potential know-how and technologies
- ✓ Providing commercial acumen and marketplace orientation
- ✓ Critical business and entrepreneurship development support
- ✓ Dedicated seed financial support for promising enterprises
- ✓ Establishing sustainable life science start-up companies

© *BioEnterprise Asia, 2002.*

As shown in Figure 10.2, the Asia-Pacific region, as a whole, was considered by participants in the Asia-Pacific IMBN survey to have an intermediate level of achievement for all parameters considered. The US and Europe were deemed to have better developed science and technology infrastructure, a more conducive cultural/regulatory environment for scientific innovation and development, better defined government policies in support of life sciences and technologies, more skilled human resources, and superior access to financial and other resources for science and technology development and commercialization. On the other hand, the Asia-Pacific region was perceived to be marginally ahead of Latin America in all parameters except perhaps human resource development, and to be substantially more advanced in all five parameters than the African region as a whole.

Comparing strengths and capabilities for each of the fundamental parameters measured among the various countries in Asia (see Table 10.1), it was generally felt that Japan was the clear leader among the Asia-Pacific

Figure 10.2   Infrastructure for Science in Various Regions of the World: Opinion Survey Conducted by Asia-Pacific IMBN Secretariat (August–December 1999)

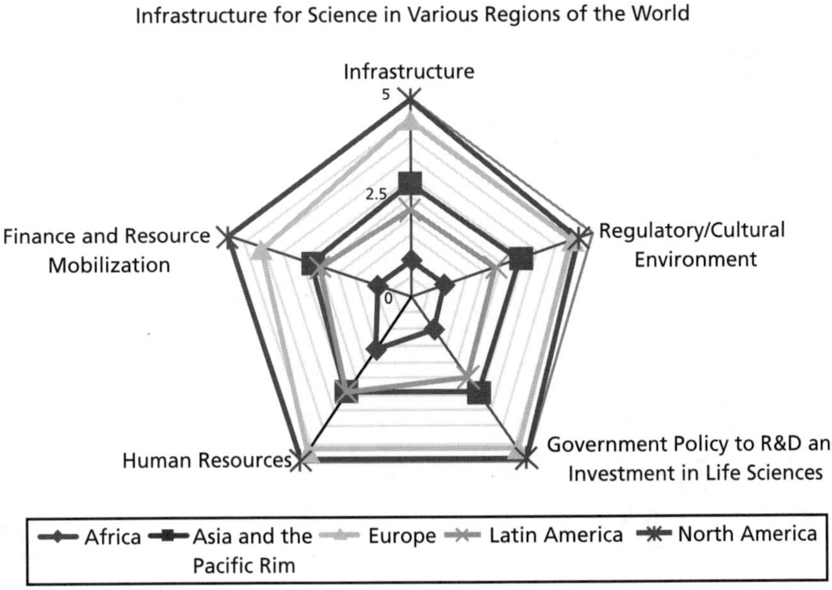

Infrastructure for Science in Various Regions of the World

Note: Twenty leading experts from around the region were invited to share their perception of life science research and development in the Asia-Pacific region compared to that in other regions. The results are based on inputs from 12 of these experts: Australia (3), Chinese Taipei (1), Japan (3), Korea (1), Philippines (3), Singapore (1).
Source: Asia-Pacific IMBN, 2001.

Table 10.1 Survey Results: Perceived Strengths and Capabilities in Life Sciences and Biotechnology for Selected Asia-Pacific Economies

	Infrastructure development		Regulatory and cultural environment	Government policy	Human resource	Finance/Resource mobilization		Overall ranking
	Physical infrastructure	Science infrastructure				Public funding	Private funding	
Japan	1	1	1	1	1	1	1	1
Australia	2	2	2	2	3	3	2	2
Israel	4	3	3	3	2	5	3	3
Singapore	3	7	4	4	4	2	4	4
Korea	5	5	6	5	5	6	6	5
Taiwan	6	6	5	6	5	4	5	6
New Zealand	6	4	5	7	6	8	8	7
Hong Kong	8	8	8	8	8	7	7	8
China	9	9	9	11	9	9	11	9
India	11	10	11	10	10	11	9	10
Malaysia	10	11	9	9	11	10	9	11
Thailand	12	12	12	12	12	12	12	12
Indonesia	13	14	13	13	13	13	13	13
Philippines	14	13	14	14	14	14	14	14

Note: Twenty leading molecular biology and biotechnology experts from around the region were invited to share their perception of scientific development in the region. The results are based on inputs from 12 of these experts: Australia (3), Chinese Taipei (1), Japan (3), Korea (1), Philippines (3), Singapore (1). This survey was conducted by Asia-Pacific IMBN Secretariat during the period August–December 1999.

IMBN member economies in all the parameters measured, followed by Australia, Israel, and Singapore. Korea, Taiwan, New Zealand, and Hong Kong formed the next cluster of economies in terms of perceived capabilities and strengths, followed by China, India, Malaysia, and Thailand.

Israel was perceived to be second only to Japan in terms of human resources, while funding from public sector sources was seen to be relatively weak (behind Singapore and Taiwan). On the other hand, Singapore was considered to have the second strongest public sector funding base for science after Japan, but was felt to be behind Korea, Taiwan, and New Zealand in relation to its scientific infrastructure.

Life Science Enterprises: Seeking to Translate Insight into Commercial Reality

There are already over 6,500 life science and biotechnology companies around the world working to translate scientific understanding into practical commercial reality. Of these, there are approximately an equal number of companies in the US (about 1,500) and Europe (about 1,800). While there were fewer biotech companies in the Asia-Pacific region than in the US or Europe in 2001 (about 1,200), the number had already ballooned by 2004 to nearly equal the number of such companies in the US and Europe by 2004 (about 3,200) (see Table 10.2). Nevertheless, on a per-million population basis, there remains plenty of upside potential for the Asia-Pacific region in terms of new life science and biotechnology companies in Asia (just 1.1 companies per million compared to about 6 per million in the US and 5.1 per million in Europe) – the region, as a whole, would need to increase the number of such companies some 5 times before it would have comparable numbers per million population in the US and Europe.

While the majority of US life science and biotechnology companies are over five years old, most Asia-Pacific companies are typically less than three years old[1] (European companies tend, in general, to be of intermediate age between US and Asia-Pacific companies). Hence, Asia-Pacific companies tend to still be relatively early in their developmental life cycles, and tend to have

---

[1] The situation in relation to life science and biotechnology companies in Asia is currently very fluid and dynamic – the number of companies is increasing rapidly, so the numbers presented here are almost certainly underestimates of current numbers. The original analysis was conducted in Spring 2001. Numbers had changed very substantially in several countries when we checked again in Spring 2002. For example, an analysis in mid-2002 by *Bioera*, a leading Chinese language biotechnology publication, suggested that there may have been as many as 400 or more companies that classify themselves as biotechnology or life science companies in Taiwan (defined, in Taiwan, as "bioindustry" players). The updated data we collected in Spring 2004 underscores how the sector has grown throughout the region.

Table 10.2 Life Science and Biotech Enterprises in the Asia-Pacific Region Compared to the US and Europe, 2001–2004

Region/Country	Estimated number of biotech companies (per million population) 2001	Rank 2001	Estimated number of biotech companies (per million population) 2004	Rank 2004	Fastest growth 2001–2004 (% growth)	Rank (increase in number of companies) 2001–2004	Rank (% growth) 2001–2004
Country/Region							
US	1,500 (6.0)	2	1,500 (6.0)	3			
Europe	1,800 (5.1)	1	1,800 (5.1)	2			
Asia-Pacific	1,200 (0.4)	3	3,200 (1.1)	1	2,000 (167%)		
Country							
Korea	300 (6.4)	1	600 (12.8)	2	300 (100%)	3	5
Israel	160 (33.3)	2	200 (41.6)	7	40 (25%)	7	9
Australia	150 (7.8)	3	280 (14.6)	5	130 (87%)	6	6
Japan	130 (1.1)	4	350 (3.0)	4	220 (170%)	5	4
Taiwan	120 (5.1)	5	450 (19.1)	3	330 (275%)	2	3
China	100 (0.1)	6	1,000 (0.9)	1	900 (900%)	1	1
Hong Kong	50 (7.0)	7	80 (11.2)	8	30 (60%)	8	8
Singapore	30 (6.9)	8	50 (11.5)	9	20 (67%)	9	7
India	30 (<0.1)	8	270 (0.3)	6	240 (800%)	4	2
Malaysia	20 (1.0)	10	30 (1.5)	10	10 (50%)	10	9

Source: BioEnterprise Asia, original research, 2001–2004.
The number of companies in each economy was estimated in the first quarter of 2001 and again in the first quarter of 2004.

products, services, and technologies that are only beginning to come to fruition. It is not surprising, therefore, that the market capitalization of all Asia-Pacific life science and biotechnology companies taken together is estimated to be less than 10% of that for the top 25 US companies. On the other hand, BioEnterprise Asia anticipates a tremendous growth in value and market capitalization as Asia-Pacific companies drive product, service, and technology development through the innovation pipeline and begin to capture a growing place in the global life science and biotechnology markets.

In the Asia-Pacific region, Korea had the largest number of life science enterprises in 2001, followed by Israel and then Australia, Japan, and Taiwan. On a per-million population basis, Israel had, by far, the highest number of bio-based companies (33 per million population) in 2001, with Australia, Korea, Taiwan, Hong Kong, and Singapore bunched together in a distant second placed grouping at between 6.4–9 per million.

The region, as a whole, has experienced a staggering growth in the number of biotech companies in the three years since our first survey in early 2001 (about 1,200 companies) to early 2004 (over 3,200 companies) – a clear reflection of the interest and investment that the sector has garnered. Particularly striking has been the growth in the number of biotech companies in absolute and percentage terms in such countries as China, Taiwan, Korea, Japan and India. Hence, China today has the largest number of biotech companies in the region (1,000), followed by Korea (600), Taiwan (450), Japan (350), Australia (280), and India (270). On a per million population basis, Israel continues in 2004 to have the highest concentration of biotech companies (over 41 per million population), followed by Taiwan, Australia, Korea, Singapore and Hong Kong.

Interestingly, and importantly, to reach a number per million population comparable with those in the US and Europe, Japan would still need to double its number of biotech companies (by 350), China would need to increase its number of companies by about six times (to over 6,000) and India would need to expand its number of biotech companies by as many as 20 times!

While the growth in numbers of biotechnology companies in Asia has been staggering, and is expected to continue to be significant for several years to come, it needs to be borne in mind that biotechnology is not just a numbers game – quality of innovation, and the capability to translate promising concepts into high impact market reality are clearly also very important. Most biotech companies in the Asia-Pacific region are still essentially early stage start-ups, and will inevitably face the attendant risks and high attrition rates common to start-up enterprises – as some mature and grow from strength to strength, while others fall by the wayside or are gobbled up in regional and global consolidations as biotech players merge to build their value proposition.[2]

There are fundamental differences in culture and approach to dealing with life science and technology development among the different Asia-Pacific economies. Israel, Australia, and New Zealand have long and illustrious histories of academic and scientific excellence in the life sciences. Japan began to be a major player in the 1950s, while Korea and Taiwan started to get serious about science and technology during the 1970s. Singapore and Hong Kong started to really get their scientific act together only in the mid- to late 1980s and have done extremely well in setting up several world-class institutions in the last couple of decades.

Thailand has a long history of agricultural, environmental, and public health excellence, and growing expertise in biotechnology; while Malaysia has built up capabilities not only in the medical sciences but also in agriculture and forestry research. China and India have proud traditions in innovation and a rich cultural heritage stretching back thousands of years, and have a growing base of world-class scientists who are working to build real value – not only at home but also at leading institutions and enterprises around the world. Even Indonesia, the Philippines, and Vietnam have core groups of skilled scientists and leading institutions working to establish the foundation for future life science knowledge-based economic and industrial development.

Comparative Assessment of Life Science and Biotechnology Development in the Region

This section provides a more in-depth overview of life science and biotechnology development in selected Asia-Pacific economies (in alphabetical order).

Australia

Australia has long established capabilities in life science research and development, and has several world-class centers of excellence in the biomedical, agricultural, and environmental life sciences (strong biotechnology

---

[2] Interesting differences in business model and approach are clearly distinguishable between US and European biotech companies on the one hand, and Asian players. European companies seem, by and large, to follow a US-type venture capital financed approach to product and technology development, taking years to get to products and revenues. The lack of adequate venture-based funding resources in Asia, and investor distaste for Greenfield-type projects has meant that Asian companies have characteristically had to develop business models focused on early rather than late revenue – through provision of outsourced contract services and research activities, distribution and sale of products from US and European players, consulting services, et cetera, even as they embark on medium and long-term innovation technology, product and service development efforts (see also Chapter 18 and Chapter 20).

clusters have been established around Melbourne, Sydney, and Brisbane, in particular). Several Australian states, particularly Victoria and Queensland, have made strong commitments to proactively develop their base of life science capabilities and to nurture the establishment of viable life science and biotechnology industries.

Australia is notable in the region for having the highest proportion of its life science companies being publicly listed (over 70 life science companies at various stages of development are listed on the Australian Stock Exchange and other bourses around the world) – with many companies having listed far earlier than would have been possible in other countries. The rationale given by several key players in Australia for early listing is interesting and instructive: essentially, the lack of an established venture capital industry prompted entrepreneurs to seek listing of early stage companies (especially during the heyday of the dot.com era in the late 1990s) to enable them to gain access to needed capital to drive product and technology development.[3]

Even though the Australian life science and biotechnology industry has experienced several rough patches, early listing has enabled several companies to bring nascent products and technologies to fruition, and to achieve regional and even international stature.

[*Note: BioEnterprise Asia believes that the Australian experience demonstrates the potential viability of establishing a framework for the public to invest in relatively early stage technology enterprises with promising products, services, and technologies – done right, this would allow the public to gain access to high growth investment opportunities far earlier than is currently possible in most markets; and could help accelerate productization and bringing of high potential products, services, and technologies to market. Care needs to be taken, of course, to safeguard the interests of investors, prevent abuse of the financing mechanism, and ensure that companies operate according to best practice standards in terms of disclosure and financial management.*]

Comparative Strengths

Strong history and tradition of scientific excellence, relatively low cost of scientific work in Australia compared to US or Europe, public markets open to biotech listings.

---

[3] Another explanation provided to the author by investment management colleagues in Australia is equally intriguing: that public investors tend to view biotechnology investment in the same way that mining concessions have historically been viewed – listing allows entrepreneurs to gain access to capital to enable them to explore the opportunity, and to share the rewards if "gold" is struck in the form of a blockbuster product, service, or technology.

Comparative Weaknesses

Premature listings for many Australian biotechnology companies (far earlier than would be possible in most other markets), perceived lack of strategic technology management capabilities to drive innovation development.

China

China has made massive progress since the early 1980s in building up its life science and biotechnology capabilities. Hundreds of thousands of Chinese scientists have been trained in leading centers around the world, and have established strong leadership positions in centers of excellence in the country as well as in major research institutions and corporations around the world.

Given its relatively low-cost manufacturing base, the rapid expansion of the economy, the size of the potential market, and the growing base of scientific excellence, China has become one of the most attractive countries for foreign investment in the world.

Areas of expertise and opportunity in China include traditional Chinese medicines, private healthcare services, biopharmaceutical manufacturing, nutraceuticals, as well as agribiotechnology, environmental and industrial biotechnology.

Comparative Strengths

Low-cost base, very big market, large talent pool (both home-grown and trained in best institutions worldwide), high investor interest.

Comparative Weaknesses

Weak intellectual property protection, perceived (and sometimes real) high risk of technology "leakage."

Hong Kong

Hong Kong has a strong tradition in academic medicine and biomedical research. Hong Kong seeks to establish strong capabilities in the life sciences and biotechnology – and especially seeks to be a world center for the development of health foods and modern pharmaceuticals based on traditional Chinese medicines.

Comparative Strengths

Perceived as a westernized gateway to China, strong entrepreneurial culture.

Comparative weaknesses

Lack of cohesive biotechnology and life science strategy.

India

India has a long history of producing active pharmaceutical ingredients (APIs) for the pharmaceutical industry and has an indigenous pharmaceutical industry with well over 1,000 local manufacturers of generic and proprietary pharmaceuticals. The country has several leading centers of academic and technical excellence, and a very strong base of skilled and well-trained scientists and engineers working in leading institutions and corporations in the country as well as around the world.

Rapid economic growth and the opening up of the economy, especially over the last decade, have built up a burgeoning middle class, and a growing private market for life science and biotechnology products, services, and technologies.

Building on its success in information and communication technology, India has already established a growing reputation for innovative product and technology development in bioinformatics and bio-IT, and as a low cost, high quality location for outsourcing of computer and call center services.[4] Its low-cost manufacturing base coupled with a skilled workforce also suggest a potentially important role for India in the production of generic and proprietary biopharmaceuticals, not unlike the role that the country has carved for itself in relation to pharmaceuticals. Hotspots in India include Hyderabad and Bangalore.

Comparative Strengths

Low-cost base, very big market, large talent pool (both home-grown and trained in the best institutions worldwide), strong innovation culture, high investor interest.

Comparative Weaknesses

Intellectual property protection still weak, perceived (and sometimes real) risk of technology "leakage."

---

[4] It is fascinating to observe that India's export of information technology products (primarily software and software services) grew from about US$100 million in 1990 to over US$5 billion by 2001 – a jump of over 50 times in little more than a decade. BioEnterprise Asia anticipates similar growth in life sciences and biotechnology (including health-IT and bio-IT) in India and the region over at least the next decade.

Indonesia

Indonesia is keen to be a significant player in life sciences and biotechnology, and has a strong base of institutions with traditional strengths in agriculture and public health. The Eijkmann Institute is a leading center for molecular biology research and development in the country. Strategic areas of interest include agriculture, healthcare, biopharmaceuticals, industrial and environmental application.

The country has set up a "Biotechnology Island" near Batam, and has initiated international collaborations in a range of areas including bioprospecting, fermentation technology, bioremediation, biodiversity protection, and medical biotechnology.

There are over 200 generic pharmaceutical manufacturers in Indonesia, and a substantial number of agriculture-based companies active in timber and food processing. Indonesia has strong public sector capabilities in vaccine and serum, and a growing interest in the establishment of private biopharmaceuticals manufacturing.

Indonesia's initiatives in life sciences and biotechnology have been seriously hampered by economic and political turmoil in the last decade, but long-term prospects for value creation in the sector are strong.

Comparative Strengths

Strong base of generic pharmaceutical players, rich biodiversity, strong research institutions, strong investment interest by private sector players.

Comparative Weaknesses

Lack of trained human resources, lack of translational biotechnology capabilities, strong need for technology transfer and partnering.

Japan

Japan has strong academic and research institutions that are equal to the best in the world. Japanese academic scientists typically work closely with leading companies in the country, resulting in close collaboration in taking scientific insights from the laboratory to practical application in the marketplace.

While Japan has had relatively few entrepreneurial start-ups in the life sciences and biotechnology (Table 10.2), a large proportion of Japanese start-ups are spin-offs from Japanese industrial giants with deep pockets. Such start-ups tend to be well-funded and to have access to well-established marketing and sales pipelines – hence, increasing their viability and chances of success.[5]

Comparative Strengths

Strong academic-industry links, start-ups and spin-offs generally well-funded, strategic investments by parent companies in leading biotechnology companies in the US and Europe help to provide access to new products, services, and technologies.

Comparative Weakness

Perceived lack of entrepreneurial culture amongst scientists and technology innovators.

Malaysia

Malaysia is a relative latecomer to the regional and international biotechnology scene.[6] The country launched the "BioValley Malaysia" initiative in September 2002. The core of BioValley Malaysia consists of three research institutes, each focused on a central priority area of advanced research for "converting Malaysian research into sustainable biotechnology": a genomics and proteomics institute, an agricultural biotechnology institute and a nutraceutical/pharmaceutical technologies institute.

The government intends to build a strong industry and indigenous small and medium enterprise (SME) base to grow around the BioValley's biotechnology institute nucleus. Malaysia also has a growing early stage venture capital base through strategic government efforts to set up and outsource venture capital funds to support early and growth-stage local enterprises. There is also strong support from the government for academia-industry collaborative R&D through the award of grants for product development and commercialization.

---

[5] In general, technology start-ups have historically been found to have a five-year survival rate of about 50% on average. The five-year survival goes up to over 80% in the case of spin-off companies.

[6] Coming into the arena late may be both a disadvantage and an advantage. While Malaysia (and the region as a whole) has lots of catching up to do, she can potentially learn from the mistakes of others who went before within the region and internationally. This is also true for Thailand, Vietnam, the Philippines, Indonesia, and other players now seeking to enter the modern BioBusiness arena.

Comparative Strengths

Rich biodiversity, strong institutions with traditions in agriculture R&D and biomedical research, strong government focus on building an indigenous SME base, growing funding base.

Comparative Weaknesses

Lack of trained human resources (both scientifically and for technology management), perceived need for greater access to cutting-edge technology.

New Zealand

New Zealand has a rich tradition in scientific excellence through the work of individual scientists and the efforts of the country's network of Crown institutes – with expertise especially in the agricultural sciences, as well as the biomedical sciences.

While several promising life science companies have been established, there is real concern about the lack of capability to translate promising concepts into practical application, and the lack of an established venture capital funding base.

Comparative Strengths

Strong scientific tradition, well-established network of agriculture-focused Crown institutes.

Comparative Weaknesses

Lack of translational biotechnology capabilities, insufficient venture capital funding support.

The Philippines

The Philippines has established several strong research groups in the biomedical, agricultural, and environmental sciences. There is substantial interest in capturing the wealth of the economy's rich biodiversity (both forest and marine).

There is need for access to cutting-edge technology and for skilled managers of science to drive the innovation development pipeline.

Comparative Strengths

Rich biodiversity (in forest as well as marine ecosystems), strong base of potential private investors.

Comparative Weakness

Lack of trained human resources.

Singapore

Singapore started getting serious about life sciences and biotechnology in the mid-1980s and has leaned strongly on foreign talent to support its investment in R&D and human resource development. Singapore has established several leading centers of life science excellence including the Institute for Molecular and Cell Biology and the Genome Institute of Singapore.

The Singapore government is investing heavily to fuel the development of the biotechnology industry – especially in the biomedical sciences. Some US$1.1 billion (S$2 billion) has been earmarked to attract corporate biomedical research centers to Singapore from around the world. By 2010, Singapore aims to be the key business base for 15 world-class companies, and a regional center for clinical trials and drug development.

Singapore is already a world-class manufacturing hub for pharmaceutical bulk actives with several projects in Tuas Pharma Park, and is working actively to expand its base in biological and biotechnology manufacturing.

The centerpiece of Singapore's life science push is Biopolis, a two million square feet (185,000 square meters) biomedical complex of seven buildings that brings together key government agencies, publicly funded research institutes and the R&D laboratories of pharmaceutical and biotechnology companies.

The translational skills and infrastructure needed to help bring scientific discovery into commercial application are still being established.

Comparative Strengths

Recognized centers of scientific excellence, attractive base for multinationals, strong financial sector, strong information technology capabilities, responsive government with proactive policy and regulatory framework, genetically diverse population (with potential value for clinical trials and pharmacogenomic studies).

Comparative Weakness

Lack of translational biotechnology capabilities.

South Korea

Korea has established strong research and development capabilities in life sciences and biotechnology. The country has identified seven basic areas for biotechnology development including biomaterials, healthcare, agri-fishery and livestock, food technology, and bioengineering.

The government has committed to injecting US$13.33 billion (16 trillion won) between 2001 and 2007 to build up the country's biotechnology industry with the goal of having Korea reach the top seven countries in the world in terms of competitiveness in biotechnology by 2010. The nation's public sector R&D investment budget alone has grown by 40–50% annually since 1998, reaching over US$270 million (323.8 billion won) by 2001.

The government has constructed the Bio-Venture Support Centre and the Korea Biotechnology Industrialization Centre. The Korea Research Institute for Bioscience and Biotechnology (KRIBB) is well established as a national center of excellence for conducting biotechnology research.

Korea has a vibrant biotechnology start-up environment with substantial investment and support from government, industry, and academia, as well as an established small private investor and venture capital funding base. The stock market is generally very receptive to biotechnology investment opportunities.

Comparative Strengths

Strong academic-industry-government links, strong small private investor base to support early stage start-ups, strong entrepreneurial culture.

Comparative Weakness

Too many "me-too"-type initiatives (overly competitive entrepreneurs with little product/technology differentiation).

Taiwan

Taiwan has established a strong research and development base in the life sciences and biotechnology with several centers of excellence.

The government has committed US$1 billion toward the formation of over 100 local biotechnology companies; proactively provides monetary awards for scientists-turned-entrepreneurs; and supports nearly 75% of the cost of all public and private sector research projects through grants. While the government technically owns all patents from publicly funded research, intellectual property laws have been modified to support the transfer of technology and the development of the biotechnology industry.

Heavy emphasis is being placed on technology incubators as crucibles for innovation and technology development – the country already counts over 70 incubators. One such incubator, the Industrial Technology Research Institute (ITRI), alone spends about US$500 million annually on technology innovation in partnership with the private sector, technology transfer from academic and research institutions to industry, and the spin-off of innovative companies – life sciences and biotechnology are becoming an increasingly important focus for ITRI and other technology accelerators/incubators in the country.

Comparative Strengths

Strong entrepreneurial culture, substantial small private investment base to support early stage start-ups.

Comparative Weakness

Weak corporate R&D culture.

Thailand

Thailand considers biotechnology as an important sector of opportunity – driven by domestic need for biotechnology products. The government sees the potential value of biotechnology in helping to achieve enhancements in productivity, given the importance of the agriculture and food sector in Thailand.

The Thai government has identified two areas of focus for life science and biotechnology investment: improved agricultural productivity and improvement of public health. The government also supports R&D in environmental technology and toxicology to reduce the effects of chemicals in the environment on human health, while developing strategies for coping with pollution and waste management concerns. It also actively supports programs to develop human, livestock, and aquatic diagnostic and therapeutic products focused on diseases endemic in the region.

Still, the industry is very much in its infancy in Thailand. Several products are in the pipeline, but few have reached commercialization. The life science industry includes amino acid production for feed, hybrid seed production, plant tissue culture-based propagation, secondary production of antibiotics, and production of animal vaccines. Most technology used by the private sector is imported.

The government is building an 80-acre Science Park about 20 kilometers from Bangkok, providing incubator units, pilot plants, greenhouses, and accommodation. Between 2001 and 2006, the government intends to spend 0.5% of its budget on R&D – and targets R&D investment by private industry amounting to 0.25% of sales revenues.

Comparative Strengths

Strong applied agriculture base, expertise in toxicology, growing pool of excellent scientists, strong university-linked and private research groups.

Comparative Weakness

Lack of expertise in translational biotechnology including product development and commercialization.

Vietnam

Vietnam has several leading institutions focused on public health and vaccinology. Vietnam's priorities in life science and technology development have focused primarily on agricultural technology and food biotechnology as well as healthcare. Vietnam currently spends about 2% of its annual budget on funding R&D activities.

Areas of focus include the development of hybrid varieties of crops such as maize. Several promising life science technology companies have been established with a focus on developing tools for diagnosing infectious diseases in humans and in agriculturally important species.

Comparative Strengths

Rich biodiversity, strong scientific and technically skilled human resources.

Comparative Weaknesses

Underdeveloped infrastructure, lack of investment resources.

Conclusion

Box 10.2 is an "Academy Awards"-type listing issued by BioEnterprise Asia based on our perspective on how each economy has performed in making things happen.

Box 10.2   The BioEnterprise Awards: Life Sciences in Asia-Pacific

- Most successful in generating private entrepreneurial investment for early-stage start-ups: **Korea and Taiwan**
- Most effective in generating spin-offs from existing major corporations: **Japan**
- Most active public market for biotechnology: **Australia**
- Most successful in attracting MNCs and foreign talent: **Singapore**
- Most successful in attracting foreign venture capital investment: **China and India**

Source: BioEnterprise Asia, 2002.

Countries in the Asia-Pacific region stand to benefit substantially from new developments in the life sciences and biotechnology – not just as consumers of products, services, and technologies, but also as potential contributors to the development of such capabilities and technologies.

To capture the value proposition of these opportunities, there is need to strengthen capabilities and resources, to invest in innovation, and to put in place a supportive environment to facilitate entrepreneurship. Rather than work in competition with each other, there is real scope and potential for countries in the region to work together to address problems and issues of common concern; to identify areas of potential synergy and complementarity; and to share expertise, resources, and facilities to help achieve regional life science and biotechnology growth and wealth creation.

Key Points

1. Many Asia-Pacific economies have already made substantial investments in the beginning to lay the foundation for capturing value from the life sciences and biotechnology.
2. There has, nevertheless, been relatively little success to date in developing viable indigenous life science sectors in most economies in the region – the translation of innovative concept to practical application has been very limited.

3. This has been largely due to a lack of public and private sector understanding of the challenges of taking promising life science and biotechnology concepts and insights through the innovation development pipeline to practical commercial reality, and a lack of managers of science and savvy entrepreneurs.

4. Substantial value can be created if governments, industry, and academia, within and across the various Asia-Pacific economies, work together to create lasting value by:
    −   investing in building physical and scientific infrastructure
    −   expanding the region's base of trained human resources and expertise
    −   putting in place the necessary laws, regulations, and working guidelines to encourage responsible and world-class science and safeguard the intellectual property rights of innovators
    −   creating conducive environments to facilitate innovation and entrepreneurship
    −   strategically encouraging both private and public investment in life sciences and biotechnology innovation and value creation

5. The most successful crucibles for life science and biotechnology innovation and entrepreneurship will be those that most successfully integrate their capabilities and resources to ensure that the necessary smart money is made available to smart people with smart ideas who capitalize on innovation by being plugged into smart alliances and partnerships throughout the region and internationally (see also Chapters 5 and 11).

Section C

Issues and Challenges in BioBusiness

*All progress is based upon a universal innate desire on the part of
every organism to live beyond its income.*

Samuel Butler

Section C examines the issues and challenges in capturing the value and
potential of BioBusiness.

Chapter 11 examines what it takes to develop world-class entrepreneurial
enterprises.

Chapter 12 examines the ethical and social concerns that we need to
proactively address as we seek to capture the value of BioBusiness.

Chapter 13 examines intellectual property considerations for successful
bioinnovation and bioentrepreneurship.

Chapter 14 discusses the policy and regulatory considerations.

Chapter 15 explores the challenges in meeting human resource needs.

Chapter 16 examines the challenges in meeting funding requirements.

Chapter 11

Creating World-class Organizations and Entrepreneurial Enterprises

One of the secrets of life is to make stepping stones out of stumbling blocks.

Jack Penn

Summary

Today's "Summit" opportunity is tomorrow's "Valley" opportunity; hence there is need to continually innovate to add value and enhance knowledge input to technology. The concepts of innovation and entrepreneurship are thus fundamental to the new knowledge-based economy. Asia-Pacific organizations, institutions, and enterprises stand to make the greatest impact, and to capture maximum value, when they operate according to best practice standards internationally and are plugged in to the latest developments through collaboration, strategic alliances, and partnerships with leading players in academia and industry throughout the world.

Introduction

BioBusiness, the business of biology, has been practised since time immemorial. From the development of crop-fields, animal farming, selective breeding, and the birth of molecular biology, to the present era of DNA chips and computational biology, BioBusiness has been undergoing an increasingly rapid metamorphosis.

The past several decades have seen the beginnings of a true revolution in the bio arena, mainly through new insights and the establishment of an ever-growing knowledge and insight base. This revolution can, in part, be attributed to recent advances in, and growing maturation of, innovative new technologies (not just in the life sciences, but also in engineering and information technologies).

Compared to other knowledge-based industries like electronics and information technology, the life science innovation and product development cycle has generally taken substantially longer, with more focus being placed on intellectual property generation and management as a basis for assessing expected future value through the development of a pipeline of new products, services, and technologies.

BioBusiness constitutes no less than 25% of the gross domestic product (GDP) of the global economy (see Table 3.1, pg 38 and Box 11.1), accounting for over US$9 trillion in value in 2001. Unfortunately, most BioBusiness activities today, especially in developing countries in Asia, Africa, and Latin America, generally fall in the "Valley" areas of the BioBusiness landscape (see Figure 4.1, pg 48), and generate relatively low returns (see also Table 5.1, pg 61). There is a need to rethink these sectors and to innovate and transform them to ensure higher economic returns through developing and providing products, services, or technologies for which the market is prepared to pay a premium – whether this be agriculturally-related, service-oriented, or manufacturing-based BioBusiness.

Box 11.1   Some Key Insights for Establishing Successful and High Value-added "Summit"-focused BioBusiness Environments and Enterprises

BioBusiness already constitutes a substantial proportion of economic activities in most societies around the world (see Table 3.1, pg 38) – about 25% of global GDP (over US$9 trillion) can be attributed to BioBusiness. Some 40% of global workers are engaged in BioBusiness activities.

The problem is that the bulk of BioBusiness activities today are "Valley"-type opportunities – where inputs and products are "commoditized" and low value-added (see Figure 5.1, pg 63 and Table 4.1, pg 50). Hence, the vast majority of workers engaged in BioBusiness today live in developing countries and are engaged in subsistence-level agriculture or low wage raw material processing-type activities (in some countries, over 70% of the population is engaged in low value-added agricultural activities).

New insights in the life sciences, and new tools for biotechnology and bio-IT provide an unsurpassed opportunity to rethink traditional BioBusinesss activities, and transform "Valley"-type activities into "Summit"-oriented activities where innovation and knowledge-based input in response to market opportunity and need result in the generation of products, services, and technologies that are in high demand and are, therefore, able to command a high value-added premium.

At the same time, it makes strategic sense to develop scientific competence and build technological capabilities, and to keep abreast of technological innovations in new scientific areas. While such innovations may currently be "Cloud" or "KIV" opportunities (primarily because no one has yet figured out how to make money from the use of these technologies), it is clearly prudent to keep up to date so we are prepared to reap the benefits when the opportunities become "Summit" opportunities. Still, it does need to be borne in mind that more than a few "Cloud" opportunities may never make the transition to becoming "Summit" opportunities as they might never prove to be commercially viable.

To capture and maintain a leadership position in developing "Summit" opportunities, it is necessary to fully understand how the R–D–A translation process works (see Figure 4.2, pg 54) to translate insights and concepts into practical reality.

Specifically, it makes sense to strategically and proactively manage the five component phases of the innovation pipeline to ensure successful R–D–A translation. As defined by BioEnterprise Asia (see Figure 4.3, pg 55), these key phases include:

- Concept
- Technology validation
- "Productization"
- Business case validation
- Market entry and growth

Managing the innovation pipeline requires strong scientific and technology management capabilities (especially in relation to the first half of the innovation pipeline, from concept to "productization") as well as strong market insight and business development capabilities (to take innovations from "productization" to market entry and growth). Hence, successful innovation management clearly requires multi-disciplinary skills and inputs.

Based on our own experiences and insights, and our analysis of critical success factors for life science innovation-oriented environments in bioclusters and enterprises around the world, BioEnterprise Asia has identified four critical factors that appear to be consistently found in, and necessary ingredients for, successful and sustainable BioBusiness hotspots (see also Chapter 5). These include:

- Smart people
- Smart ideas
- Smart money
- Smart alliances and partnerships

The world stands today at the dawn of a life science revolution of epic proportions that promises to completely transform our lives and practically every sphere of human activity – BioEnterprise Asia estimates that economic activities accounting for 50% or more of global GDP could be impacted by innovations and development in the life sciences and biotechnology.

Our analysis shows that biotechnology currently accounts for less than 0.5% of global BioBusiness activities (see Table 3.1, pg 38). In our assessment, biotechnology has only recently begun to emerge from the latent phase of its life cycles as the science was being validated and the technologies became increasingly mature. We are entering the rapid growth phase of this exciting technology sector that promises to radically alter many existing sectors even as it spawns new ones across the entire sphere of human economic and social activity.

We anticipate rapid growth of biotechnology in the post-genome era as it transforms and expands the BioBusiness landscape over the next several decades (see also Figure 11.1 which shows how the maturing of life science technologies and growing acceptance of biotechnology products in the marketplace have fueled revenue generation in leading biotechnology players in the US).

Asia-Pacific economies can choose to proactively drive BioBusiness value creation in the region and internationally by establishing and nurturing world-class institutions, organizations, and enterprises that are well-placed to generate

Figure 11.1   Cumulative Revenues of Five Leading US Biotechnology Companies (1980–2001)

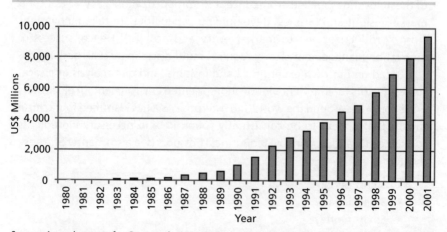

Source: Annual reports for Genentech, 1980–2001; Amgen, 1981–2001; Biogen, 1983–2001; Chiron, 1985–2001; Genzyme, 1985–2001. Reproduced with permission from an illustration in the BIO website – www.bio.org.

innovative intellectual property and develop cutting-edge new products, services, and technologies in response to market opportunity and need (see also Box 11.2). Or we can take a more pedestrian approach and be bystanders hoping to pick up some crumbs as leading US and European players capture value from life science innovation and entrepreneurship – just as most Asia-Pacific economies found themselves doing during much of the information and communication technology revolution. The choice is ours.

Box 11.2   World-class: A State of Mind?

Asia-Pacific countries have built up truly world-class institutions – ranging from Tokyo University to Jawaharlal Nehru University to Seoul National University to Chulalongkorn University to the National University of Singapore – that are equal to, if not better than, the best in the West. In the life science arena, the Asia-Pacific International Molecular Biology Network (Asia-Pacific IMBN) now counts over 260 members who were selected on the basis of their excellence in science – none of these scientists would be out of place at Oxford or Princeton. These and many other individuals in the region are thought-leaders in their respective fields, and are internationally regarded for their achievements.

Unfortunately, in too many countries in the region, we seem to be trapped in a post-colonial mind warp where ideas and opinions coming out of Western institutions and corporations are given greater reverence while potentially more brilliant ideas and insights coming out of locally-based scientists, entrepreneurs, institutions, and enterprises tend too often to be neglected and left to fester. This, in my mind, is a reflection of insecurity and a fundamental lack of belief in ourselves and our own capabilities – I call this the "post-colonial" mindset.

Even greater cause for concern is when investors in the region (both public and private) all too often fail to take the lead to make modest "smart money" investments to help validate and bring local and regional innovation and technology to fruition (and, thereby, to help fuel the development of future global leaders from the Asia-Pacific region) while throwing money to make follow-on investments in sometimes grossly over-priced investment opportunities touted by big name players in the US and Europe (see also Box 16.1, pg 248 and Table 16.1, pg 251).

World-class is an attitude thing – if I don't believe I am the best (and my opinions matter), why should anyone else? Until and unless we start treating the bright and brilliant who choose to stay in their home economies to make a difference (or who choose to return to their home economy/region after international exposure) with the same respect we do those based in leading institutions in the US and Europe, we will always be second best. And we will continue to wonder why our most outstanding and independent minds choose to leave and find more receptive environments elsewhere.

Opportunities and Challenges for Creating Value in Asia

Luck is when preparation meets opportunity.

Neil Peart

Over the last several decades, governments in the Asia-Pacific region have invested heavily in building up scientific infrastructure and in human resource development by encouraging their best and brightest to study and conduct research at leading institutions throughout the world.

Today, Asia-Pacific scientists are highly regarded for their knowledge, skills, and capabilities. Walk into any major institution in the world (Harvard, Stanford, Cambridge, MIT, and so on) and you will find top-notch scientists in leadership positions with names like Kumar, Kim, Lee, Hassan, Singh, and Sato.

There are those who still speak of the movement of leading scientists and professionals from less developed countries to established centers in countries like the US, Europe, and Singapore as the "brain drain." I see such movement more as a "brain flux" in that people will go where the opportunities to maximize their potential and contribution lie – at some stages in their respective careers, this may be in Western institutions or corporations, and at other stages, this would be in institutions and enterprises in their home countries or region. This is a natural and completely rational cycle.

The reality is that many Asia-Pacific economies have already been busy building up core capabilities and competencies that could potentially enable them to capture a piece of the rapidly expanding life science and biotechnology market opportunity (see also Chapter 10). The region already has a growing base of world-class scientists and institutions that can potentially play a leading role in making things really happen (see Box 11.2).

The region also has a rapidly expanding portfolio of promising enterprises with innovative technologies that hope to compete in the international marketplace, and potentially become multinationals of the future. There are already nearly as many life science enterprises in the region as there are in the US and Europe (Table 10.2, pg 150) even though the region really did not get into the arena until relatively recently.[1] Current trends suggest that the sector can anticipate substantial growth in value and market capitalization in the coming years as relatively early-stage companies mature and bring increasingly innovative products, services, and technologies to market while demonstrating increasingly robust revenue generating capabilities.

It should be borne in mind that not all of these enterprises will succeed. Indeed, it is generally assumed by some venture capital investors, based on past experience with their investment portfolios, that just 1 in 7 or fewer start-ups is likely to make it big, while most of the rest are unlikely to survive for five years or more.[2]

Enterprises in the Asia-Pacific region face a myriad of issues and challenges (Box 11.3). The biopreneur has to face not only the challenges common to all other entrepreneurs and technopreneurs, but also problems inherently associated with the life sciences – prolonged time to get concrete output from investment in research and development (ranging from months to several years), the relatively slow and inefficient clinical and field testing process for new products and technologies arising from the rigorous and demanding product registration and approval process, the substantially higher emphasis placed on intellectual property as a driver of future value, and so on.

Nevertheless, our experience at BioEnterprise Asia has been that it is entirely feasible to maximize the likelihood of success, and minimize the risk of failure, by ensuring (among other things):

- A solid science and technology base. In our experience, there are usually five to eight years (or more) of insights from scientific research and technology that go into establishing a life science or biotechnology business venture. This compares with less than a year for many dot.com ventures of the late 1990s

---

[1] It can be argued that biotechnology started being taken seriously by the government and investors (and came of age in valuation terms) in the US in the early to mid-1980s, in Canada in the early 1990s, in Europe in the mid-1990s, and in Australia around the turn of the millennium. The author believes that we are already in the earliest stages of a similar coming of age in Asia.

[2] It can be argued that the success rate of investment by some professional venture capitalists (VCs) has been particularly low because they often base investment decisions on selection criteria that unwittingly select for failure. Companies that fall outside the sphere of interest of such VCs, the relatively low to medium technology players with products, services, and technologies that are more tuned to market needs, are more likely to survive and thrive than the high-tech and "sexy" investments that professional VCs are typically attracted to. Cutting-edge sexy opportunities (like much of nanotechnology for example) tend, more often than not, to be relatively high risk "Cloud"-type opportunities since, in most cases, no one has yet figured out how to make money from them – or if there will prove to be significant market demand for products, services, or technologies based on such opportunities.

- A clear understanding of the challenges and needs for successfully driving technology and product development from concept to market
- A strong focus on outputs and the need to generate revenue and cashflow from product sales, service provision, and technology partnering sooner rather than later
- Strong strategic alliances and partnerships with leading institutions and technology players in the region and internationally

In the long term, it should be borne in mind that the value of any enterprise, and its portfolio of new products, services, and technologies, is not dependent on venture capitalists or financial markets, but on market acceptance and demand.

Box 11.3   Issues and Challenges Faced by Life Science Enterprises in Asia

Life science companies operating in Asia face a number of challenges including:

- Lack of knowledge and understanding regarding issues and challenges facing life science enterprises amongst prospective investors
- Lack of management and business development expertise and capabilities
- Lack of resources for research and development
- Lack of access to cutting-edge technology for new product and service delivery
- Lack of access to world-class strategic technology and market development partnerships and alliances
- The need to span the "investment gap" between promising technologies at the concept/technology validation stage, and the point at which investors typically enter investments in Asia, when a product is either close to market, or already available for sale
- Analysts in Asia are not familiar with the technology, and find it difficult to understand requirements for successful exploitation of their long-term commercial potential

Moving Things Forward: The Case for BioPartnering

The man who gets the most satisfactory results is not always the man with the most brilliant single mind, but rather the man who can best coordinate the brains and talents of his associates.

W. Alton Jones

Taking BioBusiness opportunities through the innovation and development pipeline requires a much wider range of expertise and capabilities than any single individual could possibly possess. To a large extent, making things happen depends on defining strategic research and development priorities (Box 11.4) and identifying and working with partners with the necessary skill and understanding to help drive product and technology development, and to maximize value creation (Figure 11.2).

Box 11.4   Defining Research and Development Priorities for Asia-Pacific Organizations and Corporations: Focus on Strategic Research

Given limited resources, how should Asia-Pacific players invest their precious R&D dollars?

I believe strongly that investment in science and research should focus on clearly defined goals and be targeted at generating useful outputs that can potentially make a difference in people's lives. As a physician and a scientist, I have always believed that generating more and more information and data for its own sake is useless and essentially "noise" that threatens to overwhelm us if we don't put it to good use to help solve real problems.

The tired old differentiation between basic and applied research has, in my opinion, been a red herring that has held back the development of science by creating arbitrary and artificial boundaries.[3] For too long, we were led to believe that basic science – whether in physics, chemistry, or biology – was somehow purer and more superior than the applied sciences focused on dealing with real-life issues and concerns. There are even leading scientists whom I have encountered who consider applying scientific insight to solving real-life problems and concerns to be a bastardization of the science.

Rather than get hung up about whether a scientific pursuit is supposedly basic or applied, I prefer to think about R&D in process terms – whether it is focused on new knowledge generation to increase understanding ("discovery" research) or on solving problems and developing new products, services, or novel technology platforms ("strategic research").

Importantly, both discovery and strategic research cut across old disciplinary and sectoral boundaries, and require integration of both basic science and applied science and technologies. Such integrative skills and interdisciplinary capabilities are, unfortunately, still in relatively short supply in much of the scientific world – given the rigid manner in which scientists

---

[3] Some would argue that there is no such thing as basic research – there is only "applied" research, and "yet-to-be-applied" research.

have classically been trained. The challenge and the opportunity is to be able to cut across traditional disciplinary boundaries to zoom in on what is important for solving our problems and concerns, to mine the global databases for what is known, to define what remains to be known, and then to conduct the necessary research to fill in the gaps in our understanding as we work to solve our societal and economic problems and concerns by developing products, services, and technology solutions that can make a difference.

I believe this is the most cost-effective and high-impact manner for world-class institutions and enterprises to operate. The new insights we have gained in molecular biology (including genomics and proteomics), and the tools of life science research and biotechnology, for example, enable us to focus on creating real value and benefit for society in real-time – be it developing diagnostic tools or therapeutics against a disease which is devastating our societies (such as HIV, Hepatitis C, dengue or SARS); developing more nutritious crops; cleaning up polluted rivers and canals in Bangkok or Jakarta; or extracting precious metals from mineral ore.

The power and impact of strategically focused science was well-illustrated by the concerted manner in which scientists, institutions, national and international organizations, and corporations around the world worked together to identify the coronavirus causing SARS, reveal its genome, and develop diagnostics, therapeutics, and vaccines against the disease. With a focused, directed approach, we were able to move at an unprecedented pace to bring the disease under control within months of its emergence in 2002/2003.

One can just imagine how such an urgent, directed, strategic approach would contribute toward solving the many other life science and BioBusiness-related problems and concerns that confront humankind – in the Asia-Pacific region and beyond.

Focusing on the various component phases of the innovation development pipeline (see Figure 4.3, pg 55), it is clear that we need to work with very different players as we move from concept to technology validation to "productization" to business case validation to market entry and growth.

During the early stages, biopartners are likely to include universities and individual scientists, as well as potential technology partners with platform technologies that can facilitate product and service development. When we enter the "productization" stage, we move toward partnering with clinical trial centers, contract research organizations (CROs) and big pharma. And as we get closer to market, partners will include market and business development players including potential distributors in markets of interest. Along the way, we need to protect our intellectual property, enter into a whole range of legal

Figure 11.2   BioPartnering: Capturing the Value Proposition for BioBusiness

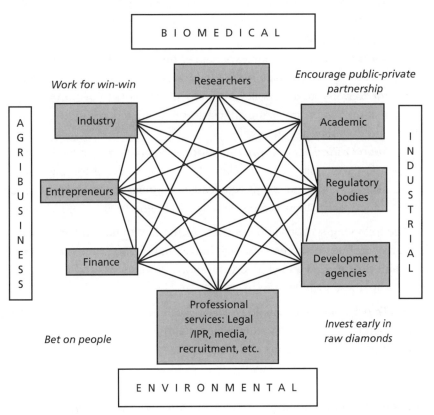

© BioEnterprise Asia, 2002.

agreements, develop brand equity, raise financial investment, interact with media and prospective investors, and so on – thus requiring us to work with even more partners to maximize value creation and capture.

Making things happen, hence, depends on governments, investors, and entrepreneurs working together to create lasting and sustainable value together with partners throughout the value chain. To create truly world-class organizations and enterprises, we need to ensure that these are well plugged in to developments around the world – and that there is opportunity for the interchange of people, ideas, technologies, and capabilities that are strategically relevant to the organization, institution, or enterprise and its priorities/objectives. As discussed in Chapter 5 and outlined in Box 11.1, the most effective biotechnology clusters, organizations, and enterprises share four critical success factors in common:

- ***Smart people*** – who are in abundant supply in the Asia-Pacific region
- ***Smart ideas*** – again, our experience is that there is no shortage of smart and even radical ideas and concepts that have the potential to transform the BioBusiness landscape if they could be validated and brought to fruition
- ***Smart money*** – in our experience, this is usually the area where Asia-Pacific economies really tend to falter because of the tendency for "cover-your-ass" policy-makers and investors to avoid perceived risk-taking by investing in yet-to-be validated technologies and "productization" concepts
- ***Smart alliances and partnerships*** – again, there is a tendency for Asia-Pacific players to be relatively weak in terms of forming strong alliances and partnerships with leading partners who can play a critical role in technology and product development.

The following sections address some of the key trends and approaches that can contribute to success and high impact in building value for the long-term, and thus truly world-class organizations, institutions, and enterprises. Specifically, these include:

- Translational biotechnology: DIY or technology partnering/licensing?
- Getting "virtual" to capture regional and international strengths
- The role of incubators and accelerators
- Bioclusters in Asia

Translational Biotechnology: DIY or Technology Partnering and Licensing?

In taking promising concepts and insights through the R–D–A translation pipeline (see Figure 4.2, pg 54 and Figure 4.3, pg 55), we can either choose to develop the products and tools we need ourselves, or we can work with others who have already developed insights, applications, and tools that could facilitate our efforts to generate products, services, and technology solutions.

Both models obviously make sense depending on the specific circumstances: our philosophy at BioEnterprise Asia is that it makes no sense to reinvent the wheel if this can be avoided. If others have gone before us and have developed part or all of the technology capabilities needed to solve our problems or address the opportunities that are of interest, and see the value of working together to develop newer and better solutions, technology licensing and partnering is the obvious answer (see also Chapter 13).

If I have seen farther than others, it is because I was standing on the shoulders of giants.

Isaac Newton

On the other hand, if there exists a clear knowledge and understanding gap in relation to our unique problems and needs that cannot be filled by available scientific or technology solutions, or if those who have developed and own the intellectual property controlling possible solutions prove to be impossible to work with,[4] it may make complete sense to develop our own innovative product, service, or technology solutions, even if this does take longer. Each approach has its own risks and its potential rewards (see Table 11.1).

Getting "Virtual" to Capture Regional and International Strengths

To capture "Summit" BioBusiness opportunities through creating new products, services, and technologies requires substantial insights on market opportunities and needs, strategic technology management capability, and the skills and capabilities to successfully traverse the R–D–A translation pipeline (see Figure 4.3, pg 55). Success depends on a wide variety of internal and external partnerships: in-house research and development processes and functions, research collaborators, multi-site field studies conducted in collaboration with

Table 11.1 Comparing Implications of Technology In-licensing and Partnering Versus Development of Proprietary Technology Solutions

Approach	In-licensing and technology partnering	Develop own technology solutions
Developmental timelines	Generally shorter	Generally longer
Need for in-house competence and expertise	Generally lower	Generally higher
Investment	Generally lower	Generally higher
Own intellectual property generation	Generally lower	Generally higher
Potential returns on investment	Generally lower	Generally higher
Risk of failure	Generally lower	Generally higher

---

[4] This could be for a variety of reasons – for example, if prospective partners demand exorbitant terms for licensing and use of their tools and technologies, or perhaps if they have unrealistic expectations regarding ownership of jointly developed intellectual property.

academic and research institutions, service providers, marketing and distribution partners, and so on (see also Figure 11.2).

The organizations and enterprises that most successfully harness strategic partnerships and alliances across disciplinary and geographical boundaries to drive the translation of actionable knowledge to bring highly valued and needed products, services, and technologies to market will be the ones that are most likely to achieve world-class leadership in their respective fields.

Imagine a company that builds on strengths and capabilities available throughout the region, for example:

- **R&D** in centers throughout the region in collaboration with partner institutions – in strategic alliance with leading scientists and institutions in the region and beyond (Australia, New Zealand, Singapore, Japan, Korea)
- **Manufacturing** in low-cost, high quality bases (Malaysia, Thailand, Vietnam, India, China)
- **Clinical trials** in collaboration with partners throughout the region (Singapore, Hong Kong, Thailand, Malaysia, Indonesia, the Philippines)
- **Marketing and Distribution** throughout the region and beyond controlled by regional headquarters: one for Southeast Asia (Singapore or Kuala Lumpur), one for Northeast Asia (Shanghai or Hong Kong), one for South Asia (Hyderabad or Mumbai) and one for Australasia (Sydney, Melbourne or Brisbane)

Such a networked enterprise is not only conceivable, it is entirely achievable. An innovative enterprise needs to achieve optimal competence in a wide range of disciplines where cutting-edge skills and capabilities are in short supply. Rather than attempt to invest in bringing all necessary competencies in-house and greatly increasing related overheads and costs on headcount that is not fully utilized, a smart strategy is to supplement in-house capabilities and resources with external alliances, partnerships, and outsource contractors for multiplier benefits (see also Boxes 7.5, pg 112 and 7.6, pg 114).

Operating as a virtual organization (in that the partners are legally separate entities but still function intrinsically as part of the project team) helps ensure that the enterprise can operate with both flexibility and speed in response to changes in the marketplace. It also enables the organization to remain lean without having to take on excessive overheads and potentially redundant specialized personnel who are really not needed on a full-time basis, and who bring the best value when tapped as needed to solve problems and make things happen on behalf of the enterprise.

The Role of Incubators and Accelerators

Access to strategic technology management capabilities, and to mentoring and business acceleration resources, can be invaluable in helping promising institutions and companies to create sustainable value and maximize their likelihood of success. The historical evidence of the impact and significance of incubators and accelerators in countries like Canada, Israel, and Australia in ensuring increased viability and mitigating business execution risk is overwhelming – where just 1 in 7 businesses, on average, are generally estimated to succeed, incubated and accelerated companies have a 50% or higher likelihood of success.[5]

Growing interest in spawning technology start-ups has led to strategic support for technology business incubators in North America, Europe, Australia, Israel, and Japan.

Traditionally, business incubators have been operated primarily by public sector municipalities and academic institutions. The National Business Incubation Association (NBIA) of the United States estimates that only 10–12% of the 1,000 or so existing incubators in North America are private or for profit. Further, only 25% of all incubators are focused on technology-based ventures. Even fewer incubators or accelerators focus on the life sciences.

In the Asia-Pacific region, the concept of business incubators and accelerators as partners in value creation for technology business enterprises is gaining recognition and there are proactive initiatives underway to establish and support such facilities and capabilities in the various economies of the region. While Australia and Israel have proactively supported technology incubators for over a decade, there is increasing interest and support for incubators in other economies, especially Korea and Taiwan.

While there is a predominance of incubator and accelerator support for information technology, communications, or manufacturing companies, business incubator and accelerator management and venture development support for start-ups operating in the area of healthcare, life sciences, and related technologies is still relatively rare. Adding to this is the reality that the region has been a relatively late entrant into the modern life science and

---

[5] On average, the likelihood of any life science start-up surviving to IPO or acquisition is generally thought to be between 10% and 15%. Research in Australia shows that companies supported by business incubators and mentor relationships have a 50% or higher likelihood of surviving, compared to 5% for non-incubated companies there (J. Gardner and A. Kenyon: *Business Incubators in Australia – An Evaluation*). The experience in Israel is similar: Of 592 "graduate" companies of incubation programs from 1991, 52% survived by January 2000. (IMBN report on Israel, 2000).

biotechnology arena so trained human resources with expertise in science and technology management are in short supply, and the investment and venture capital industry lacks experience and exposure to the sector.

To be successful, a biotechnology incubator or accelerator needs to understand the issues and challenges confronting new enterprises (see Boxes 11.3 and 11.5) and be committed to working with entrepreneurs and client organizations (whether start-ups or growth-phase enterprises) to:

- Evaluate the commercial potential of their intellectual property and technology, and help define a long-term intellectual property management strategy to maximize value creation
- Develop and validate strategic business and implementation plans
- Co-found (if necessary and appropriate) and establish early operations for the businesses with which it works, including bringing together world-class scientific and technical directors and advisors, and identifying and recruiting appropriate staff
- Obtain start-up and follow-on investment
- Identify and facilitate strategic alliances with international partners (both corporate and academic), and help negotiate technology partnering and licensing opportunities
- Define market entry and development strategies for products, services, and technology platforms being offered by the company
- Raise investor interest and support
- Provide on-going strategic and management input

Box 11.5 Life Science Enterprises and Incubators/Accelerators

It can be a very complex undertaking to get a new life science enterprise off the ground – in addition to dealing with the usual corporate, governance, management, and resource mobilization issues, life science enterprises also have to worry about the need for innovative R&D, protection of intellectual property, technology licensing and partnering issues, working with academic and technology partners for mutual benefit, regulatory issues and concerns, revenue generation to ensure cashflow, and the relatively long development cycle before products can be brought to market (especially in relation to drug development).

Few start-ups have the knowledge, experience, and expertise to deal with these and other issues and concerns. Many would-be entrepreneurs, scientists and innovators who are keen to join such start-ups find the challenges, uncertainty, and risk of entrepreneurship too daunting – and choose to remain within the fold and relative security of salaried jobs in government, academia, and industry until it is clear that the enterprise is viable and funding is in place. Worse, too many early-stage enterprises have flawed business models that prevent them from capturing true value in the marketplace. Hence, only 1 in 7 start-ups have historically been able to effectively make the transition from dream to reality. To succeed, they need access to mentors and advisors with the knowledge, strategic management skills, contacts, commitment, and passion to work through the inevitable challenges they will face.

A business accelerator, with the right mix of domain knowledge, experience, insight, strategic management skills, and contacts, can make all the difference by providing the mentoring, advice, and hands-on management capabilities that can enable entrepreneurs to traverse the otherwise treacherous seas to success. BioEnterprise Asia operates through a network of world-class scientists, managers, and entrepreneurs who have made their own mistakes, and have built up a substantial storehouse of experience and insight across the region and beyond which the co-entrepreneurs we work with can tap as needed. This helps shorten learning curves, minimize execution risk, and maximize value creation through helping to establish strategic alliances and capturing business development opportunities.

In our experience, most business concepts developed by scientists are raw gems which need substantial work to bring out their potential (see Figure 4.2, pg 54) – more often than not, the business model is wrong, and the business (while it might look good on paper) would not be able to make it in the real business world.

Also, few scientists are able to build up the knowledge base and business management team they need for their companies to succeed – there tend to be major gaps in terms of strategic management skills, business development skills, product development skills, alliance building skills, investor management skills, marketing and sales skills, and so on.

A good incubator or accelerator can make all the difference by refining business strategies and building operational models that would work, filling gaps in management, helping to raise funding support, and driving product, service and technology development.

It is important, though, that the incubator or accelerator does not indiscriminately select client enterprises without ensuring that there is a clear match between the goals and objectives of the founders and those of the incubator or accelerator (see also Box 11.5). In our experience, there needs to be clear alignment of strategic focus and business intent for the accelerator to maximally benefit client entrepreneurs and their enterprises. Box 11.6 outlines

> **Box 11.6 BioEnterprise Asia's Selection Criteria for New Enterprises and Technologies**
>
> - High growth potential targeting unmet needs and opportunities in the life science marketplace (with a global market perspective and a strong focus on the Asia-Pacific region)
> - Potential to build world-class scientific and management team that recognizes the benefits of mentoring and strategic alliances
> - Product, service or technology platform portfolio with the potential to generate revenue within 12 to 18 months (focus on intellectual property creation and R-D-A translation)
> - Excellent candidate for merger, acquisition or IPO within three to five years (to provide liquidity and exit opportunities for investors)

key criteria used by BioEnterprise Asia in evaluating prospective enterprise and technology opportunities to determine their fit with our capabilities and competencies and our level of interest in bringing them into our technology business acceleration program.

In our experience, technology companies are most successful when they have a clear focus on developing products, services, and technologies in response to market opportunities and needs. As a technology business accelerator, we are not afraid, where appropriate and necessary, to proactively put together the people, technology, and resources to set up new enterprises seeking to capture "Summit" opportunities. To maximize the likelihood of success, and to minimize execution risk, we work closely with entrepreneurs and companies in our acceleration program to ensure that they understand the need to meet our rigorous due diligence checklist (Table 11.2), which is essentially consistent with best practice due diligence requirements of prospective investors in technology competitors.

Table 11.2 Key Technology, Business Model, Financial, and Human Resource Considerations for BioBusiness Enterprise Success

Technology	Market	Financial	Management
Ownership of technology	Market opportunity	Funding requirements	Management capabilities
Technology licenses	Market size growth	Revenue projections	Track record and references
Competitive status of technology	Market penetration strategies	Potential grant funding	Commitment
Technology pipeline	Competitor analysis	Other financing sources	

Bioclusters in Asia

A biocluster is a concentration of life science and biotechnology-related institutions, laboratories, and businesses. There are already estimated to be some 400 science and technology parks around the world that either already boast strong bioclusters, or are keen to establish such bioclusters. Internationally recognized bioclusters include, in the US: the Bay Area, Boston and Cambridge, San Diego, and Seattle; in the UK: London, Cambridge, Oxford, and Central Scotland; in Germany: Munich, Frankfurt, and Heidelberg; in Scandinavia: Medicon Valley and in Japan: Tsukuba Science Park.

Typically, local and state governments establish bioclusters as a way to help promote the development of technology-related businesses and to fuel local economic development. Governments are generally prepared to fund the construction and provision of purpose-designed buildings, and to provide a range of incentives and support services and infrastructure to facilitate development and success of the biocluster.

The presence of one or more established academic or research institution often serves as the nucleus for the biocluster. The institution(s) can serve as a useful source of collaboration and partnership, and can spin off a range of high potential companies or technologies for licensing by start-ups and support companies in the biocluster. The concepts and ideas that drive start-up companies are usually drawn from academic institutions and laboratories working closely with colleagues in industry to translate insights and findings through partnering and appropriate licensing arrangements.

Venture capitalists and financial securities players help provide the smart money to drive development of promising technologies down the innovation development pipeline – often supported by strategic public sector grants and seed funds. A whole range of supporting players can be involved in the process: from equipment manufacturers to technology partners, process technology consultants, CROs, intellectual property and legal firms, accounting firms, incubators and accelerators, and so on.

Key hotspots with existing or planned bioclusters in the Asia-Pacific include:

Australia: Brisbane, Melbourne, Sydney
China: Shanghai, Beijing
Hong Kong: Hong Kong Science Park
India: Bangalore, Hyderabad (Genome Valley), Mumbai, Delhi
Indonesia: Bioisland (Batam)
Israel: Kiryat Weizmann Science Park (Rehovot), Jerusalem, Haifa
Japan: Tsukuba, Tokyo, Yokohama, Osaka
Malaysia: BioValley (Selangor), Penang, Sarawak, Johore

Singapore: BioPolis, Science Parks
South Korea: Seoul, Taejon, Pohang
Taiwan: Hsinchu (Industrial Technology Research Institute), Taipei
Thailand: Thailand Science Park
Vietnam: Ho Chi Minh City

Managed with vision, bioclusters can play a very critical role in driving life science and biotechnology development, and in helping to transform local economies. There is a danger, nevertheless, that, if there is lack of emphasis on best practices, isolated bioclusters will not be able to attract a critical mass of people, technologies, money, and alliances or partnerships, in which case, they would be in real danger of becoming white elephants.

In our experience, the truly enlightened players tend to establish strong incubation or acceleration capabilities to ensure that start-ups have access to state-of-the-art facilities and shared resources, and minimize risk by gaining access to experienced advisors and mentors. Additionally, they often manage and attract substantial seed funding resources to enable the necessary smart money investment to facilitate successful innovation and enterprise development (see also Figure 4.3, pg 55 and Box 16.1, pg 248).

Bioclusters in the Asia-Pacific region should work proactively to attract the best and brightest, and to ensure that they, and the institutions and start-up enterprises with which they are associated, are well plugged in to the international life sciences and biotechnology community, and are capable of achieving the critical success factors for world-class bioclusters. They would also do well to consider the development of a sound branding and marketing strategy to differentiate themselves so they can make the greatest impact (see also Chapter 13).

Conclusion

Institutions and enterprises in the Asia-Pacific region are well placed to play world-class leadership roles in helping to drive life science and biotechnology development by proactively working to strengthen their ability to translate insight into practical applications. To be most effective, they would benefit greatly from having a clear understanding of the R–D–A translation process, and of how to effectively manage each phase of the innovation development pipeline.

Tremendous value will be created in the BioBusiness arena over the next several decades as innovative technologies mature and come to fruition. The institutions, enterprises, bioclusters, and economies that capture the most value will be those that most successfully create a confluence of enlightened investment (*smart money*) in bioinnovation (*smart ideas*) and bioentrepreneurship (*smart people*) – and which work in synergy with key players around the world (*smart alliances and partnerships*) to translate dreams into reality.

Key Points

1. The Asia-Pacific region is well placed to establish world-class life science and biotechnology organizations, institutions, and enterprises.
2. There is a role for both the public and private sector in facilitating successful translation of research and development insights to practical application and commercial reality.
3. Facilitating successful innovation and helping entrepreneurs grow and succeed creates wealth for society – those societies that provide the most fertile ground for entrepreneurship and innovation will yield the most benefits.
4. Asia-Pacific entrepreneurs and enterprises that seek to be world-class will need to be creative and innovative in implementing best practice solutions to maximize their likelihood for value creation and minimize risk. Smart approaches include tapping into opportunities for technology partnering (including technology transfer and licensing relationships) as well as establishing "virtual" organizations and enterprises that enable close partnership between in-house and external partners (including, as appropriate, advisors, collaborators, market development partners, and so on) to achieve strategic organizational and enterprise objectives and goals.
5. Entrepreneurs can be made – with the right mentoring and support (this works best in the context of a close working alliance between government, academia, accelerators and incubators, bioclusters, investors, and industry partners).

Chapter 12
Ethical and Social Concerns

*It has become appallingly obvious that our technology has
exceeded our humanity.*

Albert Einstein

Summary

*Science and technology make their biggest impact when there is clear
alignment between the dreams and aspirations of scientists, and the values,
priorities, and needs of society. We already have in hand, given the life
science tools and technologies that have been developed thus far, the
potential to radically alter life as we know it, and to create new hybrid
species and life forms that have never existed in nature. We will soon have
the ability to make multiple genetic copies of ourselves and of other species
through cloning, if we do not already. We will also, in the foreseeable
future, be able to insert desirable traits into practically any organism of
interest, including humans.*

*It is imperative that we seek to use the tools, knowledge, and capabilities
we possess responsibly – for the good of society, and for our future
generations. To ensure that professionals engaged in biotechnology and
BioBusiness operate in accordance with best bioethical practices, it may be
worth establishing a code of conduct for life science professionals.*

Introduction

Ethics can usefully be defined as the branch of philosophy concerned with
how we should decide what is morally wrong and what is morally right.
Ethical conclusions need to be based on reasons; take into account historically
established ethical principles; be based on consensus; take account of minority
interests; and be open to the possibility of change in the face of new
understanding and experience.

The simplest way to determine if an action would be right or wrong is to
consider what its possible consequences might be. Traditionally, ethics has

188

concentrated mainly upon actions that take place between people at any given point in time. In recent decades, however, moral philosophy has widened its scope by taking into account interspecies and intergenerational issues.

Ethical decisions can be taken at a number of levels, from the individual to the international. Some general ethical considerations that relate to the application of modern tools of life science and biotechnology include:

- How to weigh the potential benefits against the possible costs?
- Do the processes involve the taking of ethically unjustifiable risks?
- Do the processes themselves constitute an "unnatural" interference with Nature, particularly in breaching natural species boundaries and violating the integrity of species?
- What is ethically wrong with interfering with Nature?
- From a religious viewpoint, is modern biotechnology to be interpreted as "playing God" or as collaborating in the on-going work of creation?
- Do these questions suggest any significant ethical differences between modern biotechnology and traditional techniques?

Ethical Best Practice Standards: Finding the Lowest Common Denominator?

Few issues are discussed with such controversy and sometimes violence as those of ethical and moral concern. In judging what is right or wrong, most people are influenced by their ethnic, cultural, and religious backgrounds; their individual experiences; their personal needs and wants; and professional or economic pressures they may be facing at any given point in time (see also Box 12.1). They are also influenced by their upbringing, their education, their openness (or otherwise) to new ideas and experiences, and by all they may have read or been exposed to along the way.[1]

Yet cultural background, personal interest, and professional training differ, and thus so do opinions about what is ethically right and wrong. Similarly, perceptions of risk can also differ substantially (see Box 12.2). Is it possible to define common ethical principles for all humanity?

Few people are likely to disagree with statements such as: "Do not do to others, what you would not want to be done to you." There are, therefore, usually very few ethical disagreements about things that are generally perceived to benefit at least some, while hurting nobody.

---

[1] Exposure today can come from a variety of sources including the media through TV, radio, newspapers, magazines, movies, video games, and the Internet.

Box 12.1   Eastern Versus Western Approaches to Dealing with BioEthical Concerns

There may well be a fundamental difference between classical thinkers of the East versus those of the West[2] in understanding ethical concerns and the "rightness" or "wrongness" of particular behaviors or actions.

To grossly oversimplify things, Easterners tend to view our ethics and actions in "relative" terms, where the potential implications can be viewed as a full spectrum of shades of gray. Who is to say if something is entirely right or entirely wrong? Doesn't the context of an action determine how right or wrong it is rather than what the action itself is? With such a perspective, the Eastern mind can, for example, justify the murder of a tyrannical ruler as being morally right if the context is justifiable, or perhaps the use of genetically modified crops to help the poor feed themselves and escape the poverty trap, and so on.

Westerners tend to view issues in "absolute" terms, where it is either black or white, with a clear sharp line dividing the two. There seems to be, in the Western mind, the need for clear rules or principles, and a fundamental belief that a clear line exists to distinguish between an action or an ethical perspective being right or wrong, sin or not. This very simple difference in worldview creates all kinds of interesting situations.

Unfortunately, different Western thinkers draw the line at different points of the spectrum. So a religious thinker may be a lot more conservative in deciding where he or she draws her line, while a scientist might believe that the line should be drawn closer to the cutting edge of what we can scientifically validate, and so on. Hence, not only do different "authorities" have different ideas about where the line should be drawn, they often have an evangelistic desire to impose their views on others and on society. All of this makes for great public debate in the Western tradition, which many in the East find very intriguing but amusing because, in the greater scheme of things, these controversies and debates are often just little storms in a teacup.

The Eastern approach, in such a context, would be to recognize that different views exist, that there is a whole spectrum of perspectives that should be taken into account but that we really do not know enough today to come to any conclusions. So why not proceed cautiously and make sure we don't

---

[2] Clearly, the contrast made here is a gross oversimplification. Nothing, in my experience, is ever as easy to categorize as it might first appear. By Western thinking, I refer to thinking associated with classical Judaism, Christianity, and Islam that has tended to influence Western ethical and moral precepts – these are all religious and cultural philosophies sharing common roots and emanating from the same small area in the Middle East. Many ancient Greek philosophers as well as modern post-Christian thinkers and intellectuals in the West tend to share a relativistic worldview in common with Hindu, Buddhist, and other philosophies that have greatly influenced Eastern thinking.

do anything dumb in the process? This is, essentially, the type of practical and pragmatic approach which many in Asia would take in thinking about and managing ethical issues and concerns, for example, in relation to human cloning or the introduction of genetically modified foods.

Box 12.2   Risk Perception and Reality

It is essential to understand the dynamic and evolutionary nature of risk perception in relation to bioethical dilemmas. The reality is that the more we know and understand about an area of concern, the less uncertainty there will be and the less of a dilemma it becomes. It is generally the fear of the unknown, and our all-too-human tendency to focus on worst-case scenarios, that often accentuate concern regarding the dilemma.

Rather than allow ourselves to be paralyzed into inaction every time we are faced with a new life science or biotechnology-related dilemma, the smart thing to do is to recognize that we are dealing with just such a dynamic and evolutionary process, and that the only way to resolve concerns is to do more science (not less), so that we can build up sufficient knowledge and understanding of the potential impact and significance of the area of concern to make a proper reasoned assessment. While we work to increase our understanding of the risks that may be involved, and the likely benefits and negative implications, we should have clear, responsible guidelines on how we go about working to resolve the dilemma.

A key element in the process is working with the media to ensure that all issues are properly understood, and that unrealistic benefits or alarmist concerns and perspectives are quickly dispelled. Every effort must be made to ensure a well-informed public that sees public policy-makers, scientists, and corporations acting responsibly and in a trustworthy manner.

The problem is that almost everything we do in the life science and biotechnology arena potentially affects others, so we cannot avoid a trade-off between the rights of some versus those of others. Hence, many ethical issues concern a conflict of interest between different groups: the interest of minorities versus majorities, or the rights of individuals versus the progress and stability of society. Should there be special protection for traditional ways of living, for example, even if this means increasing sacrifices for the modern majority? Are traditional values of a society more important than individual freedoms?

Another dimension of complexity in seeking to find consensus on dealing with ethical dilemmas comes when there is need to take account of the interests of those who cannot directly express their interests: the intellectually handicapped; the person in a coma; the unborn child; other species that share the world around us; the environment; future generations.

Ethical and Social Considerations in BioBusiness

New developments in the life sciences and biotechnology raise a variety of important ethical issues and concerns that will need to be addressed by every society. In the agricultural sector, the potential risks and benefits of genetically modified organisms have aroused considerable controversy.

In the biomedical arena, a range of issues have raised ethical and moral concerns: How long should lives be artificially prolonged in cases where death seems inevitable? Should women have the right to abort if they choose to do so? How much should we be prepared to spend to save a life when financial resources are limited? Do we really want to know if we have the genes that make us highly susceptible to a fatal disease if there is no cure available? Should human cloning be allowed? Should the confidentiality of our medical information be protected?

Other ethical and moral issues relate, for example, to the protection of intellectual property. In the pharmaceutical industry, for instance: is it ethical to maintain patent protection and to sell a potentially life-saving drug at prices that may be prohibitive for patients who need it most?

The following sections will address a range of pertinent ethical issues and concerns including:

- The use of genetically modified organisms in agriculture
- Ethical issues in healthcare: Focus on human cloning
- Safeguarding of personal genetic information
- The need for a scientific hippocratic oath or a code of conduct for life sciences

The Use of Genetically Modified Organisms in Agriculture

Opponents to the use of genetically modified organisms in agriculture, such as environmentalist groups and consumer associations, tend to focus on two areas:

- ***Safety considerations*** – that genetically modified organisms might be dangerous for human consumers
- ***Environmental considerations*** – that the introduction of genetically modified plants and animals into the environment could lead to a chain of effects that cannot be controlled by humans

Proponents of the use of genetically modified organisms, including some research organizations, genetic seed producers, and some philanthropic organizations, often argue that necessary safety testing and environmental studies have already been done, and that these indicate little or no safety or environmental danger.

They often point out the reality that nature itself often conducts genetic engineering experiments of its own to create genetically modified organisms, for example, the SARS virus as well as other infectious diseases that have caused epidemics and even pandemics throughout human history and killed millions, or new mutations leading to cancer or other genetically-linked diseases. The products of nature's experiments can be far more detrimental than anything produced by responsible scientists in the laboratory under strict guidelines to ensure safety and benefit.

Also, the argument is often used that the availability of high-yield and disease-resistant genetically modified food will help to feed rapidly growing populations, especially in developing countries (see also Box 5.1, pg 63 and Box 8.1, pg 118), while eliminating or greatly reducing the need for chemical fertilizers, insecticides, and herbicides which can be toxic and hazardous to both humans as well as the environment.

BioEnterprise Asia raised the issue of genetically modified organisms to a group of 12- to 15-year-old students participating in a BioCamp in December 2002. Their opinions and perspectives provide illuminating insight into the way young people today think about this ethical dilemma (see Box 12.3 and Table 12.1).[3]

Box 12.3   Children Speak Out: Singapore Kids Share Their Views on Genetically Modified Organisms

Singapore, 12 December 2002. Seventy-one students participating in a week-long "Learning from Experiments" BioCamp held at Temasek Junior College in Singapore shared their views on genetically modified organisms/food

---

[3] Young people of today will be the leaders of tomorrow – it is, therefore, important to get a sense of how they think. It should be borne in mind, nevertheless, that the cohort sampled here is a group of bright urban kids from throughout Singapore who have benefited from several days of exposure to issues in life sciences and biotechnology during their BioCamp session. Clearly, their views should not be taken as representative of the thinking of all young people in Asia. Nevertheless, their reactions and perspectives should be of interest to all who seriously want to ensure that we prepare future generations to deal responsibly and effectively with the moral and ethical dilemmas that will inevitably confront them – we have a responsibility to help them to develop the knowledge and skills to think for themselves rather than to seek to impose our prejudices and worldviews upon them.

through a vote in a "National Referendum" after participating in "National Debates" to explore the potential benefits and risks associated with the development and use of genetically modified foods, and to consider if the public has a right to know if genetically modified organisms are present in their environment or the food they eat.

The Scenario
The tools of life science and biotechnology are increasingly being used to create genetically modified organisms for agriculture and to satisfy human curiosity.

While some consider such use of modern biotechnologies to be a natural extension of classical biotechnology, others consider such work unnatural and potentially very dangerous. There is growing polarization of perspectives throughout your country, and, indeed, throughout the world.

Your government has decided that the best way to resolve concerns and issues relating to genetically modified organisms and to come up with suitable guidelines for R&D as well as for sale of products derived from genetically modified sources would be to first hold a series of national debates to enable diverse views and perspectives to be heard, and then run a national referendum to enable each person to share their perspectives and suggestions before formulating national guidelines and policies for genetically modified organisms.

You have been invited to participate in consultations and debates at the grassroots level leading up to national debates. Essentially, the debates will address two major subjects of concern in relation to genetic modifications:

- Regional debates to address the issues surrounding the assertion that "The potential benefits of GM outweigh potential risks"
- A national debate addressing the issues surrounding the assertion that "The public has a right to know if they are being exposed to genetically modified organisms and foods"

The Findings (see Table 12.1 for details)
While the students are generally open to research and development work being carried out on testing and developing genetically modified organisms, they expressed concern that genetically modified organisms might pose a threat to public safety and to the environment. They also generally feel that additional and special guidelines and regulatory requirements should be in place to minimize potential risks associated with genetically modified organisms.

While the students see potential benefits from the development and use of genetically modified organisms, they are not convinced that the benefits outweigh the risks. They expressed openness to the prospect of genetically modified organisms being developed and used to increase agricultural yields and resistance to disease, but expressed strong concern that rogue nations and terrorists should not be given access to the technology to create virulent strains of organisms.

At the same time, they expressed pro-business perspectives – supporting the notion that companies and scientists who develop novel genetically modified organisms have the right to benefit from their work.

The students strongly expressed the perspective that people have the right to know if genetically modified organisms are being released into the environment or are present in their food, and that foods containing genetically modified organisms should be labeled. One debater, in the course of the "National Debates," tried to make a case for not requiring disclosure or labeling so business interests and farmers growing genetically modified crops and foods are protected – but other participants responded negatively to such a perspective in favor of more openness and disclosure so that the public can choose for themselves.

[Note: In a curious departure from its usual emphasis on openness and transparency, official US policy does not generally support labeling of genetically modified foods. The European Union, on the other hand, is generally strongly in favor of labeling to enable people to know and to choose. In Asia, several countries, including Japan and Korea, have strong labeling requirements. Other Asian countries, including Singapore, do not appear to have strong views on the labeling issue.]

Overall, the students demonstrated substantial sophistication in understanding the issues and concerns involved with the release of genetically modified organisms into the environment. The complexity of the subject, and their concern that we still do not have all the answers, may help account for the relatively high prevalence of "undecided" votes in response to several questions raised in the "Referendum."

[Note: The student voters, who constitute a representative cross-section of 12- to 15-year-olds in Singapore, were participating in a five-day "Learning from Experiments" BioCamp program. BioCamp is an innovative learning experience providing children with the opportunity to gain a working understanding of the opportunities and challenges posed by new developments in the life sciences and biotechnology. The program covers key aspects of the life sciences including consideration of the diversity and the genetic basis of life, as well as introduces key principles of biotechnology and its application. BioCamp 2002 was jointly organized by Temasek Junior College (a premier pre-university college in Singapore) and BioEnterprise Asia.]

Table 12.1   Summary Results of BioCamp Survey on Genetically
Modified Foods (2002)

Assertion	Agree (%)	Disagree (%)	Undecided (%)
Research leading to the development of genetically modified organisms/foods should be allowed in your country	69	7	24
Newly developed genetically modified organisms/foods pose no threat to public safety in your country	17	56	27
There is little or no risk that genetically modified organisms might transfer their altered genes to wild relatives	16	59	25
There is little or no risk that genetically modified organisms will upset the balance of populations or reduce biodiversity in natural ecosystems into which they are released	12	56	32
Food from genetically modified crops or livestock are likely to be safe to eat	29	21	50
The potential benefits of genetically modified organisms/foods outweigh any potential risks	20	38	42
There is no need for additional or special safeguards to restrict the release of genetically modified organisms/foods into the environment (above and beyond safeguards already in place for protection of the environment and for food safety)	18	62	20
There is no need for the public to know if a given food is genetically modified or not	6	78.5	15.5
Producers of genetically modified crops and livestock should be required to label their products as being genetically modified so that the public knows and can make its choices accordingly	70.5	4	25.5
Companies and scientists have every right to benefit commercially from creating genetically modified organisms	29	19	52
Would you consider it to be acceptable to develop genetically modified organisms/foods that can provide higher yields of products of commercial interest	68	19.5	12.5

Table 12.1 (continued)

Assertion	Agree (%)	Disagree (%)	Undecided (%)
Would you consider it to be acceptable to encourage "field trials" and testing of newly developed genetically modified organisms in poorer countries before they are allowed for release in more developed countries	39	53	8
Would you consider it to be acceptable to release newly developed genetically modified organisms/food without first ensuring that they pose little or no risk to the environment or to naturally existing organisms	7.5	85	7.5
Would you consider it to be acceptable to enable rogue nations and terrorists to use genetically modified organisms to make deadlier tools for biowarfare and bioterrorism	6	81	13

Note: Results derived from responses to "National Referendum" questionnaire by 71 student participants of BioCamp's "Learning from Experiments" program held in December 2002. The participants came from different schools throughout Singapore and were aged between 12 and 15 years. BioCamp is an innovative life science education program organized by BioEnterprise Asia in collaboration with Temasek Junior College.
Source: BioCamp, 2002.
© BioEnterprise Asia, 2002.

Ethical Issues in Healthcare: Focus on Human Cloning

New advances in healthcare and the biomedical sciences have introduced a number of important new ethical challenges and concerns. These range from concerns regarding the use of stem cells (see also Box 14.2, pg 229), to concerns regarding human cloning, to concerns regarding confidentiality of personal genetic information, to equity issues, and concerns in relation to access to proprietary drugs and vaccines.

Human cloning has raised its own ethical questions and concerns since scientists and science fiction writers first raised the possibility. The issue has taken on increased urgency since the cloning of Dolly, the sheep, and a growing clamor of claims by maverick scientists and fringe pseudo-religious groups that they have either already cloned, or will soon be cloning, humans.

BioEnterprise Asia raised the ethical and social issues surrounding human cloning to a group of 10- to 12-year-old participants in a BioCamp in Singapore in December 2002. Boxes 12.4 and 12.5, and Table 12.2 provide intriguing and interesting insights into the way in which young people in Asia today address this dilemma (see previous footnote).

Box 12.4   Children Speak Out: Singapore Kids Share Their Views on Human Cloning

Singapore, 5 December 2002. Sixty-seven students participating in a week-long "Discovery and Fun" BioCamp held at Temasek Junior College shared their views on human and animal cloning through a vote in a "National Referendum" after participating in a "National Taskforce" to explore the potential benefits and pitfalls of cloning.

The Scenario
The leader of your country has made a great contribution to your country.

There is a growing movement seeking to use new developments in life sciences and biotechnology by attempting to clone the leader so future generations can benefit from his capabilities. However, there is also much controversy regarding human cloning and its implications – and many in the country are questioning the soundness of seeking to clone the leader on moral grounds even if human cloning does become technologically feasible.

At the same time, a growing range of issues and concerns in relation to both potential benefits and potential pitfalls of human cloning have arisen that call for urgent national consideration.

[Note: Many societies around the world condemn any experimentation on human tissue, and have banned the use of public funds to support research on human embryonic tissues and human cloning. Such actions have not deterred a fascination with the subject, and appear to be ineffective in preventing those who choose to work privately on such initiatives from doing so or from moving their work to countries that do not restrict such research and development. Already, maverick scientists around the world are claiming that they are either working to create human clones or have already succeeded in creating such clones.]

Being a wise and benevolent person, your leader has decided to establish a "National Taskforce" to weigh the potential benefits and the potential pitfalls of human cloning, and to hold a "National Referendum" on the subject.

The Findings
While voters are generally open to the idea of cloning animals, they feel human cloning should not be allowed in their country.

They are generally in favor of the idea of cloning great leaders and Nobel laureates, but strongly oppose providing "evil" leaders or scientists with the technology to make copies of themselves.

While they are open to the idea of families cloning members who have been tragically lost, or to the possibility of using cloning technology to clone lost pets, they generally oppose allowing the wealthy to make clones of themselves just because they can afford it. On the other hand, they strongly endorse the idea of growing organs and tissues that may be needed by people.

[*Note: The student voters, who constitute a representative cross-section of 10- to 12-year-olds in Singapore, were participating in a week-long "Discovery and Fun" BioCamp program.*]

Box 12.5   Potential Benefits and Pitfalls Identified by Student "Taskforce on Human Cloning" at BioCamp

Some potential benefits
- Can potentially be used to create a superhuman race (eugenics)
- Creation of spare body parts
- Recovery of loved ones
- Pet banking – to make clones of much loved pets
- Reproduction of own good qualities
- Cloning for conservation of endangered species
- Cloning of extinct species
- Can create clones of aggressive people to fight wars
- Can be used to bring important people back to life
- Infertile couples could have children with cloning
- Parents who have lost their child in an accident would be able to clone the child who was killed
- Farmers can clone their strongest and healthiest farm animals so they are less likely to contract diseases
- Can clone intelligent scientists to increase research talents
- Can increase human productivity in factories by cloning people who can work well in those environments

Some potential pitfalls
- Cloning is not natural
- Loss of human diversity if there are too many clones of the same people
- No unique sense of identity for the clone – which may lead to psychological problems
- Bad clones created for evil purposes
- Humans would be acting like God
- Cloning may be against some religious beliefs
- Would be bad to have clones of the same leader ruling all the time – should give a chance to new talents
- Would not be good to create farms of human clones to be murdered for organs

- Clones could be treated as slaves or inferior persons
- Greedy scientists could produce clones to make more money
- Clones may be discriminated against

Note: Results derived from responses to "Potential Benefits/Potential Pitfalls" questionnaire by 67 student participants of BioCamp's "Discovery and Fun" program held in November/December 2002. The participants came from different schools throughout Singapore and were aged between 10 and 12 years. BioCamp is an innovative life science education program organized by BioEnterprise Asia in collaboration with Temasek Junior College.
Source: BioCamp, 2002.

Table 12.2 Summary Results of BioCamp Survey on Human Cloning (2003)

Question/Assertion	Yes/Acceptable (%)	No/Not acceptable (%)	Undecided (%)
Do you believe that whole animal and human cloning research should be allowed in your country?	36	48	16
Do you believe that whole animal cloning (not including human cloning) should be allowed in your country?	52	36	12
Do you believe that human cloning should be allowed in your country?	22.5	67	10.5
Would you consider cloning to be acceptable to enable society to benefit from the capabilities of a great leader or leading thinker (for example, a Nobel prize winner)?	55	24	21
Would you consider cloning to be acceptable to enable an evil leader or evil scientist to make copies of themselves?	4.5	94	1.5
Would you consider cloning to be acceptable to enable families to make copies of much loved pets?	55	34.5	10.5
Would you consider cloning to be acceptable to enable families to make copies of beloved grandparents or parents who have been tragically lost?	58	27	15
Would you consider cloning to be acceptable to enable families to make copies of beloved children who have been tragically lost?	61	31.5	7.5
Would you consider cloning to be acceptable to allow anyone who can afford it to make copies of themselves?	7.5	73	19.5

Table 12.2   (continued)

Question/Assertion	Yes/ Acceptable (%)	No/Not Acceptable (%)	Undecided (%)
Would you consider cloning to be acceptable to grow organs and tissues that may be needed by people?	82	9	9

Note: Results derived from responses to "National Referendum" questionnaire by 67 student participants of BioCamp's "Discovery and Fun" program held in November and December 2002. The participants came from different schools throughout Singapore and were aged between 10 and 12 years of age. BioCamp is an innovative life science education program organized by BioEnterprise Asia in collaboration with Temasek Junior College.
Source: BioCamp, 2002.

Safeguarding of Personal Genetic Information

Our growing understanding of genetics and genomics, and how our genes affect health and disease, has meant that we are beginning to have an increasing ability to determine the risk and likelihood of different diseases (for example, cancer or heart disease) based solely on studying a person's genotype.

Further advances in genetics and genomics promise to enhance our ability to personalize medical care and improve health by ensuring early management and even prevention of diseases of concern in persons with high risk, as well as to develop drugs that are customized to ensure best healthcare outcomes for such individuals. Similarly, new insights into genetic influences on personality, intelligence, criminal behavior, drug and alcohol addiction, and a growing variety of traits are being recognized every day.

At the same time, there is growing fear and concern that individual genetic information may be misused and even abused – when, for example, people may be selected (or rejected) for specific jobs on the basis of their genotypes, or people with high risk of specific diseases might be asked to pay high premiums by insurance companies (or worse, be excluded from coverage).

There is clearly need to resolve concerns and issues relating to the use and abuse of personal genetic data, and to come up with suitable guidelines for enabling better understanding and management of disease while ensuring that individuals are not discriminated against because of their genetic make-up.

Formulating national guidelines and policies for the management of confidentiality of, and access to, personal genetic data requires appreciation and understanding of a range of perspectives including:

- Personal genetic and genomic information of individuals can enable better understanding of health and disease, genetic influences on personality, intelligence, criminal behavior and other social traits
- There is need to protect confidentiality when conducting research using personal genetic and genomic information of individuals

Some governments (for example, the government of Iceland) have established DNA databases for their populations. While the benefits of such databases for research and development are likely to be substantial, there is clearly concern regarding the risk of abuse, especially in societies where individuals or authorities with access to relevant data may not be so scrupulous in safeguarding the confidentiality of others.

It is possible to conceive of many ways in which genetic and genomic information might be used and abused including:

- Universities and academic institutions might use personal genetic data to help profile prospective students, and to determine their suitability for various courses of study
- Employers might wish to use personal genetic data as one measure for determining the suitability of a candidate for employment
- Insurance companies might want to use personal genetic data: to determine the suitability of an individual for insurance coverage; to determine what restrictions there might be to coverage; and to determine what premiums to impose to cover the risks associated with genetic traits and predispositions to disease

There is clearly need to balance the interests and concerns of society for better understanding and managing disease with concerns of the individual regarding privacy and confidentiality of personal genetic information.

BioEnterprise Asia conducted a series of brainstorming sessions on the use and abuse of personal genetic information with participants from workshops on life sciences and biotechnology and on bio-IT between 2001 and 2003. Some observations and recommendations from these sessions give useful food for thought for those economies seeking to formulate guidelines for safeguarding personal genetic information:

- Any genetic or genomic information collected from a person (including DNA samples and information available in medical records and DNA databases) should be treated as the personal property of that individual
- Nobody should be allowed to perform any genetic test on a person or collect the person's genetic material without first obtaining permission from that person

- Individuals have a right to know if any organization (public or private) is collecting their personal genetic and genomic data, and how this information is being used
- Nobody (including governments) has the right to obtain or gain access to, or use, a person's genetic and genomic information without his/ her permission
- Nobody (including governments) has the right to disclose anyone's personal genetic information without his/her permission
- Governments may not use personal genetic data of citizens without first obtaining their permission every time they wish to use the information

Most would agree with the assertion that individuals should not be discriminated against because of their personal genetic and genomic make-up. One potentially very powerful approach for protecting the rights of individuals, especially in relation to possible discrimination by insurance providers, would be to take the view that we cannot hold a person responsible for his/her genes. So it makes sense to pool risk associated with gene-based defects and susceptibility, while making the individual directly responsible for health aspects over which they do have direct control (for example, exercise behavior, smoking, blood pressure and blood glucose regulation with medication, and so on).

Hence, this would allow for a social security system that helps to protect the public for health expenses arising from genetic contributions to disease over which they have no control, and a personal protection component in which insurance premiums are adjusted according to their behavior in mitigating risk – few countries, if any, have any guidelines or rules in place for how to deal with such circumstances.

There is clearly opportunity and need for countries around the region and internationally to respond to rapidly changing reality and to make a strong stand in favor of protecting individuals while enabling society to benefit best from the data and information that can be gleaned from studying their genotypes and phenotypes.

The Need for a Scientific Hippocratic Oath or Code of Conduct for Life Sciences

Today, we live in a time when new knowledge and growing capabilities place more power in the hands of the individual life scientist and innovator than has hitherto been dreamt possible – in fact, those of us with the knowledge and the skills to manipulate the genetic code, and potentially design organisms with new traits and characteristics of our choosing, will be primarily limited only by our imagination.

We can either choose to use the knowledge and power we have to solve problems and bring benefit and wealth to society, or to respond to greed, naked self-interest and the desire to destroy and even terrorize.

How does one who possesses such power decide how to use it (or, more importantly, how not to use it)? How do we prevent new knowledge and insights, and new tools, from being manipulated by despots and terrorists?

There is a characteristic ivory tower mentality prevailing among many scientists that their work is "ethically neutral" – that they are simply pursuing the generation of new knowledge and insight for its own sake, and that they, therefore, have no responsibility for how the knowledge they generate is used. While this is a convenient "escape hatch" to avoid taking moral responsibility for both the positive and negative use to which one's discoveries and contributions are put, the question needs to be asked if scientists should take a moral stance, and refuse to allow their efforts to be used in ways that may be detrimental or destructive.

J. Robert Oppenheimer, who coordinated the Manhattan Project leading to the development of the atomic bomb, reportedly felt intense guilt with the loss of innocent lives when bombs were dropped on Hiroshima and Nagasaki in 1945.[4] He was concerned, after the fact, that he had "blood on his hands." But he did nothing to stop the development and use of the bomb.

On the other hand, Josef Rotblat played a key initial role in the Manhattan Project with the US and its allies because he feared that Adolf Hitler would produce an atomic bomb first. He reportedly always hoped that the bomb would never need to be used. When it became clear to him that Hitler and his fellow Nazis had abandoned the German effort as too difficult, Rotblat became the only scientist who chose to walk out of the project and subsequently became a peace activist, despite initial ridicule and isolation from his colleagues and the military establishment. He came subsequently to be awarded the Nobel Peace Prize in 1995.

What can we say, looking at their actions with 21st-century lenses, about the ethical basis of the actions of Oppenheimer and Rotblat? Were they both ethically right? Was one of them wrong and the other right? Or did they both

---

[4] It is indeed ironic, and a sad indictment on humanity, that the most destructive "weapons of mass destruction" ever unleashed in the history of humankind were not developed or used by crazy despots or terrorist groups, but by the most powerful nation on Earth acting, by all accounts, in the interest of freedom and democracy. One can only hope, and pray, that history never repeats itself!

do the wrong thing ethically? What would you have done if you were in either of their situations?

What should a scientist do if she is involved today in a secret biotech project that might lead, for example, to the creation and unleashing of superbugs that could potentially eliminate entire populations? Should she act according to a sense of ethical and moral responsibility and refuse to carry on with the work when she realizes the potential (ab)use? Or should she follow orders/instructions because she is working for a "higher cause," whatever this might be? Should her actions differ depending on whether she is being sponsored by the US military, say, rather than by Al Queda, the terrorist organization?[5]

The reality is that there is no way we can hope to police every laboratory and scientific establishment and the work it does, or what each individual scientist or innovator chooses to do in the privacy of his or her own backyard.

Most responsible academic and research institutions and corporations in more developed countries have some form of in-house rules and best practice guidelines on ethics and ethical review processes to ensure that all officially approved scientific research and development activities meet basic ethical standards. The US government and many other governments around the world have sought to prevent work on human cloning, for example, by banning public funding for such research. But what is there to stop a privately funded laboratory from carrying out cloning experiments – as the Raelians and other groups claim to be doing?

How does one ensure that secret laboratories belonging to the military establishments of rogue nations, or to fringe terror organizations around the world, are not developing ever more pathogenic biological weapons to terrorize their own people or even the world at large?[6]

We could, and should, establish best practice guidelines for any and all life science and biotechnology laboratories operating in a country, and set up systems of audit to ensure that any and all work carried out in licensed laboratories meet ethical and safety requirements. Only laboratories that meet good laboratory

---

[5] It should be noted that despots and terrorists throughout history have always sought to appeal to "higher causes" to sublimate the despicability of the actions they have sought to perpetrate. Should individuals be encouraged to act according to their conscience and personal moral judgment, or should appeals to religious, ethnic, political, or nationalistic affiliations rule?

[6] Similarly, what is to prevent responsible governments and biotech enterprises that believe they are acting in the public interest from carrying out "classified" research to create pathogenic organisms and other hazardous biological products and then, perhaps, working to develop appropriate screening tests or antidotes? We can live in the belief that they are being developed for the "right" reasons – but will those reasons still be right when they end up in the wrong hands?

practice (GLP) certification requirements (see Box 14.2, pg 229), and operate under strict ethical and safety rules would be licensed to operate.

But what can we do about makeshift laboratories or unlicensed research establishments? The stark reality is that there is little or nothing we can do unless we operate on the basis, and hope, that each scientist or innovator will act appropriately and ethically. No number of safeguards or regulations will prevent an individual from cloning a hybrid Frankenstein monster if that is his intent – we can take away public funding, we can restrict access to other facilities or collaborations, but will this stop those who seek to work against the best interest of society in the first place? The reality is that the privately funded individual or scientific team working in a private high security laboratory could potentially do anything it wishes. At the fundamental level we have no choice but to depend on individual choices to ensure that the right things are done, and done right.

It is precisely out of such concerns that Rotblat and other leading thinkers have proposed the equivalent of a Hippocratic Oath for scientists.[7] Most of us in the medical profession, with the power we have over the lives of individual patients, are committed to working according to a code of medical ethics and conduct inspired by Hippocrates, the father of modern medicine (modern versions differ substantially from the code he established some 2,500 years ago).

Given the power that life scientists and biotechnologists have today over current and future life (and death), it seems only appropriate, and very necessary, that we should establish a similar code of conduct and ethics for the life sciences that govern the action of everyone engaged in innovation and product, service, or technology development in the life sciences and biotechnology.

The only things stopping people from doing wrong are their training, their upbringing, and their sense of right and wrong. These are all "soft" aspects that are not typically taught in academic, research or professional training programs. But the reality is that they have to be taught, the lessons have to be learnt, and a new Hippocratic Oath or code of conduct for life science professionals possibly needs to be developed so that scientists and the organizations or corporations they work for have a clear sense of what is right and wrong, and work with a sense of conscience and responsibility for the best interest of society and the environment.

As educators and as responsible members of society, we have a moral, ethical, and social responsibility to ensure that any and every individual who

---

[7] Josef Rotblat, World Conference on Science, 1999.

passes out of our academic and research institutions as a life scientist or entrepreneur, or who joins the BioBusiness professional arena in one way or another, has a keen understanding and appreciation of bioethical principles, and pledges to follow a best practice code of conduct and ethics that is akin to the medical code of practice based on the Hippocratic Oath. See Table 12.3 for some thoughts on possible elements that a good code of conduct might potentially incorporate.

Table 12.3 Possible Elements for Consideration in a Universal Code of Conduct for Life Science Professionals[8]

Proposed Element	Rationale
I acknowledge that I have a special responsibility for the future of humankind, the environment and of all forms of life on Earth. I will strive to apply my skills with utmost respect for human rights and the environment. Above all, I will seek to cause no harm	Emphasize sense of responsibility to life and the environment as fundamental obligations
I vow to practice my profession with conscience and dignity, and to uphold the noble traditions of scientific integrity and the pursuit of knowledge and truth. I will, at all times, treat my fellow life science professionals with the same professional respect and courtesies with which I would wish to be treated	Emphasize commitment to professional standards
To the best of my ability, I will contribute to education, training, and understanding of science in the public interest	Emphasize commitment to education and public awareness
I pledge to support research and development efforts that contribute to the solution of vital problems of humankind including poverty, hunger, disease, violation of human rights, armed conflicts, and environmental degradation	Emphasize commitment to being part of the solution, not part of the problem
I pledge to subject the assumptions, methods, findings, and goals of my work, including its possible impact on humanity and the environment, to open and critical discussion. I will reflect upon my work and its possible consequences and judge it according to ethical standards. I will do this even if it is not possible to foresee all possible consequences and even if I have no direct influence on them	Emphasize commitment to working openly and ethically, and to freely subject self and work to scrutiny by peers and the public

[8] This listing consists of both original elements as well as elements that have been adapted from a range of draft codes of ethics and of conduct including the Hippocratic Oath, practice codes of the American Medical Association, proposed texts for a Hippocratic Oath for Scientists, and so on. Our intention here is to stimulate debate by providing a smorgasbord of important ideas that we feel might possibly be worthwhile to consider including in a universally applicable code of conduct for life science professionals – we are not advocating that all the elements be included in such a code.

Table 12.3   (continued)

Proposed Element	Rationale
I acknowledge that curiosity and pressure to succeed may cause me to act in a manner that may be detrimental to human life or to the environment. I will not permit loss of objectivity or considerations of race, religion, nationality, policy, prejudice, or material advancement to intervene between my work and my commitment to act for the advancement of humankind and the environment	Emphasize self-awareness and recognition that several factors can potentially prejudice or bias our judgment and our actions Underline commitment to work in accordance with ethical best practices
If there is any indication or concern in my mind that I may be acting in a manner that is in conflict with my commitment to professional standards, I will abstain from further work until appropriate assessment and precautionary actions have been taken. If necessary and appropriate, I will inform the public	Emphasize commitment to subject personal actions to scrutiny from peers in accordance with best ethical practices
I pledge to enhance awareness of bioethical principles amongst my colleagues I will not keep silent if I become aware of any work that runs contrary to the best interest of human dignity or of environmental integrity. I will strive to expose those who are deficient in character or who engage in fraud or deception	Emphasize commitment to always operate in accordance with the highest ethical standards, and to maintain the highest standards by "whistle-blowing," if necessary, and exposing unacceptable practices
By the same token, I will not wilfully plagiarize or deliberately sabotage the work of other life science professionals	Emphasize commitment to operate at the highest level of personal professional integrity and respect for colleagues and the value of scientific insight and contribution
I pledge to support the open publication and discussion of scientific research. Since the results of science ultimately belong to humankind, I will conscientiously consider my participation in secret research and development initiatives that serve military, national, political, or commercial interests. I will not participate in such initiatives if I conclude that society or the environment will be injured thereby	Emphasize professional commitment to place responsibility to human life and the environment above any organizational considerations or commercial interests
I pledge not to take part in the development and production of weapons of mass destruction and of weapons that are banned by international convention	Emphasize commitment to honor best practice ethical standards, and not to allow knowledge, skills, and capabilities to be used for destructive purposes

Table 12.3 (continued)

Proposed Element	Rationale
I shall respect the law and always seek to abide by best practice guidelines that are applicable to my work, but I will not hesitate to seek changes to laws and practices that are contrary to the best interest of human dignity or environmental integrity	Emphasize respect for rule of law while recognizing that some laws and practice rules currently in place in different countries may not be consistent with operating according to best ethical practices
I will always seek to safeguard the public interest and my freedom to act independently for the benefit of society and the environment. I will not allow myself to be coerced or forced into taking any actions that are contrary to my commitments or this code of conduct	Emphasize need to safeguard scientific freedom and integrity.
I will make any attempt to coerce me to act inappropriately known to my peers and to the public	Lays down a possible approach to protect scientists from abuse or manipulation – for example, by despots or terrorist groups
I will support, honor and protect those who might experience professional disadvantages in attempting to live up to the principles of this code of conduct	Acknowledge that living up to high ethical standards can put colleagues at risk, and emphasize professional commitment to help colleagues who are under threat of persecution or punishment for standing up for their ethical responsibilities
I agree to abide by this code solemnly, freely, and upon my honor	Emphasize that the individual enters the code of conduct of the profession of his own free will

Source: BioEnterprise Asia, 2003.

Conclusion

There is clear need in every society to develop the resources and capabilities to proactively address and deal effectively with ethical and social dilemmas. In all our efforts, it is important to work to safeguard and enhance:

- Public and environmental safety
- Public understanding of the science and issues involved so as to engender objective informed debate and decisions on life sciences

and biotechnology. The power of public understanding and acceptance cannot be underestimated especially if the aim is to encourage utilization and adoption of the results of research for the public good

- Development of a conducive regulatory and cultural environment
- Training of human resources to deal effectively with such concerns. For example, investing in providing training opportunities for philosophers and ethicists facilitating the training of lawyers and other professionals who can help provide the legal and operational framework for resolving such issues and concerns in the interest of society, providing training opportunities for members of the media so they can be actively involved in the process of developing sound understanding of the issues and concerns surrounding ethical, moral, and social dilemmas

It is essential to train responsible scientists and other life science professionals to have a clear sense of right and wrong, with a clear appreciation of how they should use the powers that their knowledge and technical competence allow. We are all responsible to ensure that science is always used for the public good. It is never too early to educate people on ethics and the choices and trade-offs we need to continually make in the public interest.

Perhaps the time has come to require that life science or BioBusiness professionals undergo bioethics training, and agree to abide by an appropriate code of practice before they are allowed to enter the profession, just as those of us in the medical profession have done for over 2,500 years.

Key Points

1. There is need to establish mechanisms for considering ethical, moral, and social implications of life science and biotechnology innovation in every society.

2. There is need to engage the public and to address concerns and issues responsibly and sensitively if the potential of BioBusiness is to be maximized.

3. Given the reality that life science professionals have a growing range of capabilities and expertise to manipulate life forms that could potentially impact greatly on human life and the environment, there is need to establish appropriate codes of conduct so those who possess scientific and technological knowledge and capability use this for the public good and the benefit of the environment, and not for self-interest and detriment.

Chapter 13
Intellectual Property, Technology Licensing, and Branding Considerations

I criticize by creation - not by finding fault.

Cicero (106–43 BC)

Summary

Recognition and respect for intellectual property rights are becoming increasingly important as prerequisites for innovation and value creation in the life sciences. Societies and enterprises stand to benefit both through protecting and capitalizing on their own base of intellectual property as well as through gaining access to use proprietary knowledge and information developed by others through licensing, technology transfer, and technology partnering relationships. Strategic management of intellectual property can help incentivize the development of innovative new products, services, and technologies. Substantial value can also be created through strategic investment in cultivating and marketing a world-class brand identity and building brand equity – not just at the enterprise level through branded products, services, and technologies, but also at the institution/organization, biocluster, national, and even regional levels.

Introduction

Everything that can be invented has been invented.

Charles H. Duell, Commissioner, US Office of Patents, 1899

The honorable former Commissioner of the US Office of Patents could not have been more wrong. Much of the economic growth and development that the world has experienced in the time since he made his remark can be attributed, directly or indirectly, to technological innovation and the generation of knowhow, products, and services that build on innovation and inventiveness.

The pace of innovation is accelerating rapidly, and with this has come newer and better technologies that have greatly impacted all spheres of human existence – with ever shorter half-lives for new products or services to become effectively redundant, as anyone trying to find spare parts or software for a computer that is a few years old will soon realize.

Innovation and creativity thrives best where there is strong protection of intellectual property.[1] Innovative individuals, organizations, and enterprises work best in an environment that enables them to protect their competitive advantage and be rewarded for their investment in new product, service, and technology development. Typically, this involves obtaining and enforcing (where appropriate and necessary) intellectual property rights including patents, trademarks, copyrights, and trade secrets.

Technology- and innovation-based industries that have benefited most from intellectual property protection include media and entertainment, electronics and the semiconductor industry, the information and communications technology industry, and the pharmaceutical and biotechnology industries.

Asia-Pacific economies that seek to benefit from the life sciences and biotechnology would do well to recognize, respect, and safeguard intellectual property rights. Any perception of laxity in management of intellectual property (whether indigenous or foreign[2]), or weakness in enforcement of intellectual property rights, can be very damaging to the reputation and credibility of that economy, and can inhibit the ability of institutions and enterprises in that economy to benefit from, and create, value from innovation.

Similarly, for local and regional institutions and enterprises to be seen as viable partners for technology transfer and technology licensing, there has to be clear respect and support for the patent rights and knowhow of others (and vice versa). Only when a prospective partner is secure and certain that we will not abuse the knowledge and information that we are entrusted with

---

[1] Intellectual property (IP) can be defined as the commercially valuable output of the human intellect. An intellectual property right (IPR) is the legally enforceable power to exclude others from using the intellectual property (or to set terms on which it can be used). The category includes trademark, copyright, and patent rights, but also includes trade secret rights, publicity rights, moral rights, and rights against unfair competition.
[2] As many as 97% of the patents granted worldwide, and about 80% of the patents granted in developing countries, are produced by individuals, institutions, or corporations from more industrialized countries. This has, in the past, created concern in many developing countries that they stand to be at a disadvantage if they respect foreign intellectual property. The experience in the last decade has been that countries that are serious about capturing knowledge- and technology-based value through attracting foreign investment and facilitating product, service, and technology development partnership between local and established foreign players have far more to gain from respecting intellectual property.

will they enter into alliances with us. This requires a commitment to operate along best practice lines to build confidence, trust and long-term value.

This chapter examines three key areas of strategic importance in relation to maximizing value creation from our assets, capabilities, and intellectual property:

- Intellectual property and its management
- Licensing considerations
- Branding and brand equity management

Intellectual Property and Its Management

The new knowledge-based and technology-intensive economy provides a very unstable environment, an environment full of opportunities and challenges – as characterized by the dynamic nature of the BioBusiness landscape (Figure 4.1, pg 48). As described in Chapter 4, even if you are able to momentarily occupy a BioBusiness "Summit," and therefore command a competitive advantage to earn a premium from utilization of privileged knowledge and knowhow to develop and sell desired products and services, you simply cannot afford to rest on your laurels.

Competing technologies and products will almost inevitably be introduced by competitors when it is clear that there is real money to be made from the opportunity. Hence, for example, biotechnology or pharmaceutical companies with blockbuster products in novel categories can today expect to see "me-too" type drugs in the market within months of release of their original product.

The only way to maintain an edge is to avoid complacency and keep innovating. Interestingly, innovation, to date, has typically come in three basic forms, through:

- Development of subsequent "improved" generations of the product – with better efficacy, better safety or improved drug delivery, and more convenient dosing in the case of drug development (through, for example, the development of one-dose-a-day slow release formulations)
- Innovation in coming up with novel ways to "expand" and "extend" the life of patents
- Seeking to establish a brand identity and to maintain brand equity and associated perception of quality, reliability, and value for which consumers are often prepared to pay a premium

Generating, acquiring, and successfully managing intellectual property is central to any effort to capture value from the innovation process. The measure of success with intellectual property is not how many patents or trademarks

you can file but what value you can derive from the intellectual property.[3]
When you patent a new development, you must be prepared to defend and
enforce it – a process that can get very expensive unless you can derive real
value from the technology.

Having a good portfolio of intellectual property that includes patents,
trademarks, copyrights, and proprietary knowhow ("trade secrets") can not
only bring value from the generation and provision of new products, services,
and technologies, but can bring value in itself through strategic licensing to
partners (see Box 13.1).

Box 13.1   Strategic Intellectual Property Management

A well-developed intellectual property management strategy enables an
economy, institution, or enterprise to use cutting-edge technologies, to control
the use of such technologies by competitors, to maximize its competitive
advantage and revenues, and to obtain rights to use technologies that do
not belong to it. Considerations for strategic intellectual property
management (especially by institutions and enterprises) include:

- Identification of the technology to develop and protect. The
  institution's or enterprise's business strategy should be based on a
  clear understanding of its core competence and knowledge base
- Identification of the most suitable mechanisms for protection of
  intellectual property: patent? trademark? copyright? trade secret?
- Identification of the scope of rights to obtain: geographical coverage,
  markets of interest, cost implications
- Valuation of the intellectual property assets
- Establishment of strategic approaches to licensing of intellectual
  property for maximum value creation – both out-licensing and in-
  licensing

Knowledge is sometimes tacit in that it is difficult to codify, and hence
difficult to transfer. Codifiable knowledge is difficult to protect. Once you tell
the idea to the potential buyer, he or she might walk away without paying. As
a result, sellers of knowledge are very reluctant to fully disclose their complete
concept to potential buyers, who will in turn not be able to properly evaluate
the knowledge. Patents offer a solution to this problem. In return for disclosing
the complete invention, the owner of the patent has the exclusive right to
commercially use and benefit from it.

---

[3] IBM, for example, derives some 14% of its net income from licensing of its patented knowledge.

Even though patents sometimes work very well in creating a market for knowledge, they do not lead to a value-maximizing outcome in an economic or social sense since the value of knowledge is maximized if it is applied as widely as possible. Patent laws, on the other hand, give the patent owner a monopoly right, restricting the number of possible applications.

Despite this loss, there is good reason why most countries choose to have patent laws and respect intellectual property ownership – without the prospect of monopoly profits, there would be little incentive for research and innovation in the first place.[4]

The paradox of value creation through knowledge is therefore the constant tension between the inventors' interest in exclusive rights and society's interest in widespread application of the knowledge. This tension helps create the volatile environment of the new BioBusiness economy with all its opportunities and challenges.

Licensing Considerations

If you have an apple and I have an apple and we exchange these apples, then you and I will still each have one apple. But if you have an idea and I have an idea and we exchange these ideas, then each of us will have two ideas.

George Bernard Shaw

Licensing plays a vital role in ensuring that an organization's or company's knowledge- and technology-base is fully exploited.

Even though cutting-edge life science and biotechnology institutions and companies may thrive on innovation, intellectual property rights (IPR), and scientific talent, they rarely have all the ingredients necessary to capture the full value and benefit of their technology base in-house.

Hence, there is a need to consider bringing in and licensing the right to use other people's technology so it can effectively synergize with your own technology platforms to create new products, services, and technology (see also Figure 13.1).

Most companies simply do not have the resources, financial and human, to guide their products through the regulatory approval process since it involves dealing with regulators and managing clinical trials in many different

---

[4] Patents do have a limited lifespan, however. Eventually knowledge is expected to apply as broadly as possible. During the lifespan of the patent, the inventor is given the opportunity to recover development costs and to make a monopolistic profit to incentivize investment in new innovations and inventions.

Figure 13.1   Strategic Approach to Product, Service, and Technology
Development: Illustrative Example

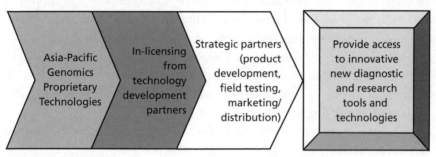

Source: Asia-Pacific Genomics, 2002.

jurisdictions, for example, working with the Food and Drug Administration
(FDA) for product approval in the US alone, while having to work with the
many regulatory authorities in other jurisdictions in Europe, Asia and other
parts of the world. It makes sense to work with reliable partners with good
local and regional knowledge to maximize effectiveness in capturing
opportunities around the world.

Many biotechnology players also lack the manufacturing capabilities and
resources to scale up production, to build marketing and distribution networks,
and to reach their target customers on their own. Again, licensing and
technology partnering arrangements may be the most effective strategy for
value maximization.

Licensing, both in-licensing and out-licensing, can play a vital part in the
corporate development and value creation effort. Licensing is not, of course,
the sole domain of developing country institutions and life science companies
– even established companies often choose to enter into licensing arrangements
with institutions and other companies to fill gaps in their own technology or
product pipeline, or to strategically supplement financial, physical, marketing,
manufacturing, or human resources needs.

There are generally many potential partners interested in licensing good
technologies since proactive technology companies are always on the lookout
for promising innovations to strengthen their product, service, and technology
pipeline.

The importance of in-licensing products to pharmaceutical companies,
for example, can be seen from a study by McKinsey in 1998 which revealed
that 14 out of 55 blockbuster drugs with annual revenues exceeding US$500
million were licensed from external sources, mostly after the technology
validation/proof of concept phase (see also Figure 4.3, pg 55).

While much depends on the quality and uniqueness of the technology developed, players keen on out-licensing products or technologies are increasingly using competitive or auction-type approaches to business development when identifying prospective licensees.

An important consideration is deciding the stage at which to license a product or technology – in general, the further the product or technology is along the development pipeline, the better the license deal is likely to be for the licensor. In considering suitable license partners, it is important to consider cultural and strategic fit, relative financial strength of the prospective partner, and what it can bring to the license arrangement other than cash.

Typical license structures would include some combination of upfront payments, milestone payments,[5] and royalties. Fair license arrangements typically ensure that the relative risks and rewards of the effort are shared between the parties.

There are characteristically four areas of interest in relation to licensing arrangements:

- Research and discovery
- Product development
- Manufacturing
- Marketing and sales

Typically, academic and research institutions or early stage biotechnology companies play the lead role in discovery and technology validation, and may provide input and support for on-going product development and testing effort (including field trials). The key role in manufacturing and/or marketing and sales are often undertaken by the licensee.

Branding and Brand Equity Management

To derive maximum benefit from a product, service, or technology offering, it is critical to differentiate one's offering from others in the marketplace. Why do people clamor to pay US$3 for a cup of coffee at Starbucks when they can get a similar cup at local outlets for US$1 or less? Why do people pay two or three times more for a Mercedes Benz than they would for a car with similar features from other makes? Why are consumers prepared to pay five times more for a product from GlaxoSmith Kline or Pfizer than they would for a similarly constituted generic product?

---

[5] These are payments to be made on reaching key measurable stages in the product or technology development process – for example, first use in man, achievement of regulatory approval, and so on.

The answer lies not in product or technology innovation, nor in superior strategies for intellectual property protection – but in intangibles that people associate with a brand. Building a brand identity and image is not easy, and it will not come overnight. It comes from years of hard work, a commitment to quality and reliability, and a commitment to be responsive to customer and market interests. It comes from a desire and commitment to give customers more than just a product or service – but an entire experience that they can fully expect when they buy into the provider and its services. Hence, innovation and commitment to building a reputation and image as a quality producer, as a reliable business partner who always delivers, as an environment that commits itself to giving the best experience, are all components of branding and building brand equity. Done right, branding can be an excellent mechanism for building value and enabling a product, service, or technology to attain premium earnings.

It is important to note, and to emphasize, that branding and building brand equity are not always focused on a single product, service, or technology. It is entirely feasible to build a brand identity for an entire company and its range of products and services, for a biocluster and the quality of scientific and technical support it offers, for a country and the experience of working in that climate or environment, or for an entire region.

Also, it is important to note that brand equity is fully intangible, and depends totally on the consumer's perceptions and expectations for buying into the brand. As the nature of the brand image is essentially intangible, the value and perception of value and the premium that the consumer is willing to pay will depend entirely on past experience, and reputation of the brand based on the experience of others. All it needs is one bad experience, one unhappy customer, one piece of bad publicity, and the entire brand development effort can start to fall apart. Hence, underlying the effort to build a brand identity for the region, for your nation, for your institutions, for your corporations, and for products, services, and technologies that come out of your country must be an underlying commitment to customer service, to reliability, to excellence – and essentially zero tolerance for failure to meet consumer expectations for best of class products, services, or technologies.

What this essentially means is that there is no place for shoddy workmanship, for poor quality control or quality assurance, for non-responsiveness to consumer demands and expectations, for a lack of reliability. Commitment to building a brand identity means commitment to building an entire infrastructure and support base for value as perceived by the end-user.

The rewards for an established brand identity are clear: an ability to command a premium compared to other product, service, or technology providers; the establishment of brand loyalty where discerning customers and clients insist on your products, services, and technologies; and the likelihood that leading players around the region and internationally will want to associate themselves with you and your product, service, and technology range.

A commitment to building brand equity requires hard work, and willingness to completely re-engineer work process and outputs from the perspective of the consumer. The beauty of building and having brand equity is that there is intrinsic value in the identity you have developed. Consumers are willing to pay extra to continue to experience what they have come to expect from your brand image, and substantial value comes to be attributed by consumers and competitors alike in your brand equity – investors are often prepared to pay a substantial premium for a piece of a world-class brand identity.

Asia-Pacific players would do well to think about branding, and about what they need to do to be able to build up brand equity for outputs from their economies. A perception of excellence can be associated with substantial value. There needs to be strong emphasis on differentiation, on moving from generic to proprietary branding, on quality, on reliable customer service, and on quality of experience.

Understanding The Brand Building Process

There are essentially four steps in the process of brand equity management that are worth considering:

- **Brand awareness.** The first step is to draw the attention of consumers and prospective customers and even investors to what you have to offer, and to begin to differentiate your offerings from those of other players. Without brand awareness, nothing happens.
- **Brand image.** Once you have captured customer or investor awareness, the rules change, expectations rise, and hype will need to be matched by substance.

    Building the brand image incorporates being understood and remembered for why you are different, for why the customer or investor should want to get involved with you, your institution, your company, or your country in the first place. The brand image embodies the character of the region, the nation, the institution, or the company; the characteristics of its product, service, and technology offerings; and the sum total of knowledge, experience, and emotional connection the consumer or investor develops in connection with your brand.

To successfully build a good brand image, it is not sufficient to pay lip service to the brand, or to put out a few slick advertisements. Much more than that, careful consideration must be given to ensuring that the entire experience that a consumer or investor has reinforces the brand image that you are working so hard to create. Every time the consumer logs on to your website, speaks to a receptionist who answers the phone, receives an email or an advertising brochure, meets an executive of the organization, or speaks with competitors or customers, the brand image is either reinforced or diminished.

Hence, it is critical that you do not even begin to raise brand awareness until and unless you can be sure that your house is in order; that all employees buy in to the need to give the right experience, and that every effort is made to reinforce your message – or else the entire exercise could end up having the opposite effect, and lead to consumer distrust and even apathy toward your brand or the image you are seeking to build. Fundamentally, you are making a promise to the consumer or investor that the brand image is consistent with the reality they can expect from working with you.

- **Brand preference.** If the consumer or investor buys in to the brand image and your intrinsic promise, and if his or her experience reinforces the image and helps differentiate your offerings from those of prospective competitors, he or she moves essentially to a preference for your offerings. In such a context, the consumer would generally choose your product, service, or technology offerings over those of other players in the marketplace. This is clearly a good position to be in, and already spells that you are well on your way toward capturing the value of the brand equity you are building. Still, it is important to remember that while the consumer or investor would prefer to use your products, services, or technology solutions, they have viable alternatives in the form of your competitors – and will choose to try these alternatives if you prove to be unavailable, inconvenient, or unaffordable. While they are prepared to pay a premium for quality, service and reliability, they will baulk at paying excessive premiums – it is critical that every effort is made to keep the customer happy and satisfied, and the whole experience consistent with their expectations.

- **Brand loyalty.** When consistent experiences clearly demonstrate their faith and trust in you and your product, service, and technology range has been well-placed, you reach an exalted status in the mind of the consumer or investor who will prefer working with you rather than any potential competitor. The consumer not only believes that you deliver what you promise in your brand image, but that the relationship between you and the consumer is a mutually reinforcing and beneficial one. Not only will consumers choose to use your products when they can, they will be prepared to actually recommend what you offer to others – creating substantial word-of-mouth marketing opportunities. When they believe they have a special relationship with you, competing branding efforts by competitors with competing products, services, and technologies are characteristically ignored.

The process of building a brand image and brand loyalty is not easy. It is a time consuming and laborious effort, that is well worth it because it builds substantial intangible goodwill, and can lead to real value creation as consumer loyalty builds up, and your reputation for quality, efficacy, and reliability builds up.

It is important to remember that consistency in positioning reinforces your brand image and enhances consumer loyalty for your offerings. Changing your message too often, or inconsistent messages in advertisements which do not reinforce the brand image do not help – in fact, they can create confusion, and an emotional disconnect, between you and your customer. Your brand gives your entire enterprise a certain personality in terms of their expectations from you – it is important that whatever interactions customers have with you, or any messages you put out, is a positive and mutually reinforcing one.

Delivering on the entire promised experience is critical for long-term growth and value creation of the brand identity – while brand equity is intangible, it is built up from providing the consumer with very tangible benefits and value. Once brand equity has been built up, it is possible to extend this to other offerings that build on the same core ideals and promise intrinsic to the brand image – this allows a broader brand franchise to be built up. The key to successful brand equity management is to build on the goodwill that has already been built up – not to keep recreating or shouting louder.

Done right, branding brings substantial returns to customers, investors, employees, and the entire enterprise. Singapore, for example, has done an excellent job of branding itself as a regional hub for life sciences and biotechnology, especially in the biomedical arena – multinational companies around the world have come to expect a high quality experience in dealing with Singapore and Singapore Inc. Thailand has done an effective job of branding itself as a healthcare tourism destination – and is successfully attracting holiday-makers from Europe and around the region to combine healthcare services and procedures with their holidays. Similarly, bioclusters around the region have started to brand themselves (BioPolis in Singapore; BioValley in Malaysia; Genome Valley in Hyderabad, etc.), and are seeking to build a brand image in the minds of prospective partners, clients, and the general public.

The importance of ensuring that hype is fully supported by mutually reinforcing action and substance is critical and essential – or there is much more to be lost than gained. Those countries, bioclusters, institutions, and enterprises that have their act together and can deliver effectively on the brand image and the intrinsic promise they create are the ones that are best placed to build long-term value.

Making things happen depends on close cooperation and a commitment to delivering on the promise from all who can play a part in determining whether the brand value is enhanced or diminished. There is clear need for partnering with policy-makers, with regulators, with municipal authorities, with utility providers, with financial institutions and others who can play a part in determining the success or failure of any branding and brand-building effort – whether at the corporate, biocluster, national, or regional levels.

In many ways, brand equity can be considered to be a strategically very important form of intellectual property, and can bring enormous value to Asia-Pacific economies that recognize the importance and value of marketing and brand development – not just at the enterprise or product/service/technology level, but also at the level of branding premier institutions and organizations, biocluster branding, national branding, and even regional branding in an effort to build up investment and support for BioBusiness activities in the region.

Conclusion

World-class players engaged in innovation and commercial development of cutting-edge R&D and the development of new products, services and technologies have much to gain from strategic intellectual property management. They would also do well to have clear licensing policies, and to work closely with collaborative and technology partners in relation to both in- and out-licensing of technologies for maximum mutual benefit and value creation.

In addition to product and technology innovation, and strategic intellectual property management through protection of intellectual property rights and licensing, it also makes sense to invest in building world-class brands and related equity for local enterprises and their products, services and technologies; for premier institutions and organizations; for bioclusters; for national

BioBusiness development efforts; and for regional commitment and support for BioBusiness development.

Key Points

1. Recognition and respect of intellectual property and intellectual property rights are essential for those Asia-Pacific economies, institutions, and enterprises that seek to operate as world-class BioBusiness players.
2. Asia-Pacific economies, institutions, and enterprises would do well to establish well-defined strategies for intellectual property management – including consideration of which products, services, and technologies to protect; how and in which jurisdictions to protect them; and how to manage the licensing of technologies.
3. There is real value that can be created from investing in cultivating and marketing local, biocluster-focused, national, and regional brand images. While this is necessarily a long-term effort based on ensuring the necessary quality, reliability, responsiveness, and experience intrinsic to the brand images are substantive rather than just hype, the tangible economic and social benefit that such branding can create are well worth the effort. World-class brands can be an invaluable form of intellectual property.

Chapter 14
Policy and Regulatory Considerations

Lead me, follow me, or get out of my way.

George Patton

Summary

There is need to establish policy frameworks and regulatory environments that facilitate and incentivize scientific and technological innovation and bioentrepreneurship. In addition to helping to ensure the development of appropriate physical and scientific infrastructure (including laboratories and science parks), there is need to provide training and skills development opportunities for scientists, life science entrepreneurs, and managers of science; to create a supportive cultural environment to incentivize and reward innovation and entrepreneurship; and to encourage the availability of smart money (both public and private) to help drive innovation and successful enterprises.

BioBusiness policies and regulations need also to take account of the dynamic nature of the life sciences and of developments in the arena; issues in relation to intellectual property and its management; and the ethical, social, and environmental concerns inherent to the sector.

Introduction

National policies and regulations form the platform and environment for the development of excellence in the life sciences and biotechnology. The approach and aims of governments and policy-makers in developing appropriate legislation and regulatory frameworks, and in participating in international forums and agreements, play a large part in helping to determine how effectively the economy, its institutions, and its corporations will be able to benefit from innovative technologies and entrepreneurial opportunities.

It is essential that all aspects of national policy – including research guidelines, product testing and registration regulations, respect for intellectual property rights, investment and trade guidelines, and so on – are developed based on a solid and reliable knowledge of the field being regulated, and are consistent with encouraging investment in, exploitation of, and application of output from the R&D process and the innovation pipeline (see Figure 4.3, pg 55). Furthermore, as most discoveries would be of potential international impact and applicability, laws, regulations, and guidelines would need to be consistent with regional and international rules (and certainly not be at variance with recognized international best practice standards).

On the other hand, given the rate of scientific progress, laws and regulations need also to evolve with changing priorities and realities, and to respond to the needs and concerns for public, animal, and environmental safety in the near and long term. Biosafety regulations, ethical guidelines, and clinical trial practices are under scrutiny: by policy-makers seeking to ensure public safety; by industry players seeking to secure regulatory approval and to build consumer confidence and larger markets; and by consumers and consumer protection groups who have faced all too many health, food, and environmental scares.

Aside from macro-level legislation, guidelines, and policies, life science and technology policy also typically involves an oversight of the governance and management of science and technology development efforts at the national, state, and even institutional levels (including the allocation and disbursement of funding in the form of strategic initiatives and national "flagship" program funding, core institutional allocations, grant funding, and so on).

Science and technology development is driven by the knowledge, capabilities, and aspirations of all who are involved in research, from research team leaders to students and technicians. Hence, scientific policy must deal also with the management and development of human resources at all levels. This typically includes, but is not limited to, systems for:

- Allocation of funding for research and pre-commercial development
- Development and maintenance of high research standards (for example, peer review, best practice guideline, and so on)
- Recruitment and development of scientists and managers of science
- Review and assessment for promotion of scientists
- Science and technology career and professional development

The challenges in developing an efficient, efficacious, and responsive science and technology policy infrastructure include:

- The need to determine research and development priorities in response to national, regional, and international opportunities, challenges, and needs (see also Box 11.4, pg 175)
- The need to balance organizational stability and operational flexibility in response to changing priorities and needs

- The need for transparent, independent, and objective review and performance audit mechanisms that help to ensure consistent R&D standards while being responsive to varied scientific interests and priorities
- The need to encourage individual investigator-driven research within the context of working to build core capabilities and competencies in response to national, regional, and international science development priorities for subsequent technology development and commercialization
- The difficulties and challenges of attracting, developing, and retaining world-class scientists and managers of science

The following sections will focus on two major areas of policy concern:

- Meeting fundamental needs for life science and biotechnology development
- Opportunity and need for public–private partnership

Meeting Fundamental Needs for Life Science and Biotechnology Development

Enlightened life science and technology development policy is critical to enable any economy to put in place the necessary fundamental capabilities and resources that serve as prerequisites for sustainable life science and biotechnology development (see Chapters 5 and 10, and Box 11.1, pg 168). These include:

- Investment in building and providing suitable infrastructure – both physical and scientific
- A supportive regulatory and policy framework
- A conducive environment that incentivizes innovation and entrepreneurship
- A commitment to human resource development
- A commitment to meeting financial and resource mobilization needs

Policies and regulations need also to take account of the critical success factors for innovation and entrepreneruship success identified by BioEnterprise Asia (see Chapter 5 and Box 11.1, pg 168). These include, above and beyond meeting the basic need for the fundamentals identified above, the need to incentivize and encourage:

- ***Smart people.*** Every effort should be made to encourage smart people to commit to helping to build the local bioeconomy and to work to bring their ideas to fruition

- *Smart ideas.* While there are plenty of smart ideas, there is need to encourage and support people with out-of-the-box ideas to test and validate their ideas, and to drive them through the innovation development pipeline (see Figure 4.3, pg 55)
- *Smart money.* Having large pools of money *per se* is not enough. Smart money focuses on investing strategically in capturing the value of bringing smart ideas to fruition (see also Box 16.1, pg 248).
- *Smart alliances and partnerships.* Those economies that are most plugged in to global trends and encourage local institutions and enterprises to establish collaborations with regional and international players stand to benefit most from new capabilities and resources (see also Figure 11.2, pg 177).

Open policies focused on value creation can have a substantial impact on making things happen. One interesting example of how open policies and a commitment to building capabilities and resources and attracting world-class scientists has been the experience in Singapore with its policy framework and guidelines for stem cell research (see also Box 14.1).

Other areas of interest and concern that will clearly impact future science and technology development include policies and guidelines for: field testing and commercial use of genetically modified organisms; clinical trials and testing of products for biomedical use; requirements for environmental and economic impact assessment as part of the evaluation and assessment of new technologies; policies in relation to technology licensing and technology transfer, and so on (see also Box 14.2).

Box 14.1   Case Study: Singapore's Stem Cell Research Guidelines and Its Success In Attracting International Scientists

Singapore laid down fairly "liberal" guidelines for stem cell research in 2002 that facilitated the establishment of a significant R&D base for stem cells and of several companies focused on such work. Singapore also attracted leading scientists from around the world to work in the republic. This prompted colleagues in the international media to ask if such liberal approaches will lead to an exodus of leading scientists from more regulated economies to economies where they had more freedom to work.

This is not the first time scientists are moving to Singapore to conduct research because they find it difficult or impossible to work in their own countries as a result of sensationalistic over-reaction to bioethical concerns in the West – brought about, in my opinion, by a combination of valid scientific uncertainty, vivid imaginations often focused on the most extreme possible scenarios on the part of religious and eco groups, political obfuscation, and a media which thrives on controversy, among other factors.

In the late 1970s and 1980s, leading *in vitro* fertilization (IVF) specialists from Australia and other centers around the world were given safe haven in Singapore and given the chance to work unfettered when it became clear that controversy and negative public sentiment, together with reactive and overly restrictive government policies, were making it impossible for them to work in their home countries. This helped Singapore become a leading international center for IVF R&D. More importantly, work in Singapore and in other centers around the world helped to dispel many of the negative myths surrounding IVF and so-called "test-tube" babies at the time.

The end result has been that IVF is today generally accepted as a procedure to help childless couples have babies. Hardly anybody talks today about the procedure being "unnatural" or of "humans interfering with the will of God" even though these were among the strongest arguments used in those days. Interestingly, many of these same arguments have resurrected themselves in relation to stem cell research and cloning. In its own way, one could argue that Singapore helped put some pragmatism and common sense into the old IVF debate – it may well do the same for stem cell work.

If US and European scientists start flocking to Singapore because asinine rules make it difficult or impossible for them to work unfettered in their home countries, law-makers and advocates for one perspective or another need only look in the mirror to identify whom to blame.

The reality is, and has been throughout history, that limiting factors to progress in science and technology have generally tended not to be scientific or technical, but rather all too human: ego, ignorance, prejudice, politics, vested interests, religious overzealousness, and a whole host of very human factors can take full credit for slowing human progress in favor of the status quo.[1]

I believe the stem cell research debate is not only a storm in a teacup, it is also rather off course. Paralysis and blockage of needed scientific validation, may, one way or the other, greatly hurt the development of promising new technologies in tissue engineering because people get so entrenched in their position they do not know how and when to back off and let things take their course.

---

[1] On a similar vein, I have to cringe every time I think about economic disparities between the haves and have-nots, about the fact that we have more than enough wealth in the world today to keep everyone happy and healthy yet hunger and disease still take such a large toll on life, and so on. Collectively and individually, we are often our own worst enemies – no matter how we try to rationalize things, we cannot avoid responsibility for failing to take proactive action to ensure greater equity when what needs to be done is so obvious to anyone who takes the trouble to objectively examine existing realities.

The fact is that embryos are NOT the only source of stem cells – that there is growing recognition that multipotent and even totipotent stem cells can be found in the cord blood of newborn babies and in adult bone marrow, for example. My prediction is that we will soon start harvesting stem cells routinely from cord blood and adult bone marrow, and much of the cause for the hang-up with stem cell research (that is, taking cells from aborted fetuses) will simply disappear.

The key is to focus on understanding the basis for our fears and concerns: what do we really know? what don't we know? how do we find answers to the questions that underlie our concerns? will these answers come from further debate, or will they come from further research?

Only by having a good grasp of the underlying reasons for our ethical dilemmas, and working with the public in a responsible, non-alarmist way while seeking to increase our base of knowledge or understanding can we dispel public concerns and begin to make reasoned assessments of the value or otherwise of any areas of interest or focus.

Box 14.2 Some Best Practice Areas that Can Impact on Success in Life Science and Biotechnology Innovation

Good Manufacturing Practice

The acronym, GMP (Good Manufacturing Practice) is used internationally to describe a set of principles and procedures that, when followed by manufacturers, helps ensure that the products manufactured will have the required quality. A basic tenet of GMP is that quality cannot be tested into a batch of products at the end of the production process but must be built into each stage of the manufacturing process.

Most countries have regulations for GMP compliance as the basis for licensing manufacturers of medicinal products and medical devices. The National Control Authority of each country is responsible for establishing procedures for assuring that products intended for use in the country meet all criteria for quality, safety, and efficacy.

Good Clinical Practice

Good clinical practice (GCP) is a standard by which clinical trials are designed, performed, monitored, audited, recorded, analyzed, and reported so that there is public assurance that the data is credible and that the rights, integrity, and confidentiality of subjects are protected.

Good Laboratory Practice

Good laboratory practice (GLP) is a quality system concerned with the organizational processes and conditions under which scientific and technical studies are planned, performed, monitored, recorded, archived, and reported.

Table 14.1 Policy Considerations in Dealing with Fundamental Needs for Life Science and Biotechnology Industry Development

Fundamental need	Issue	Recommendations
Infrastructure development	Infrastructure development varies considerably across the region. Large economies have the problem of being too big to change quickly, while small economies have the problem of higher relative costs. There is also concern regarding the risk of duplication of resources at institutional, biocluster, state, national, and regional levels as competition heats up to build and provide access to world-class physical and scientific infrastructure, while countries typically lack a critical mass of scientists	To establish infrastructure required for high quality research. This includes meeting fundamental need for physical infrastructure, and for the establishment of scientific infrastructure – including laboratory and related support needs for safety and containment, and the development of institutional capabilities and resources for world-class science
R&D culture	A thriving community of scientists is often lacking, particularly in smaller or developing economies There is typically a limitation of supportive capabilities and resources incentivizing innovation and technology entrepreneurship in Asia, compared to the comparative wealth of investment support for innovative product, service, and technology development, as well as investment in support of technology start-ups, in the US and Europe	To develop a more vibrant R&D culture that helps to incentivize innovation and entrepreneurship, facilitates academia–industry relations, and encourage exchange of scientists and innovators at the enterprise, institute, biocluster, state, national, and regional levels

Table 14.1 (continued)

Fundamental need	Issue	Recommendations
Legislation and IPR protection	The rate of scientific advancement is rapid. Legislation needs to be adaptable, and be able to evolve and respond to the needs and concerns of the public and of the scientific community. Although legislation is generally in place in many parts of the region, implementation and enforcement tends to be weak. This has led to low public awareness or confidence in molecular biology and biotechnology capabilities in each economy and, as a result, hesitation by investors and private industry to invest in R&D and early stage enterprises	Education, training, and investment in legislation development and IPR protection. Scientists and innovators need to work with entrepreneurs, policy-makers, investors, legal experts, and the media to ensure growing expertise and support in the region for innovation and enterprise development
Human resources	The shortage of skilled human resources in many economies is a key limiting factor for capturing the value and potential of modern BioBusiness

A common regional challenge is the need to increase the attractiveness of a scientific career, by developing more complete and diverse career paths to entice and reward new generations of innovative and entrepreneurial scientists

There is a dearth of science managers in the region, a major hindrance to the development of the regional life sciences industry | Cross training in academia and industry settings is becoming increasingly crucial

Need to review the current career development pathways, and encourage greater flexibility and opportunities within and across disciplinary areas, and between academia and the private sector

There is opportunity and need to re-examine education policies and curricula to ensure that modern biology is incorporated into education programs as early as the primary school level, and that more and more students can choose to be trained in the life sciences and related technologies

There is need for executive and mid-career training opportunities to enable interested managers to gain an understanding of the opportunities and challenges in BioBusiness administration and management |

Table 14.1   (continued)

Fundamental need	Issue	Recommendations
Finance and resource mobilization	Public funds for research are generally available, although quantums in some countries may not be sufficient to support world-class research and development. Also, scientists face the challenges of often opaque evaluation systems, varying funding levels and rapidly changing funding focus	There is need to ensure greater commitment to ensuring the availability of smart money to support early-stage innovation and technology development
		Economies in the region would benefit from having access to a network of trained evaluators from throughout the region and beyond that could aid policy-makers and investors in funding and policy decisions
	Another hurdle tends to be the low level of participation and interest of private investors and industry players in R&D and in commercialization of research findings in many countries	There is clear opportunity and need to encourage public–private cooperation in R&D and in commercialization of technology. Such encouragement can come from a variety of activities including providing tax and investment incentives for industry to engage in R&D; facilitating interaction and communication between researchers at institutions of higher learning and industry players; and providing grants in support of technology innovation and commercialization

Opportunity and Need for Public–Private Partnership

There is need for Asia-Pacific economies to strategically work toward putting in place policies favoring closer public–private partnership in making things happen in life science and biotechnology. Among other things, this could entail working together to facilitate early-stage innovation support, and successful commercialization to promising products, services, and technologies. The private sector can also play a pivotal role in licensing and supporting the validation of promising concepts and nascent technologies developed by scientists at research and academic institutions.

Different economies in the region are at different stages in establishing and strengthening such collaboration between the public and private sectors. Some governments, such as the Australian, Japanese, and Korean governments, have very good working relationships with the private sector. Other governments still tend to view the private sector and its motivation with uncertainty or even suspicion.

BioEnterprise Asia has studied the evolution of the nature of the relationship between public and private sectors in the region, and has identified three major phases in building up confidence for public–private partnership (see also Table 14.2):

Phase I: Traditional Phase – lack of trust, different agendas and priorities, little interest in working together

Phase II: Transitional Phase – initial fierce concern and sense of competition with the private sector, with confusion regarding the roles of the public versus private sectors; later, there are moves toward closer cooperation and collaboration

Phase III: Integrated Phase – high trust, excellent and open working relationships, people move easily across sectors and roles without

Table 14.2 Typical Public Sector Perceptions as Indicator of the Level of Public-Private Sector Cooperation

Phase	Typical perception
Traditional Phase	
Phase I: Non-recognition	"The private sector is irrelevant, they are a non-player."
Transitional Phase	
Phase IIa: Avoidance	"We don't work with the private sector. They have sold out, lost sight of our humanitarian and social mission. They only want to make money."
Phase IIb: Competition	"We don't trust the private sector. They steal our best people. We don't want to work with the private sector."
Phase IIc: Acceptance	'We need to find a way to work with the private sector but we don't know how to approach, talk or work with them. We are concerned, however, that they might attempt to subvert the national agenda."
Phase IId: Cooperation	"We encourage the private sector to work with us to meet our agenda and to share their views on national biotechnology considerations."
Integrated Phase	
Phase III: Synergy	"We work closely with the private sector to achieve national biotechnology objectives. We encourage open information sharing and consultation with the private sector. People move freely between the public and private sectors. The private sector is our partner."

discrimination, emphasis on finding the best person for each job regardless of whether they come originally from the public or private sector.

Table 14.2 outlines a useful diagnostic tool developed by BioEnterprise Asia to assess the level of public–private partnership in any given sector based on perceptions expressed by public sector players. Importantly, the level of cooperation and collaboration can vary substantially depending on sector and specific area of cooperation or partnership activity. Those economies that are most successful in facilitating public–private partnership will be best placed to establish and nurture sustainable development of life science innovation and the establishment of a viable and dynamic indigenous life science and biotechnology sector.

Conclusion

There is need to establish a policy, legislative, and regulatory framework that protects the interests of the public while incentivizing innovative science and technology (see Table 14.1). While it is critical that public safety and public health are not put at excessive risk, policy-makers and regulators should be well aware that there is a need to rethink archaic rules in response to new insights and understanding.

This is not so easy since we often need to work in the context of incomplete information, with pieces of the jigsaw puzzle being put together with time. Still, guidelines and related decisions need to be laid out sooner rather than later, as it may be too late when sufficient information finally becomes available (since undesirable actions may have already been undertaken) – for example, in relation to release of genetically modified organisms without due safety and environmental testing. Here, the governing rule should be that used by many physicians: "First, do no harm!" (see also Table 12.3).

There is clearly need for visionary policy and legal frameworks toward establishing the conducive cultural environment to facilitate, drive, and incentivize innovation and entrepreneurship development in the region. Most important of all, public policy should be based on a recognition of the critical importance of cooperation and collaboration between the public and private sectors in creating lasting and sustainable value for economies in the region and beyond.

Key Points

1. Government policies play a key role in helping to shape development of the life sciences and biotechnology in any economy.

2. Government policies impact not only the legal and regulatory framework under which innovators and entrepreneurs operate, but also help shape public investment in building physical and scientific infrastructure, human resource development and institution-building, establishment of a cultural environment incentivizing and rewarding innovation and entrepreneurship, and provision of public funding to fuel the successful translation of concept to practical reality and the establishment of viable and high growth enterprises.

3. Government attitudes and policies toward the private sector can play a key role in either facilitating or retarding public–private partnership in support of life science and biotechnology innovation and the establishment of successful high growth enterprises. There is a clear need for closer public–private partnership in building lasting and sustainable value for enterprises, institutions, bioclusters, and other players at the national and regional levels.

Chapter 15
Meeting Human Resource Needs

There is something that is much more scarce, something rarer than ability. It is the ability to recognize ability.

Robert Half

Summary

The translation of cutting-edge research and development into commercially and socially valuable innovations and enterprises requires skilled and competent individuals across the entire pipeline, from upstream R&D to productization and product development, to field-testing and evaluation, to market and business development. While the experience of the last several decades has helped fuel the development of world-class scientists and institutions in the region, there continues to be a dearth of skilled and effective managers of science who understand both the business opportunities and the scientific potential. Additionally, there is growing need for key service and support professionals, including technology-savvy legal expertise, intellectual property managers, and media, public, and investor relations personnel.

Introduction

Modern BioBusiness institutions and enterprises need to gain access to a wide range of capabilities, core competencies, and expertise to enable them to successfully drive innovative new products, services, and technologies through the developmental pipeline (see Figure 4.3, pg 55). In addition to the requisite strategic science and technology management expertise to take product, service, and technology concepts through proof of concept and technology validation through productization, there is also need for marketing and business development capabilities to take pre-commercial products through business case validation to successful market entry and development.

Along the way, there is need for access to expertise for intellectual property management, management of clinical and field tests, production process development, quality control and quality assurance, product registration, marketing and business development, and distribution channel management, among other capabilities. In addition, life science and biotechnology enterprises require access to more generic capabilities that are critical to the success of any enterprise including administrative, financial management, operational management, legal, public and investor relations, and fund-raising expertise.

The Asia-Pacific region has experienced a dramatic increase in innovation and entrepreneurial activity in BioBusiness technology-related industries throughout the region in recent years, spurred initially by the Internet "bubble", starting in the mid-1990s. Investor interest in the region is now focused on life science enterprise opportunities with high-growth potential in response to growing market demand. Companies that are able to develop and supply innovative products, services, technologies and/or supporting infrastructure in response to changing healthcare and life science needs in the Asia-Pacific region and the world are well-placed for future growth and success. However, the growth and development of such enterprises have tended to be hampered by a dearth of management skills and talent to support the translation of new insights in life science technology into successful commercial application.

Governments, organizations, institutions, and enterprises attempting to operate in the BioBusiness arena need to be fully conversant with the risks and challenges involved in taking concepts and ideas to fruition, and with how to successfully manage these risks. Yet, managerial skills and market insight required to bring a discovery from the laboratory to commercial application are in short supply and are even rarer in start-up enterprises – hence, serving as a major bottleneck holding back successful and efficient R–D–A translation (see Figure 4.2, pg 54).

The following sections will focus on a range of issues of priority interest in relation to identifying, building, and meeting human resource needs for successful bioinnovation and bioenterprise development, including:

- Understanding human resource needs for different stages of corporate development
- The critical importance of education and capacity-building
- Rethinking academia and life science education
- Innovative approaches to working with the best and brightest

Understanding Human Resource Needs for Different Stages of Corporate Development

Successfully taking a life science company through different enterprise life cycle stages requires specialized skill sets and capabilities at each stage of development:

- *Early stage companies.* Early stage enterprises need entrepreneurial-type individuals who are not afraid to take major calculated risks, and to work long hours to make the dream come true. Such individuals characteristically are prepared to work under less-than-ideal circumstances, often with minimal technical and staff support. Translating early stage enterprises to growth stage companies often depends on the vision, commitment, and passion of the dreamers, visionaries, and entrepreneurs to make things happen.

- *Growth stage companies.* Growth stage companies need to make the transition from the maverick operating style typical of entrepreneurs to become formalized corporate structures that build on the efforts of their founders to capture revenue and market share. The individuals needed to drive development of companies at this stage are the builders (rather than the dreamers and the mavericks). They help the companies successfully make the transition from the heady, idealistic start-up days to achieving the stature of mature organizations. Only a few exceptional entrepreneurial types successfully make the transition – smart entrepreneurs recognize that they must be prepared to step aside and hand over the reins to steady managers to enable the company to formalize its *modus operandi* and reach its maximum potential.

- *More mature companies.* More mature companies have solid, if somewhat ossified, operating structures and can be relatively inflexible once a particular strategic direction is set. The people who are attracted to work in such organizations tend to be big company corporate-types who want secure positions with well-defined job definitions and well-established support infrastructure. Almost by definition, managers of mature companies are more averse to risk than the maverick entrepreneurial start-up types.

Critical Importance of Education and Capacity-building

An education isn't how much you have committed to memory, or even how much you know. It's being able to differentiate between what you do know and what you don't.

Anatole France

There is growing need to re-examine biological science education curricula in our schools, and to ensure the injection of modern life science and biotechnology into education programs – starting as early as the primary and secondary school levels, but also working to incorporate fundamental knowledge and understanding of the principles of life science and biotechnology in training programs at the vocational as well as tertiary educational levels (see also Box 15.1).

Box 15.1   The Israeli Experience in Shaping Education

During the 1960s, leading scientists in physics, biology, and mathematics in Israel, in collaboration with the Ministry of Education, established a collaborative framework for the promotion of science education known as the "Center of Science Education." This government-funded organization is involved in a variety of academic and applied activities promoting science education for K-12 graders.

These activities include the development and production of teaching materials, participation in and leadership of national curriculum commissions, teacher training (pre-service and in-service), and research activity in science education. The capacity of the "Center for Science Education" to be at the cutting edge of this field was also very instrumental in the introduction of changes in the system, which are essential in this rapidly evolving field.

In 1992, the Ministry of Education appointed a commission, headed by the President of the Weizmann Institute, Professor Haim Harari, to examine the state of science and technology education, define the future goals, and recommend how these goals can be achieved. The commission made specific recommendations in a variety of topics, including:

- The strengthening of the mathematical literacy and capabilities of all students, starting with the elementary school level
- Joining science and technology education in elementary and junior high school levels (grades 1–9), rather than separating the two disciplines (this is especially suitable in this period when science and technology are so closely interrelated)

> - It was emphasized by the committee that it is mandatory not to train just the future scientist or technologist, but also the future citizen whose life will be strongly affected by modern science and technology
>
> The implementation of these and other recommendations was approved by the Israeli government in 1993 significantly increasing the budgets allocated for science and technology education and is currently widely applied.
> Source: Dr Benjamin Geiger, The Weizmann Institute of Sciences, Rehovot, Israel, Report of the Commission on the Strategic Vision for Asia-Pacific IMBN, 2000.

Traditionally trained teachers typically have little or no understanding of how to teach modern biology, and will need to be retrained and provided with the necessary resources, knowledge, and skills to enable students to gain sufficient understanding of the opportunity or potential of the modern life sciences and biotechnology, and how new developments in the arena are likely to impact on them going forward.

The gravity of the situation should be taken seriously, especially when one takes account of the very dynamic nature of this field, and the speed with which new discoveries and technologies are being made. Delays in providing the young with sufficient "bioliteracy" to make sense of developments in the life sciences and biotechnology, and their implications in social and even career terms may well slow down the ability of these societies to capture the value and potential of plugging in to the life science revolution.

Training and education in the fundamentals of the life sciences and biotechnology should not be narrowly restricted only to future professionals in the arena. Just as we treat information and communication technology as basic survival skills in this day and age, we need to emphasize basic understanding and knowledge of life sciences and biotechnology to students, even at the primary school level, to enable them for the future bioeconomy.

In an innovative experiment, BioEnterprise Asia organized a series of BioCamps – targeting 9- to 12-year-olds in "Discovery and Fun" programs, and 12- to 15-year-olds in "Learning from Experiments" programs. Even though the concepts of the genetic basis of life, of genomics and proteomics, and of how these new developments are beginning to change life as we know it has not been taught to them in schools, students as young as eight or nine had little difficulty in understanding and applying sometimes abstract concepts in the life sciences, and in appreciating the application of such technology in health and disease. With the use of age-appropriate models, simulations and experiments, students were able to participate actively and intelligently in dialogue and debates on ethical and social concerns in the life sciences and biotechnology (see, for example, Box 12.3, pg 193 and Box 12.4, pg 198).

The BioCamp experience clearly validates our perspective that children are never too young to start the education process and that failure to engage our children in understanding the life sciences and biotechnology may well leave a substantial subset of our regional population being functionally illiterate in the most important area of knowledge and insight over the next several decades.

The 21st century will certainly be dominated by societies that are technology- and knowledge-intensive. Natural resources will be less dominant as drivers of wealth creation – more important will be how we add value to natural resources to create value and benefit to society and in the marketplace. Trained human capital is critical for any knowledge-based economy. It is important, to reach prosperity, that we increase investment in life science and biotechnology education, and that we take the lead through our schools and academic institutions to catalyze the development of human resources who are well-placed to lead and support the establishment of knowledge-based BioBusiness economies.

It is obvious that developments in science and technology will have a major impact on the lives of all people – and scientific and technological literacy will be increasingly essential. There is growing need for literacy in modern life science and biotechnology for the lay man, and this need will only increase in time as BioBusiness gains an ever more pervasive influence on all aspects of our lives (see also Box 15.1).

Investment in education and skills development is, hence, a very important investment that our societies can and should make. For example, it is important to set ambitious goals in educating students at the undergraduate and graduate levels to become leaders and innovators in BioBusiness – whether in the healthcare, biomedical, agricultural, environmental, or industrial sectors. As such, academic institutions have a special responsibility for promoting science and technology education. Universities should devote effort to the development of trained science and technology expertise in their respective countries. Researchers involved in cutting-edge research and development should also be encouraged to write, develop teaching materials, and mentor young students with an interest in pursuing careers in the life sciences and biotechnology.

As has been emphasized throughout this book, modern BioBusiness is a multi-disciplinary endeavor requiring the knowledge base and skill sets of a range of trained experts and professionals. Whether one is a lawyer, a financial analyst, an intellectual property expert, or a process engineer, knowledge and understanding of the modern life sciences and the implications of modern biotechnology are becoming increasingly important for those who want to play a part in capturing the BioBusiness value potential. Hence, executive education opportunities to equip these individuals with at least a basic understanding of the vocabulary, and key concerns and priorities, in BioBusiness would certainly be very useful and beneficial.

It is also necessary to re-examine our education curricula at the vocational training and tertiary levels to endow students, regardless of their field of study, with a basic understanding of the life sciences and biotechnology – and of how multi-disciplinary research, managerial and technical support inputs are critical for successful development of a vibrant BioBusiness-oriented economy. The understanding of research management, intellectual property management and commercialization processes, and of ethical and social issues in life sciences and biotechnology, among other areas, will help equip students not only for careers in their chosen fields, but also for careers that contribute constructively and meaningfully to catalyzing the establishment of vibrant bioeconomies throughout the region.

Rethinking Academia and Life Science Education

Academia has traditionally been the preferred course for career advancement for scientists and seemed to offer, over the last several decades, the best chance to achieve stature and make a real difference professionally. While this clearly remains a viable option, interesting and challenging new opportunities abound everywhere.[1]

The old rigid traditional departmental classifications in academic and research institutions put up as barriers by specialists are being broken down as we increasingly recognize the value and potential of coming together to solve multi-faceted problems that transcend disciplinary boundaries (see also Box 11.4, pg 175).

The education of students of science can only benefit from the knowledge and expertise of scientists who are prepared to step outside the rarefied stratosphere of the ivory tower to deal with real-life opportunities and challenges. We need to start taking a non-traditional approach to education and the qualifications and prequisites of our educators. While the purist and ultra-specialist will always have their place, people who have worked in

---

[1] Don't get me wrong. There is no higher calling, in my mind, than to inspire young minds – it is exciting and very rewarding to engage actively in teaching and training future generations of scientists, and in inspiring a love for new knowledge and insight.

industry, entrepreneurs, and policy-makers have valuable insights to share with students of science, giving a much better rounded education than is currently the case in most of our institutions.

We should encourage all who are interested, regardless of whether they work in the public or private sector, to make an active contribution to training and education and sharing their knowledge – by volunteering in schools, by participating in educational programs, by taking on adjunct appointments on the faculty of academic and research institutions, and by taking on interns.

There is a great opportunity to cross-train students of different disciplines – business, management, law, engineering, public policy, and so on – in the opportunities and challenges in life science and technology development. We need managers of science – people who not only understand the sciences, but also have a good appreciation of the challenges of making things happen; people who are not only caught up in the technical beauty of new ideas and technologies, but who are keen to see these applied to making life better, and to changing things for the better. Such individuals will play the greatest role in facilitating the translation of scientific and technological insight into practical, commercial reality (see Figure 4.3, pg 55).

What we need most of all to fuel the life science and technology revolution are people who are true innovators and pioneers in spirit and action. People who do not feel hide-bound to follow the doctrines of specialty but are prepared to challenge scientific and technical dogmas to come up with newer and better ways of doing things. This applies whether we speak of individuals who will take up management careers, engineering, or IT, or even law, political science, or the humanities. The better we understand the way things work, the more effective we can be in finding newer and better ways to do things, to create value, and to make a difference.

The opportunity and need to rethink our education curricula to enable such individuals to flourish is critical.

Innovative Approaches to Working with the Best and Brightest

Mediocrity knows nothing higher than itself, but talent instantly recognizes genius.

Arthur Conan Doyle

Asia has a desperate need for managers of science – people who understand the promise and potential of the science, the technological issues and challenges in translating insights through the innovation development pipeline to the market, and the opportunities and challenges in market and business development. Access to individuals with the requisite skills and experience can greatly mitigate execution risk and increase the likelihood of success of life science innovations and enterprises.

Rather than insist on rigid working conditions that make it difficult, if not impossible, to gain the services and input of leading scientists, entrepreneurs and managers of science, much more can be gained by working out flexible win-win relationships with committed players who are prepared to play a part in helping to drive technology and human resource development by engagement on a part-time or advisory capacity. Institutions should, for example, encourage adjunct attachments and allow leading players in industry and around the world to be affiliated with the institution. This way, these leading thinkers can be engaged to share their knowledge and experience, and to contribute their insight toward helping the institution to develop its R&D program, help train students and future captains of industry, and facilitate the identification of leading future innovators and entrepreneurs. The best part is that many leading experts would welcome the opportunity to maintain an affiliation with emerging institutions and prospective centers of excellence – and would do this for a token honorarium and perhaps some space and facilities for students and their research activities. Both sides win.

Similarly, enterprises would do well to invite leading thinkers and industry players in the country and internationally to serve on their science and technology advisory boards, and be actively involved with their efforts as part of their "virtual" project management teams (see Chapter 11). The more savvy the advisor or consultant, the more plugged in to state-of-the-art development and work in the region and beyond, and the better connected to licensing and partnering opportunities, the better. The right advisors can play a very proactive role in helping to drive scientific, technology, and market development, and in facilitating strategic alliances and partnerships that can create substantial value for the enterprise.

Conclusion

Most countries in the Asia-Pacific region needs to train and develop the human resources that will drive and support value creation in the life sciences and biotechnology. While there is clear need to have trained professionals today, it will be even more critical to ensure that future generations of children have literacy and understanding of modern biotechnology and bio-IT.

Each child should be trained to understand and appreciate the implication of modern biology and the life sciences. The skill sets and knowledge base required are quite different from those for classical biology. We need to train our teachers to teach children, and to develop new curricula that are responsive to changing realities.

It is also necessary and appropriate to provide orientation and life science education for professionals in many fields of work that are potentially complementary to the life sciences and biotechnology.

We live in a world of inequity today – the haves and the have-nots, the literacy divide (between the literate and the illiterate), and the digital divide (between the computer literate and the illiterate). Let us learn from the mistakes of the past to ensure that every living person on this planet has at least a basic understanding and appreciation of the BioBusiness arena, and how they can apply and use this information in their daily lives and for improving their livelihoods.

For the sake of our future generations, we cannot afford to create a *biological divide,* for it is only by harnessing the innate creativity and inventive spirit that is in each of us that we will be fully able to exploit and capitalize on the opportunity and potential of BioBusiness.

Finally, it is important to recognize that world-class scientists and managers of science are in short supply throughout the region and beyond. Rather than create rigid working rules demanding that leading thinkers and implementers dedicate themselves 100% to working with any institution or enterprise, there is substantial value that can be created by encouraging flexibility through adjunct, advisory or consultative roles so the knowledge, insight, and experience of these leading thinkers can be tapped for the maximum benefit of the institution or enterprise.

Key Points

1. Asia-Pacific life scientists are equal to the best in the world. The brain drain is a short-term illusion. Over the longer term, we really have a brain flux where the best and brightest go where they can make the biggest impact.
2. For successful innovation and enterprise development in BioBusiness, there is need for both strong science and technology management capabilities, as well as for market and business development capabilities. There is, hence, tremendous need for managers of science. There is also strong need for supporting professionals including lawyers, intellectual property specialists, and effective financial managers. There is also need to provide

executive education and training to enable these professionals to support life science and biotechnology enterprises more effectively.

3. Awareness of the fundamentals of modern life sciences and biotechnology and of how it will impact us and our lives is critical, and should start from rethinking our primary and secondary school education curricula. Just as we now have an economic divide, a literacy divide, and a digital divide, we need to ensure that we do not unwittingly create a *biological divide* between those who understand the opportunity and potential of new BioBusiness innovations and their impact on our lives, and those who don't.

4. Institutions and enterprises need to recognize that world-class capabilities in life sciences and biotechnology, and in the management of science, are rare. Rather than insist that talented individuals commit themselves rigidly to single institutions or enterprises, cutting-edge institutions and enterprises will benefit most by offering opportunities for leading thinkers to work with them on an adjunct or advisory basis so they can benefit from the knowledge, insights, and capabilities that the leading thinkers and implementers possess.

Chapter 16
Financing Considerations

The greatest mistake you can make is to be continually fearing you will make one.

Elbert Hubbard

Summary

Smart people with smart ideas can find it very difficult to succeed in translating their insights to innovative products, services, and technologies through the innovation development pipeline without access to smart money (whether provided by the public or private sector) that recognizes the value and potential that is being created. Societies seeking to establish sustainable and high growth life science and biotechnology industries focused on "Summit" opportunities would be best served by ensuring that innovators and entrepreneurs have access to needed funding, resources, and facilities to take their initiatives through proof of concept through productization to enter the marketplace.

Introduction

Countries throughout the Asia-Pacific region have invested heavily in life science education and research over the last several decades. Such investment has resulted in a growing base of internationally recognized scientists and academic centers of excellence, and a substantial portfolio of intellectual property and know-how (see Chapter 10). There has, however, been relatively little success in translating much of this know-how into commercial application despite the obvious potential of some lines of research.

There is great need in the Asia-Pacific region for targeted funding to support the identification and nurturing of high potential technologies and technology business enterprises. A proactive, market-oriented stance is vital to explore new business directions and to establish exciting new companies that are responsive to market opportunities and needs.

The following sections will address areas of key funding interest and concern, including:

- Funding for bioinnovation and bioenterprise development
- Sources of funding for entrepreneurial enterprises
  - Family and friends
  - Angel investors
  - Formal funding from venture capitalists and strategic investors
  - Initial public offering (IPO) and post-IPO trading

Funding for Bioinnovation and Bioenterprise Development

Investment requirements at different stages of enterprise and technology development typically vary quite considerably. Early stage enterprises and technologies generally require a relatively small investment quantum. At the same time, early stages of enterprise and technology development necessarily involve net expenditure to bring products, services, and technologies to fruition and, hence, typically operate under negative cashflow circumstances until the enterprise is able to generate revenue.

Investment in BioBusiness innovation and entrepreneurship is essentially an investment in the future. Traditionally, basic life science research and development was funded by governments while applied research in the life sciences was left to major industry players (see also Box 11.4, pg 175). This framework left little room for entrepreneurship funded by individuals, angel investors, or venture capital, and concomitant limited success in the commercialization of R&D results from public institutions. It is increasingly being realized that there is a place for both public and private smart money funding in support of innovation and entrepreneurship development (see also Box 16.1 and Table 16.1), and that greatest success is achieved when the public and private sectors work closely and cooperatively together (see Table 14.2).

Box 16.1   Differentiating Smart Money from "No Brainer" Money from "Dumb" Money

Some authorities focus just on total access to capital when examining financing for technology innovation and entrepreneurship – for example, how much available money is there for technology investment from venture capitalists and institutional investors, access to grants, and so on. These are important and do give a sense of how much support there is to help fuel venture growth, at least once operations have reached critical mass to interest venture capitalists. Experience has shown that it is very important to differentiate between "smart" money, "no brainer" money, and "dumb" money.

"Dumb" money would be money that goes blindly into an investment opportunity on the basis of rumor or whim with no understanding of the people or capabilities behind the opportunity and no due diligence – unless one is extremely lucky, such investments are usually lost.

"No brainer" money is investment money that goes in for the obvious opportunity with relatively low risk perception (for example, the usual pre-IPO investment opportunity that Asian investors sought throughout much of the 1990s in the region and in the US and Europe): put money in six months before the IPO, see a two- to three-fold gain when the public enters the frenzy, and sell off the investment at its peak, laughing all the way to the bank. This has been the standard formula used by many conservative investors – and can nearly be a sure thing to bring returns when the stock market is on a bull run. "No brainer" money investment tends to be short-term, low-risk investments based on following trends and herd-mentality opportunities.

"Smart" money investment, on the other hand, is strategic investment focused on giving innovators the chance to validate new technology and bring it to commercial application long before it is generally seen as an attractive investment proposition by the market at large. Such investments tend to be perceived as "high risk" investment (you would have this perspective if you did not understand the arena nor know what you were doing!) and do take somewhat longer to come to fruition. But they can lead to tremendous upside (30 times or more) when the opportunity does start to capture the attention of other investors and the public, and enter the conventional wisdom as being a "hot" pick (essentially, "no brainer" money investors then start to jump in). An illustrative example of smart money investors would be those who bet on Bill Gates and Steve Jobs when they were still basically long-haired geeks, before Windows or Apple meant anything to anyone other than holes in walls or fruits.

As we examine the technology innovation development pipeline (Figure 4.3, pg 55), it is clear that five distinct phases can be discerned: from concept to technology validation to productization to business case validation to commercialization and growth. Smart money is critical for jump-starting innovation, and translating dreams to reality. Smart money investors share the dreams of the innovators. They help fuel the first half of the five-phase pipeline: from concept to productization (by productization, we mean the development of a product, service, or technology to the level where it is essentially mature enough and ready to enter the market through sale, service provision, or application of the technology – and hence has the prospect of being a revenue generator) when the venture is still a net "cash burn" enterprise, and the prospect of revenue might still seem a long way off. Access to smart money is, in my opinion, the X-factor in investment, and the key differentiator between successful innovation-based value creation and sham me-too attempts at value creation.

While "no brainer" money is generally available when an opportunity becomes a sure thing, getting it translated from a dream to a sure thing requires smart money. If you look at different technology and biotechnology clusters, this is where you start seeing the differences between the ones that will one day be leaders, and those that are content to serve as a base for other people's ideas and other people's sure things. Here is where I see Korea and Taiwan really taking off, also Australia and Israel (and here is where Germany was transformed from being a sleepy biotechnology backwaters before the mid-1990s to becoming a regional, if not global, force when the government made a strategic investment to fuel innovation and the establishment of the knowledge economy[1]).

Germany and the US both provide important examples of countries that used different strategies to fuel innovation: Germany is typically perceived as a player driven by public funding, while the US is typically raised as an example of privately driven innovation.

Germany does represent a very interesting case where the government realized that smart money was not coming from the private sector, and it decided to make a strategic smart money investment in fueling and supporting the development of the innovation economy.

Importantly, even though the US is generally perceived as being a VC and rich private investor-driven environment, the reality for many US technology companies has been that the role of the very smart money investment by private investors who started the company has been relatively much smaller than the critical grant-funding and contract technology development opportunity provided by enlightened strategic players like the National Institutes of Health (NIH), the US Department of Defence, and the National Aeronautics and Space Agency (NASA). Classically, a quick look at the average US biotechnology company's books will show that income from these grants and contracts, to effectively fuel technology validation and productization, can greatly outstrip equity investment into the company – often by a factor of 4:1 or higher. Public smart money, therefore, plays a much more significant role in the US than is generally appreciated or understood.

---

[1] It has become fashionable among people who should know better to parrot glib remarks that Germany's push to establish an innovation economy has been a dismal failure because a significant proportion of Germany's new biotech enterprises have had difficulty obtaining follow-on funding. Before rushing to judgement, it is advisable to consider the alternative: how would Germany's biotech capability and IP base have evolved if no funding had been made available to allow for innovation and enterprise development? Strategic investment has provided Germany with a strong life science and biotech base that is today recognized as being among the best in the world – my hunch is that time will bring very substantial returns on investment for Germany.

Making things work for life sciences and biotechnology requires strategic investment in value creation; and it does not matter whether the smart money comes from the public or the private sector.

Table 16.1   Characteristics of "No Brainer" Versus Smart Money

Characteristics	"No brainer" money	Smart money
Perceived risk	Low	High
Expected returns	High	Very high
Time lines	Short-term	Long-term
Innovation quotient	Low (follow the pack)	High (innovation leader)
Economic value-add	Low	High

Compared to spending by traditional big governments or major corporations with deep pockets, private equity financing of innovation and start-up enterprises tends to start at a disadvantage as chronic shortage of funding and a never-ending search for new investment may add significant financial risk to the science and technology risk that is faced by all players (see also Box 16.2). On the other hand, private equity financing of bioentrepreneurship and bioenterprise development is very focused on direct commercialization of scientific findings – a strong market focus can greatly facilitate success in moving innovative products, services, and technologies through the innovation development pipeline (see also Figure 4.3, pg 55).

Life science and biotechnology innovation is not necessarily expensive or high-risk. In fact, it can be quite affordable and relatively low-risk for people who know what they are doing, and how to do it. I would argue that *failure to invest* in innovation and life science enterprise development is much more expensive and risky (from both an economic development and a value creation perspective) than making the investment.

One mechanism for managing risk and increasing the likelihood of investment success is to provide for low cost (or no cost) access to purpose-designed laboratories and shared facilities for technology validation, while strategically providing access to mentors and acceleration capability through innovative grant provision and strategic investment in the development of such capabilities (see also Chapter 11). Several countries, internationally as well as in the region, including Australia and Israel, and increasingly Korea and Taiwan, have traditionally invested in providing access for innovators and entrepreneurs to such capabilities.

> **Box 16.2   Different Types of Risks That Need to Be Managed in Technology Enterprises**
>
> - **Science/Technology risk.** This is where the underlying science or technology driving an innovation or entrepreneurial initiative simply does not measure up compared to competing technologies and solutions – and the products, services, or technologies developed from the use of such science or technology prove to be uncompetitive in the marketplace.
> - **Execution or operational risk.** This is where managers fail to successfully translate and bring viable products and services to market, or fail to deliver a standard of performance or product output that the market is seeking.
> - **Market risk.** This is where the market is either not interested in the product or service, or demand or interest is low so the product, service, or technology simply does not generate a significant market to begin with. Another scenario would be where market interest and attention shift from the offerings to newer and better products or technologies – as happens, for example, when the product turns out to be of fad interest only. Market risk can be managed by good market sensing and monitoring.
> - **Financial risk.** The risk that money invested in a project or initiative will be lost because the initiative fails to come to fruition or to achieve financial sustainability before the money runs out.

Professional venture capital firms in the US and Europe have been critical players in fueling investment and growth of life science enterprises at their earliest stages. Smart money has been willing to invest, often at a very early stage, in smart people with completely out-of-the-box ideas. Asian venture capitalists, on the other hand, have tended to be risk averse, have little domain knowledge, and take a more cautious approach to investing – preferring to follow big name investments, almost inevitably in the West.

The reticence of investors in Asia-Pacific economies to identifying and supporting early stage, world-class opportunities in the region is one of the biggest stumbling blocks to life science entrepreneurship development in the region. The same people who have money thrown at them in the West would be hard pressed to get the support they need to bring their ideas to fruition in Asia.

Countries like Canada, Australia, Israel, and Germany decided relatively early to make a bet on investing in life science technology and innovation and have taken an "enlightened" public-sector approach to facilitate technology and enterprise development through grants, commercialization support, and investment at the very earliest stages of starting up. These economies have seen substantial growth of their indigenous life sciences sector and are beginning to see good returns on investment – recent estimates suggest that every public dollar invested in life science innovation support and entrepreneurship returns US$3.50 or more in terms of new job creation and income to the state through taxes. Asia-Pacific governments would do well to learn from this experience.

In recent years, Taiwan and Korea have invested strongly in providing innovators and entrepreneurs with access to incubation and technology business acceleration facilities and services – and their investments have started to pay off handsomely. For example, Taiwan has built over 60 incubators since the mid-1980s; these have been nurturing a growing variety of technology companies, including a growing range of BioBusiness-oriented companies.

Sources of Funding for Entrepreneurial Enterprises

Moving entrepreneurial technology enterprises through the various stages of enterprise development typically requires access to different informal and formal sources of funding at each stage (see Figure 4.3, pg 55). Typically, early enterprise development is either self-funded or supported by friends and family. As the enterprise reaches the proof of concept stage, it typically taps into angel investors or even formal venture capital funding to bring its initial product, service, or technology offerings through the productization stage and to market. After it starts to generate significant income and enters the rapid income growth stage, it typically considers listing as a potential source of further funding to fuel expansion and further growth (a viable alternative would, of course, be a trade sale of the enterprise to a strategic corporate investor).

Family and Friends

Family and friends are, of course, the most informal way to fund a new company. This has been the traditional way in which new enterprises in the Asia-Pacific economies have been started up for generations. From the investor's perspective, having an entrepreneurial friend or relative has some advantages, as there is generally less risk of being cheated, and the investor can evaluate the personality and commitment of the entrepreneur much better than any outside party could.

However, there should be very clear understanding by all parties regarding how the returns should be divided if the venture is successful, and conversely, what should happen if the venture fails. Investors should also be aware that early stage investment is typically an investment with extremely low liquidity.

On the other hand, the potential returns when the venture goes well could be very high. Investors lucky enough to invest at the "friends and family" stage in a high growth, successful technology enterprise investment opportunity that eventually goes public or is acquired by a leading international player can typically expect to recoup 20 times their initial investment or higher.

From the entrepreneur's perspective, failure of the venture could result in a substantial loss of face and a breakdown in communications between the entrepreneur and his/her friends and family. Many friendships have ended, and relationships soured, when things do not pan out as well or as quickly as everyone had hoped. On the other hand, providing friends and family with an investment opportunity that brings substantive returns will generally mean that they would be eager to invest in the entrepreneur's next venture.

Angel Investors

Angel investors are normally wealthy individuals, often with relevant experience in the field. Usually they feel personal excitement about being part of a start-up, and they aim to add value through their experience. In contrast to family and friends, angel investors characteristically invest substantially larger sums – depending on the nature of the business, and their level of commitment to it. For businesses that compete internationally, an angel investment could range from several hundred thousand to a few million US dollars. Most business angels have a clearly defined exit strategy, usually at IPO or acquisition.

Individuals who are considering becoming angel investors should have considerable net worth. Investing a substantial part of their capital in only one firm is not a well-diversified portfolio. While recognizing the potential for very high upside with the right investment, angel investors should be prepared to lose all their investment.

Many life science start-ups are founded by scientist innovators who may not have the necessary knowledge or skills to successfully operate a business (unless they have access to the right mentors, advisors or work with an incubator or accelerator). Ideally, angel investors should have some domain knowledge of the life science sector and a clear sense of how they can potentially contribute to building value in moving the products, services, or technologies to be offered down the innovation development pipeline (see Figure 4.3, pg 55).

Another invaluable way in which angel investors can support the enterprise is through bringing in potential market and business development partners, as well as prospective follow-on investors. This not only allows them to evaluate the opportunity better, but also helps the young enterprise to succeed. Sometimes, the entrepreneur may not need further technical assistance, in which case a strong relationship of trust between the investor and the entrepreneur can often replace domain knowledge.

Formal Funding from Venture Capitalists and Strategic Investors

Formal rounds of funding are generally the domain of professional financial investors, particularly venture capital (VC) firms. These firms generally employ teams of professional experts who evaluate the fundamentals of the prospective investee company. Different VC investors like coming in at different stages: some specialize in seed stage investments and are keen to provide maybe a couple of million dollars in investment; others see themselves as growth stage investors and typically do not want to come into an investment opportunity unless it is seeking, say, US$10 million or more. VC firms usually choose to come in on an investment opportunity only after proof of concept and technology validation or, more commonly in Asia these days, after productization when the company is likely to be within months of bringing in revenue (Figure 4.3, pg 55).

There might be one or several formal rounds of funding, and capital involved might range from a few million US dollars to tens of millions of US dollars or more. In addition to VCs, strategic investors are another group that typically come in to investment opportunities at the formal funding stage. In contrast to venture capitalists, strategic investors are typically large corporations that operate in fields related to that of the investee, and are generally interested in the firm's technologies and products rather than seeking quick financial gain. They might, for example, be a pharmaceutical or medical products company that sees potential synergy between the products and technologies being developed by the start-up and its own range – they might even be considering the possibility of acquiring the start-up.

IPO and Post-IPO Trading

The nature of investment changes considerably once a company goes public. An IPO offers the private investor who did not have the chance to come in at the "friends and family" or angel-investor stages, the opportunity to participate directly in the enterprise opportunity, avoiding the risks and resource commitment of angel investors, and the need to invest through financial intermediaries such as VCs. Investors at the IPO and post-IPO stages in publicly listed companies have the option to cash out or buy additional shares at the current market price at any given time, giving them good liquidity (a luxury that early stage smart investors do not typically have to begin with – but early investors stand to gain multiple times their original investment, a proposition that post-IPO investors typically do not have).

The IPO offers an "exit" opportunity for early stage investors in the enterprise – allowing them to sell their shares for cash. Merger or acquisition of promising companies with strategic investors offers a viable alternative "exit" route for early "friends and family" and angel investors.

Taking Things Forward

Financing in support of innovative life science and biotechnology concepts can come from a variety of potential sources – typically public sector funding through grants helps to fuel early stage development, while private sector funding tends to come in after proof of concept and technology validation. The bursting of the dot.com bubble followed by economic turmoil, the Iraq war, and the SARS outbreak created an investment gap for technology enterprises in the Asia-Pacific region – investors were only prepared to come in relatively later in the process, often choosing to come in after productization or shortly before products are released into the market (see Figure 4.3, pg 55).

This left many early stage companies in economies throughout the region with innovative and promising products, services, and technologies starved of cash at the crucial proof of concept and productization stages. The picture was essentially similar whether one spoke of Israel or Australia or of any other Asia-Pacific economy. The pendulum has begun to swing, and at the time of writing in late 2003, there is growing evidence of returning investor confidence and interest in helping to fuel further growth of promising life science and biotechnology enterprises.

To increase our efficiency in translating exciting concepts to innovative offerings in the marketplace, and improve the success of promising life science and biotechnology enterprises, there is need for more smart money – whether from the public or the private sector – to help innovative new products, services, and technologies successfully traverse the innovation development pipeline (see Box 16.1 and Table 16.1).

Strategic smart money investment promises to bring substantial returns to investors and to the societies that are enlightened enough to invest in laying the foundation for life science innovation and enterprise development. These societies can expect to see long-term economic benefit through job and wealth creation.

Key Points

1. Research has traditionally been funded by the public sector, while commercial development has tended to be funded by major corporations.

2. There is a growing opportunity in the Asia-Pacific region for public–private partnership to fuel life science and biotechnology innovation and entrepreneurship development.

3. Smart money investment in smart people with smart ideas by both the public and private sectors can not only help to bring new innovations to fruition (including the commercialization of publicly funded research), but can be critical in helping to support the development of high growth, high potential enterprises that can generate substantial economic benefit through job and wealth creation.

4. Private funding is essentially complementary and not competitive with public sector funding. Establishing mechanisms to facilitate and incentivize private-sector investment in life science and biotechnology R&D, innovation, entrepreneur development, and enterprise growth can be critical in helping to fuel value creation in Asia-Pacific economies.

Capturing the Value

Be the change you want to see in the world.

Mohandas K. Gandhi

Section D examines the opportunity for action facing Asia-Pacific economies eager to capture a piece of the growing pie of value that the life sciences and BioBusiness have in store. Laying the right foundation today will place the region in a very strong position to make a substantial impact in driving the BioBusiness agenda forward.

Chapter 17 examines public policy opportunities to ensure that Asia-Pacific countries are able to capture the value potential of BioBusiness.

Chapter 18 examines entrepreneurial opportunities for those who are prepared to take their chances to identify and build true value in the arena.

Chapter 19 addresses investment opportunities for those who want to help fuel the BioBusiness revolution.

Public Policy Opportunities

I start with the premise that the function of leadership is to produce more leaders, not more followers.

Ralph Nader

Summary

Traditionally, the government in each country (whether national, state, or local) would take the lead to put together large-scale infrastructure and development programs, usually working in cooperation with international agencies and funding institutions with an interest in supporting such initiatives. Characteristically, governments generally underwrite programs and initiatives before they reach the stage where they become interesting commercial opportunities, at which point close cooperation between government and private enterprise is often the best way to move things forward. Wherever possible, governments should seek to facilitate strategic alliances and partnership between institutions and enterprises across national boundaries, and to work nationally, regionally, and internationally to promote and support technology innovation and entrepreneurship development as drivers of BioBusiness development.

Introduction

Where self-interest is suppressed, it is replaced by a burdensome system of bureaucratic control that dries up the wellspring of initiative and creativity.

Pope John Paul II

Many Asia-Pacific economies (including Japan, Korea, Israel, Chinese Taipei, Australia, Singapore, China, Hong Kong, Malaysia, and Thailand) have identified the life sciences as a priority growth sector, and have invested substantially in building the infrastructure and the human resource expertise to make things happen (see also Figure 17.1). Their efforts have begun to pay off handsomely

Figure 17.1 Gross Expenditure on R&D (GERD) in Selected Economies (% of GDP)

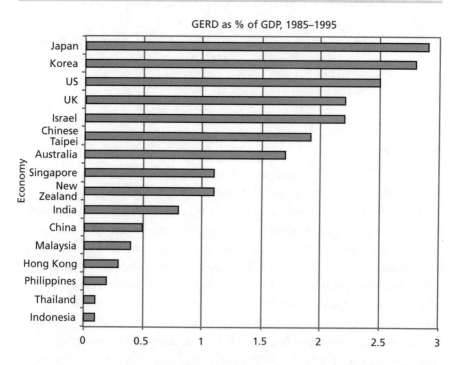

GERD as % of GDP, 1985–1995

in terms of the establishment of a strong science and technology base as represented by a growing pool of world-class scientists and centers of excellence in the region.

However, the intellectual property and know-how developed by these scientists and institutions have tended, thus far, to have found limited commercial and social application. There are two key limiting factors:

- The dearth of managers of science in the region with the requisite knowledge and understanding of the life sciences and business processes to successfully drive innovative products, services, and technologies down the developmental pipeline (see Figure 4.3, pg 55).

- The relative lack of smart money investment in support of innovation and technology commercialization in the region (see Box 16.1, pg 248).

The application of modern biotechnology in the Asia-Pacific region is still in its infancy – leaving vast opportunities waiting to be tapped. While the region has nearly as many life science enterprises as the US and Europe (see

Table 10.2, pg 150), most are still relatively immature; the market capitalization of all biotechnology enterprises in Asia today is estimated to be less than 10% that of the top 25 US companies. As their products, services, and technologies move through the innovation development pipeline, it can be expected that there will be substantial increases in market capitalization and value of these Asia-Pacific enterprises.

How can the potential of BioBusiness be realized for the benefit of the region? Clearly, an environment of partnership and cooperation between government, industry, and academia, and a commitment to establishing world-class institutions, enterprises, and bioclusters should be in place before a country can fully reap the benefits of a flourishing life sciences and biotechnology economy (see Chapter 11). In this chapter, we will discuss the following issues:

- Public policy and the generation of wealth from BioBusiness
- Building infrastructure for science and technology
  - Physical infrastructure
  - Scientific infrastructure

Public Policy and the Generation of Wealth from BioBusiness

The life sciences and biotechnology offer the opportunity and potential for countries and cities that take an enlightened approach to establish a viable framework for attracting investment and a strong and vibrant life science and technology industry sector.

Wealth creation clearly does not come simply from a policy decision to abandon low value-added sectors in favor of higher value-added sectors. While it is rational and worthwhile to continually seek to reach the summit in our various economic and commercial activities so we can generate more wealth and thus pay better wages to workers, bringing this about requires investment in a range of key areas including:

- Development of appropriate infrastructure, both physical and scientific/ technical
- Establishment of a conducive policy and regulatory environment – including a framework for public–private partnership for entrepreneurship and enterprise development
- Development of, and access to, trained and skilled human resources through education and the provision of appropriate training and skills development opportunities, as well as proactively facilitating the active engagement and participation of world-class life science professionals in the work of local institutions, enterprises, and bioclusters

- Availability of funds for strategic investment via both enlightened public-sector investment through the provision of grants and financial incentives in support of innovation, enterprise, and biocluster development, as well as private investment through encouraging equity investment and the establishment of a framework for cooperation and partnership in shared funding of projects and initiatives
- Development of mechanisms for consideration and management of ethical, legal, social, and environmental implications (ELSEI) through the establishment of ethical review processes and the development of appropriate good practice guidelines that are responsive to concerns and needs of society (see also Chapter 12).

Developing innovative products, services, and technologies from scratch within the framework of law in any country consumes time, energy, and money in addition to access to good facilities and trained expertise. Stakeholders would need to have patience and would need to seek sufficient funds for completing the R&D work. Before an innovator or enterprise initiates such work in any economy, an important aspect to consider would be the economy's government policies and incentives for investment and growth of entreprencurial enterprises.

Research is a long-term, capital-intensive activity that should not be subject to the vagaries of changes in government administration. Governments are best served when they recognize and acknowledge the need for stable incremental funding for research. In addition, governments are well-advised to develop quality driven, user-friendly, transparent, and objective means for fund administration.

The development of funding policies and budgets should also keep in mind:

- The need for balance between discovery and strategic research
- The need to attract, develop, and retain world-class scientists
- The need to encourage and support application and commercialization of research findings
- The socio-economic costs and potential benefits from research findings and their commercial and social application

More than just focusing on the highest "Summits" in the BioBusiness landscape, there exist innumerable opportunities to bring incremental benefit and value creation by taking advantage of new insights and understanding that are being generated through R&D activities in the country and internationally to create jobs and eliminate poverty. These include:

- Introducing innovative and needed new technologies and capabilities through technology transfer opportunities
- Increasing agricultural yields through cultivating more productive varieties of crops and introducing new techniques in agriculture, and expanding the range of agricultural production in response to market interest and demand in the region and internationally
- Introducing new approaches to improving public health and healthcare services through the introduction of appropriate technologies for health
- Protecting biodiversity and environmental integrity

Such innovation can make a substantial difference in raising previously "Valley" activities up the slopes toward the "Summits" (see Figure 4.1, pg 48).

Eliminating humankind's most devastating challenges, such as ensuring essential food and income growth for poor sustenance-level farming communities and the urban poor, and preventing infectious disease using vaccines, have tended to be seen in the past as low-margin "Valley" BioBusiness opportunities. Increasing innovation and growing recognition of the value-added that such innovation can bring in terms of improving health and well-being, raising economic productivity, and increasing opportunities to generate income will undoubtedly lead to stronger interest and support for such efforts.

Building Infrastructure for Science and Technology

Regional infrastructure for molecular biology and biotechnology can be examined from two perspectives – physical and scientific.

Physical Infrastructure

A reliable and well-maintained physical infrastructure (power supply, transportation networks, telecommunication networks) is a basic requirement for economic growth, science and technology development, and for facilitating application of research findings.

In addition to the large-scale public infrastructure, the development and management of industrial parks and incubator facilities by public and private entities are also important factors for increasing the rate of development of excellence in science and the application of scientific discoveries. While clustering of high-tech activities would help to minimize costs in terms of common facilities and to promote interaction amongst scientists, it is important to remember the basic rules of estate management and responsiveness to market interest and demand so as to avoid the proliferation of "white elephants."[1]

Scientific Infrastructure

The construction of research buildings and facilities is often seen as a key step to developing scientific and technological excellence. While the need for well-equipped modern buildings still exists, it is becoming increasingly evident that in addition to individual research facilities, there is also the pressing need for access to powerful and reliable information and communication networks, the need to coordinate and maximize utilization of equipment and other research facilities, and the need to facilitate cooperation and collaboration amongst life science professionals, institutions, and enterprises both within and across national boundaries. This holds true at institutional, national, regional, and international levels.

In modern biological laboratories, aside from space and basic equipment, access to central and shared facilities for work such as large-scale sequencing, genomics, bioinformatics and computational biology, development of transgenic animals, electron microscopy, peptide and oligonucleotide synthesis, mass spectrometry, and x-ray crystallography, can greatly facilitate the efforts of institutions and enterprises to generate innovative and world-class output. Clearly, more than just building such capabilities, careful attention needs to be placed on their maintenance and upkeep.

Scientists working in areas with possible biomedical applications should have ready access to collaborations with medical facilities. Similarly, access to clinical trial capabilities and resources, land for field tests (for agribiological products), together with clear guidelines for ensuring safety and minimizing potential risks, should be available.

Yet, it is questionable if all such facilities should necessarily be established within an institution or even within an economy if usage is likely to be low. There is little to be gained from blindly duplicating resources and facilities that are already available in other institutions and facilities elsewhere just because it is prestigious to have them. The fundamental approach should be

---

[1] There sometimes appears to be a pre-occupation in some economies with building buildings and equipping them with expensive equipment and facilities – often to serve more as a "showcase" without due consideration of the actual need or potential utilization of the facilities.

to identify the need, and then to gain access to facilities and capabilities wherever they may be (in other institutions or corporations in the country, region, or internationally) through strategic collaboration and outsource partnering relations. Still, it may prove worthwhile and necessary to invest in big ticket facilities and capabilities as a strategic move to build interest and value.

Conclusion

Nothing will ever be attempted if all possible objections must first be overcome.

Samuel Johnson

Policy-makers in the Asia-Pacific region stand at a major threshold in BioBusiness-related economic and social development. New developments in the life sciences and biotechnology in the post-genomic era promise to revolutionize our lives and our livelihoods over the next several decades in ways we are only now beginning to imagine. While the revolution has already started, it is still very early days yet – products, services, and technologies based on new tools and technologies still capture less that 0.5% of the global BioBusiness sector (see Table 3.1, pg 38). As more and more new technologies mature, we will see "Cloud" opportunities being translated into "Summit" activities at the same time as more and more "Valley" activities are transformed through the injection of new knowledge and new technologies toward becoming "Summit" opportunities (see Figure 4.1, pg 48).

Policy-makers can be leading players – even visionaries – in putting in place the necessary groundwork to enable their communities and countries to proactively capture a piece of the growing life sciences and biotechnology pie. They can do this by bringing about the necessary changes in their society to ensure sustainable livelihoods for their people, and by ensuring that appropriate strategic investment is made to build the necessary science and technology infrastructure; that their populations are bioliterate (through investment in providing creative education and skills development); that policies and regulations incentivize and support product, service and technology development, and a culture of innovation and entrepreneurship in a spirit of public–private partnership; and that sufficient financial resources from both the public and private sectors are made available to fuel successful R–D–A translation and value creation through the innovation development pipeline.

They can also seek to ensure that they create favorable conditions for a confluence of smart people with smart ideas together with smart money and smart alliances and partnerships with leading public and private sector players throughout the region and internationally. Just as we have recently been reminded by the SARS pandemic that disease knows no boundaries, we need to also recognize that the same goes for world-class science and technology. We can no longer afford to be parochial or insular in our approach to helping our societies gain access to the tools and technologies that will help us and our populations climb up the value-added ladder to first escape the poverty trap, and then to reach for the summits of development and wealth creation.

The road ahead will not be easy. There will inevitably be stumbles and mistakes made along the way – but the mark of our character is not going to be the number of times we fall, but how we pick ourselves up and go on to build from strength to strength.

If you don't make mistakes, you aren't really trying.

Coleman Hawking

Knowing what we already know about the opportunities and potential that the age of biology will bring, it is already entirely possible for us to develop a clear roadmap with well defined milestones – for each village, for each rural district, for each town or city, for each state or province, for each country, and for the region – to capture value from the revolution.

We need to remake ourselves and our societies. We must be open and candid about the challenges and risks that lie ahead, and we must ensure transparency in our policies and our processes. Most of all, we must seek to harness the energies and potential of all who can help us achieve our goals and objectives – across disciplinary, sectoral, national, and regional boundaries. Together, we can build synergies and operate to create value far more effectively than we ever could apart (see Box 17.1).

Box 17.1   Biotech Is More Than Just Costs and Competition

31 May 2003. Last Saturday, the *Business Times* ran an article on the push for biotechnology on both sides of the causeway [linking Singapore and Malaysia].

The danger of presenting the issue in an "us versus them" style is that it does not do enough justice to the commitment and effort by both countries to build viable and sustainable life science industries.

I have long worked to promote biotechnology innovation and entrepreneur development in both Singapore and Malaysia (and, indeed, throughout the Asia-Pacific region). As part of my efforts, I have worked with scientists, entrepreneurs, policy-makers, angel investors, and venture capitalists in both countries to establish promising technology enterprises, as well as with multinational corporations and international biotech companies with state-of-the-art technologies seeking to establish high-growth Asia-Pacific operations.

These are still early days for biotechnology in Asia – and indeed globally. The next three to four decades will be a time of explosive growth of new knowledge, insights, technologies, and opportunities. There is much that can and should be done, and those of us working at the cutting edge of life science technology innovation are at the forefront of helping to build several exciting industries of the future.

It would be a real pity if the immense opportunities biotech offers are reduced to a mere comparison of costs involved in taking a pharmaceutical drug through the development pipeline and its related likelihood of success – "US$650 million" and "1:5,000 chance or less of making it" respectively – as the article did. The reality is that biotech has applicability in all dimensions of life. BioEnterprise Asia estimates that 40% or more of the activities that currently contribute to the GDP of any Asia-Pacific country can be substantially impacted by new insights and developments in biotechnology – whether these relate to improved approaches to diagnostics or disease management; to improvements in agriculture; to the development of biofuels and new biomaterials (including bioplastics); to the development of newer and better approaches for cleaning up the environment and managing our wastes, or to the development of newer and more cost-efficient industrial processes.

While developing innovative solutions to these other concerns may not sound as sexy as developing the next blockbuster drug (or, perhaps, *tongkat ali*), they are much less risky and more likely to drive economic development and wealth creation for our societies. Biotech is only high-risk when you do not know what you are doing. Few, if any, would stake their future on taking one early-stage drug and trying to drive it through the development process. There is substantial value to be generated for those who have the knowledge and skills to find solutions to the myriad of problems and concerns our societies face – and the cost of validating new technology insights, creating exciting new products, and bringing such innovations to market can be surprisingly low for those who actually know what they are doing.

I believe, we can all be winners in biotechnology and the life sciences if we invest strategically in innovation and building to create maximum value. The pie is not only big enough for both Malaysia and Singapore to capture biotech opportunities without having to compete, but it can be expanded many times over if the countries in the Asia-Pacific focus instead on working complementarily to identify synergies and core competencies to build on the strengths that we possess as a region.

We need the vision and the foresight, especially during these challenging economic times, to rise above petty sibling rivalries to invest in building a strong and vibrant base for technology entrepreneurs to grow and thrive in our region.

Source: G. Shahi, The Business Times, Singapore, 31 May 2003
Reproduced with permission from The Business Times

Key Points

1. Policy-makers can play a critical role in facilitating BioBusiness and the establishment of the local bioeconomy by helping to create fertile ground for future success.
2. The first thing that should be done is to fix what is broken through ensuring literacy and education to provide opportunities for skills enhancement and career development, and to meet basic public health needs.
3. At the same time, there is need to build the foundation of scientific development by emphasizing the availability of necessary fundamental needs:
   • Infrastructure (both physical and scientific)
   • Human resource development
   • Enlightened policy framework
   • Conducive cultural environment encouraging innovation and entrepreneurship
   • Encouraging the availability of funding and necessary resources to support research and development
4. Policy-makers who appreciate the prerequisites for industrial success will recognize the need to encourage, in their economy:
   • Smart people (local as well as international people who are committed to helping the economy achieve maximum potential)
   • Smart ideas (encouraging local scientists, innovators, and entrepreneurs to think outside the box; and committing to testing and evaluating their ideas for further development)
   • Smart money (encouraging the availability of both public and private money to support early stage innovative technologies and promising local life science and biotechnology enterprises)

- Smart alliances and partnerships (encouraging greater cooperation and collaboration among local scientists, innovators, and enterprises; between public and private entities; and with collaborators and partners in the region and internationally)

Chapter 18
Entrepreneurial Opportunities

Only those who dare to fail greatly can ever achieve greatly.

Robert F. Kennedy

Summary

The coming of age of cutting-edge life science and biotechnology tools and technologies, an increasing focus on developing innovative products, services, and technology solutions in response to market opportunity and need, and growing understanding of how to minimize execution risk and maximize returns on investment are creating tremendous opportunities for innovation and entrepreneurship in the Asia-Pacific region and internationally. Asia-based scientists, innovators, and entrepreneurs stand to create substantial value and economic benefit for themselves and their societies. To fully capture the opportunity and potential, they will need to work closely with academic and research institutions, governments, prospective investors, and the best brains in business in the region and beyond to translate their dreams to reality. We are limited only by our imagination.

Introduction

There is opportunity practically everywhere you look across the BioBusiness landscape. BioBusiness already constitutes over 25% of global GDP (see Table 3.1, pg 38). The BioBusiness arena currently covers a wide range of existing sectors (see Box 1.1, pg 2), and promises to expand its reach to include many more existing sectors that did not traditionally depend on innovative input from the life sciences and biotechnology, as well as to create entirely new industry sectors over the coming decades.

In every sector one cares to look at – from public health and healthcare services, to fisheries (and ornamental fish breeding), to agriculture, to food production and processing, to environmental protection, to industrial processes, to fuels and energy supply, to plastics, to waste management, to pollution control – you will find low value-added "Valley" opportunities, knowledge-intensive, high-market demand and high-premium "Summit" opportunities and great ideas but uncertain "Cloud" opportunities (see Figure 4.1, pg 48).

The would-be innovator or entrepreneur is essentially spoilt for choice when seeking to identify exciting innovation opportunities in life science and biotechnology. So many problems to solve, so many opportunities to capture. Where should one focus one's energies and efforts? How to create an unfair advantage and capture the value proposition?

The first step might be to seriously examine what it is you, as a prospective innovator or entrepreneur, want to do with your life. Being an entrepreneur might be perceived as glamorous – but it involves making a very serious commitment to investing your blood, sweat, and tears to translate an idea, a dream, a vision, into reality while working inhumane hours against substantial odds.

If you choose your focus wisely on building on your talents and strengths, and are able to deal effectively with the inevitable challenges and failures along the way without losing your commitment and passion for wanting to realize your dream, you may just have a chance to succeed.

Success is the ability to go from one failure to another with no loss of enthusiasm

Winston Churchill

Translating Dreams to Reality: Considerations

When we work with would-be entrepreneurs at BioEnterprise Asia, one of the first things we do is to acquaint them with the *Pessimism-Time Curve* (see Figure 18.1).

It is entirely normal that when entrepreneur-wannabes first sit down to start hatching their entrepreneurial game plans, there is an infectious degree of enthusiasm and optimism – we call this the *uninformed optimism* stage, the optimism of the uninitiated.

As they get deeper and deeper into the initiative and begin to realize the challenges and obstacles they will face – legal, financial, technology management, intellectual property management, personality conflicts, and so on – the level of pessimism and concern inevitably increases, and a state of *informed pessimism* sets in. This is the high risk stage in getting the enterprise off the ground. It is the stage where would-be entrepreneurs and members of their team are likely to get cold feet, where they realize how good they have

Figure 18.1   The Pessimism-Time Curve

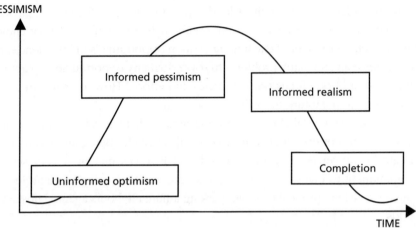

it with cushy jobs and a regular income, perhaps – and where some of their original team of associates and would-be partners are likely to back off because they do not really have the stomach to deal with the seemingly insurmountable challenges that confront them.

The whole venture is in great danger of falling apart before it even starts unless some members of the entrepreneurial team are able to pull themselves over what we call the "latent energy of pessimism" hump to begin seeing the prospect of light at the end of the tunnel. They then enter the *informed realism* stage where they can see a way forward, and begin to get a handle on exactly what it will take to bring their efforts to successful *completion*.

[*Note: We at BioEnterprise Asia often advise prospective entrepreneurial partners in our acceleration program that one of our key purposes as an accelerator is to help provide the necessary mentoring and advice to enable entrepreneurial teams to tunnel through from uninformed optimism to informed realism without having to go through the pain of informed pessimism and possibly dropping out.*]

There is always risk that something will go wrong and things will not pan out as originally conceived by the founders. In fact, it is highly unlikely that every aspect of a new project or enterprise initiative will evolve as originally planned – more often than not, the business direction will need to be modified to suit new realities and circumstances. And the people involved with the enterprise, and the skill sets they bring to the table, will necessarily change as products, services, and technologies move through the different phases of the innovation development pipeline (Figure 4.1, pg 48).

After a prospective entrepreneur has latched on to the dream she wants to realize as an entrepreneur,[1] she would then be well-advised to contemplate Figures 4.2 and 4.3 to gain insight into and understanding of the process of translating the dream to reality, and an appreciation of the five phases of the innovation development pipeline: from concept, to proof of concept or technology validation, to productization, to business case validation, to market entry and growth.

Is the entrepreneur dealing with an existing product, service, or technology that has already been validated and productized, perhaps in a different market? Here, the entrepreneurial team will need to focus on developing and validating an effective market and business development strategy for capturing the value of the enterprise. Or is this a novel product, service or technology development effort where there will be a need to traverse the entire innovation development pipeline from concept to reality (see Figure 4.3, pg 55)? Whatever the case, it is important to consider what needs to get done in driving the product, service, or technology most effectively to market entry and growth.

Along the way, the entrepreneurial team would do well to also consider BioEnterprise Asia's due diligence checklist covering technology (and related products and services), market considerations, financial needs, and human resource considerations (see Table 11.2, pg 184).

The entrepreneurial team should also consider what it takes to build a world-class operation (see Chapter 11), and to consider the necessary challenges in the course of their implementation efforts. Among other things, this will include the need for value-added strategic alliances and partnerships to facilitate their efforts, and consideration of the various biopartners with which the entrepreneurial team will need to work to maximize value creation. Box 18.1 summarizes some of the market issues and concerns to be taken account of as products, services, and technologies are brought to market.

Box 18.1   Recommendations for Responding to Challenges of the New Marketplace in Asia

- Segment the markets and target your customers
  - Regional strategies focused on megacities are more effective than national coverage
- Adapt cost structures to local markets

---

[1] This could be an original dream, someone else's dream, or a dream that we create together. The important thing is that they have adopted the dream as their own, and are deeply committed to bringing it to fruition.

- Embrace new technologies
- Strengthen the case for your products
  - Pharmacoeconomic/cost-effectiveness analysis
- Shorten time to market to maximize returns
  - Global trial and "clinical trial" approach to negotiating product entry
  - Strategic market entry and development (plan ahead!)
- Accelerate integration and return to full operational effectiveness after merger and acquisition (M & A), where applicable
- Work for win-win with the public sector and policy-makers

Focus on Entrepreneurs

Entrepreneurs come in all shapes and sizes. Some have years of educational experience. Others are drop-outs from school. Some are really young; others may be older and may be in the midst of transitioning from one career to another. Entrepreneurs characteristically have one trait in common: they believe intensely in what they are doing, and are willing to risk everything to make their dream come true. To be most effective and successful, they will need to put together a team of individuals with complementary skills and capabilities that is prepared to work together to move things forward.

Few scientists-turned-entrepreneurs make world-class business leaders. In most cases, it actually makes sense for them to hand over the reins of power to professional managers and other colleagues who are better equipped and more capable of getting things done when the venture moves from early stage to being a more mature enterprise – and move to a strategic advisory role, rather than play a direct management role, in supporting on-going development (see Chapter 15).

On Selecting Investors

A company at the earliest stages has several options for financing itself. If it has access to products and services that are ready for market in their own right, bringing them to market and generating revenue from these products and services is clearly the way to go. Revenue generated early can then help support longer term product and technology development efforts (see also Box 18.1).

In most cases, however, a technology business enterprise would not initially be in a position to fund itself through product or service revenues, and will need to somehow obtain the necessary cash injection to drive its prospective product, service, and technology offerings through the innovation development pipeline (see Figure 4.3, pg 55). It will need to bring in investors and biopartners to help it raise the necessary financial support (either in the form of grants, equity investment, or both).

Taking innovative concepts through the early stages of innovation development, whether they are licensed from local academic and research institutions or conceptualized in-house in the start-up, requires smart money investment to enable them to make the cross-over from dream to reality – for proof of concept and technology validation, and to begin the productization process. The amounts required at the early stage, typically US$500,000 or less, can make all the difference in increasing the value proposition of the enterprise (see Figure 4.3, pg 55) once the right vision, and the strategic, management and scientific development capabilities and partnering relationships are in place. Such smart money funding, which usually lasts from several months up to about a year, can play a key role in minimizing risk and maximizing potential for value creation for the company.

Technology start-ups characteristically subsequently need funding beyond "proof of concept" to enable them to capture the scientific and technical potential of validated products, services, and technologies that they are working to productize. This would come in bigger-seed stage investment chunks of about US$1.5 to US$3 million or more, depending on the product and the effort required to take it through the various development and testing stages. This level of funding would help them develop their revenue-generating potential from the products, services, or platform technologies being developed.

If the product being developed is a prospective drug, the start-up will need to consider how it expects to cover the costs involved in taking the product through the various stages of clinical development.[2] This could raise funding needs for productization by a factor of tens of million of US dollars or higher. Typically, start-up companies have therefore tended to choose to license out promising molecules to big pharma or biotech players, so the cost and responsibility of further development is transferred to the partner in exchange for upfront payments, milestone payments, and the promise of royalties when the drug eventually enters clinical use. The advantage of an out-licensing strategy, if an interested partner can be identified, is that this could lead to significant early revenue generation for the start-up[3] from licensing fees, so it

---

[2] BioEnterprise Asia considers clinical development of new drugs as part of the productization stage of innovation development – see Figure 4.3, pg 55.

[3] The alternative would be a very substantial net expenditure if the start-up tried to run the clinical development effort itself. The investment climate in Asia is not generally conducive to investors pumping in tens of millions of dollars or more to support early-stage clinical development of novel drugs through phase I or phase II.

can conserve its resources to develop new innovative products, services, and technology platforms for its pipeline.

Importantly, start-ups typically need access to soft loan facilities to help them tide over the inevitable emergencies and cashflow concerns as they drive technology and product development. Such funding tends to be severely lacking in many Asia-Pacific countries unless guaranteed by the founding entrepreneurs' already over-stretched personal resources (and adding to the already considerable risks and challenges they face in getting their enterprises off the ground).

The very real gap in funding at this very early stage can be a major bottleneck for successful innovation. BioEnterprise Asia describes this as the "investment gap" – between the expense and need to take promising concepts through technology validation through productization in the innovation development pipeline (see Figure 4.3, pg 55), and the reality that private investors, especially post-dot.com bust, tend to only be interested in coming into the investment after productization, when the product, service, or technology platform is either close to market or already generating revenue from sales (see also Box 16.1).

The public sector can play a major role (as it has in countries like Canada, Germany, and Israel – and increasingly Taiwan and Korea) by making grants and helping to underwrite loan facilities for, start-up enterprises, and providing access to mentoring and incubation support to ensure that funds allocated are used wisely and effectively. The public sector can also proactively incentivize smart money investment by private players in innovative R&D (through tax credits and other incentive instruments), and by encouraging the establishment of a public market for shares in promising early-stage technology enterprises.

The reality is that countries that have invested most in building up a strong base of indigenous life science small and medium enterprises (SMEs) have tended to see the greatest returns in terms of translating locally developed technology innovations from academic and research institutions, as well as in job creation and economic growth from high technology enterprises. Investing in facilitating innovation and entrepreneur development is clearly enlightened self-interest from the perspective of the governments – and it provides an opportunity for the established private investors to better understand how to mitigate risk and maximize returns in early-stage investments through actively participating in helping to mentor young companies and encouraging incubation and acceleration support.

Making Things Happen

It is not the horse that draws the cart, but the oats.

Russian proverb

Innovators and entrepreneurs contemplating life science and biotech business opportunities today have a wide range of "Summit"-oriented options and possibilities to choose from – whether they are interested in healthcare (Chapter 6), biomedical life sciences (Chapter 7), agricultural life sciences (Chapter 8), environmental or industrial life sciences (Chapter 9), or other areas of potential BioBusiness opportunity. There is value to be created, and money to be made, by those who know what they are doing, and how to do it (or who work with people who do, including mentors, advisors, and technology-savvy accelerators or incubators).

Rather than take on high-risk, long-term projects that can take many years to come to fruition and can cost hundreds of millions of US dollars to capture (as with classical Western drug development efforts through the FDA pipeline), BioEnterprise Asia proposes adopting a "hot" start-up strategy for first-time entrepreneurs, given the reality that investors in the Asia-Pacific region tend to be much more interested in quick returns and are averse to investing in greenfield ventures requiring many years of investment in R&D before they generate any returns (see Box 18.2). Such an approach minimizes execution risk by enabling the enterprise to avoid having to bet everything on the success of a single product or service under development, for example, while enabling early revenue generation – which, in itself, reduces dependency on outside investors while making the company more attractive to investors at the same time.

Things are likely to get very exciting for life science and biotechnology innovators and entrepreneurs in the Asia-Pacific region over the next several years and decades. It is to be fully anticipated that investors (both public and private) will be increasingly interested in making smart-money investments in innovative and high-potential entrepreneurial enterprises in the region given: the strong base of centers of research and development excellence in the region; growing understanding, interest and support for successful life science and biotechnology innovation and entrepreneurship; increasing market capitalization of region-based BioBusiness companies as their products, services, and technologies reach market, and they start to experience significant revenue growth; and increasing investment in biocluster development in the region.

Box 18.2   "Cold" Versus "Hot" Start-Ups

BioEnterprise Asia's experiences with advising, mentoring, and supporting the start up of new enterprises over the last several years have led us to develop the concept of "cold" versus "hot" start-ups.

As we see it, a cold start-up is typically based on pre-validated technology freshly spun out of an academic or research institution environment. While driving product, service, and technology development for such start-ups can be very worthwhile and bring substantial value over the long term, it can be difficult to raise funding support for the initiative in the post-dot.com era as investors have tended to be risk averse and are typically not familiar with the technology or its potential.

On the other hand, "hot" start-ups build on validated technologies licensed from leading partner institutions or enterprises. These start-ups can potentially seek to capture low hanging fruits that can deliver revenue and positive cashflow within a reasonable time window of, say, 12–18 months (for example, by licensing third-party technology, products, or services to begin with), while developing proprietary products, services, or technologies over the medium- (say, 24–36 months to revenue) to long-term (say, more than 36 months to revenue). The medium- to long-term offerings can either be based on work done in local or regional institutions, or can be developed in-house in the start-up.

Investors, especially during times of economic uncertainty, tend to be much more comfortable with the relatively short time-to-money in "hot" start-up opportunities, and are therefore keener to make early investments in such enterprises.

Hence, to increase the viability and likelihood of success, we increasingly advocate that entrepreneurs in the Asia-Pacific region build a "hot" start-up strategy unless strategic investors are committed to providing long-term funding in support of "cold" start-up business strategies.

Key Points

1. There is a growing range of technology innovation and entrepreneurial opportunities in BioBusiness across a whole range of exciting sectors – from healthcare, to biomedical sciences, to agriculture, to environmental and industrial life sciences and beyond. We are still at the dawn of the biotech era – substantial value will be created over the next several decades.

2. Entrepreneurs would do well to identify and focus on "Summit" opportunities in response to market interest and demand for products, services, and technologies of interest.

3. To fully capture the value proposition of entrepreneurial opportunities, entrepreneurs need increasingly to work with partners in academia, government, investors, technology partners, service partners, and so on. Given investment realities in the region, entrepreneurs are advised to focus on "hot" rather than "cold" start-up opportunities until they have access to sufficient resources to be able to comfortably drive "cold" opportunities.

4. It is anticipated that the Asia-Pacific region will see a substantial increase in valuation of life science and biotechnology companies around 2004/05, and that this will lead to a surge in private equity and public market investment interest in local and regional players. The timing for those contemplating starting up entrepreneurial enterprises in the life sciences in the region could not be better.

Chapter 19
Investment Opportunities

The harder you work, the luckier you get.

Gary Player

Summary

Investment opportunities in the life sciences and biotechnology are becoming increasingly available across the entire BioBusiness landscape. There are clearly far more raw diamonds that are waiting to be mined, shaped, and polished than there have been resources invested in helping to bring them to market thus far. Prospective investors are therefore spoilt for choice, and have a wide range of potential products, services, and technologies across the BioBusiness landscape to choose from. The greatest value will be created by smart investment in technology concepts and ideas that successfully traverse the innovation development pipeline and find strong market interest and demand in the region and internationally. Investors who learn how to separate raw diamonds from gravel, and are prepared to go in early to help drive the development of promising technologies and ideas will be the ones who will benefit most from the life science and biotechnology revolution.

Introduction

Any investment is a trade-off between risk, expected returns, and liquidity. Generally, the relative importance of each aspect of the trade-off depends on the stage of development of the investment opportunity. As a rule of thumb, the earlier the stage of development, the higher the perceived risk, the lower the liquidity, but the higher the expected return (see also Table 16.1, pg 251).

It is important to note, though, that the willingness to take high risk indiscriminately will NOT automatically be rewarded with high returns. On the contrary, it is probably the fastest way to lose your money if you do not know what you are doing, and why.

Early stage investment requires investors to be particularly diligent in evaluating the fundamentals that have been addressed throughout this book.

The reality is that there are some bad technology and business concepts out there (what we at BioEnterprise Asia call *gravel* as opposed to good, high potential ideas which we call *raw diamonds*; see Figure 4.2, pg 54).

Take the effort to go out and find smart investment opportunities if you have a good understanding of the technology arena and the potential of the products and services that are being developed, a good sense of the market opportunity, and the ability to recognize a "raw diamond" when you see one (see also the key technology, business model, and financial and human resource considerations for BioBusiness enterprise success outlined in Table 11.2, pg 184).

Otherwise, make investments through intermediaries, such as incubators, accelerators, venture capitalists, or fund managers, who can assist you in benefiting from private equity investment opportunities in promising high growth BioBusiness enterprises that you would otherwise not be able to gain access to (unless you are lucky enough to be able to identify and invest in the opportunity when it is still in the "friends-and-family" or angel investor stage). Alternatively, invest only in relatively low risk, established companies that are already listed.

Biotechnology and the Stock Market

The main purpose of the stock market is to make fools of as many men as possible.

Bernard Baruch

The history of the public markets for life sciences and biotechnology has been fraught with boom and bust cycles – there have been major speculative growth cycles with peaks in the mid-1980s, early 1990s, mid-1990s, and early 2000s. These cycles have been driven by feeding frenzies and media over-hype, and have had very little to do with the value that has been created across the life sciences and biotechnology arena. While it is great to make lots of money by catching a boom cycle and cashing out before the market crashes, these roller coaster rides have had very little to do with real value creation in life sciences and biotechnology, which has been increasing at an accelerating pace (see, for example, Figure 11.1, pg 170), and will continue to do so over the coming several decades.

Attempting to value life science and biotechnology companies can be difficult under any circumstances given the reality that most such companies have traditionally gone for extended periods with little or no revenue generation or cashflow.[1] Investors have, therefore, sought to value them on the basis of projected future income and the portfolio of intellectual property and products they have in their pipeline.

While the stock market typically thinks in terms of days, weeks, months, or even quarters, the actual development of profitable life science and biotechnology products, services, and technologies can take years, if not decades. In the US, companies like Genentech used the first "Biotech Boom" of the 1980s to fill their coffers, and than go back to the lab to develop their products, to push them through the clinical development process and finally reach the product market in the 1990s. Without the intermediate booms, it would likely have been impossible for Genentech, Amgen and other major biotechnology players to raise sufficient cash to turn them from R&D companies into the vertically integrated players they now are.

The market in Asia is typically not as supportive of innovative, high cash burn opportunities with no immediate revenues as the US and European markets have been. Hence, Asia-Pacific players need to take a substantially different strategic course to capture and build long-term value – they need to focus on both early revenue generation and long-term proprietary product, service, and technology development (see also Box 18.2, pg 280). Hence, strategic alliances and partnership with leading US and European players can be invaluable in helping Asia-Pacific players get products to market quickly as they continue to build their own portfolio of promising products, services, and technologies.

Making Smart Investments in the Asia-Pacific Region

A pessimist sees the difficulty in every opportunity; an optimist sees the opportunity in every difficulty.

Winston Churchill

Assessing the value and potential of life science and biotechnology enterprises can be usefully accomplished by examining the technology, market, financial, and human considerations for BioBusiness enterprise success identified by BioEnterprise Asia in its in-house due diligence checklist (see Table 11.2, pg 184).

---

[1] A favorite in-house joke at BioEnterprise Asia is that typical biotech companies with no revenues and no prospect of revenues in the foreseeable future were dot.coms long before there were dot.coms. Given the investment climate in Asia, we have avoided involvement in such opportunities, focusing instead on "cold" and "hot" start-ups (see Box 18.2, pg 280).

There is a growing niche for private equity financed bioentrepreneurship in Asia. This is largely because the traditional academic and research framework has not favored successful translation from basic research into application (see Figure 4.3, pg 55), since it has been typically difficult for researchers from public research institutions and universities to cross over to commercially oriented research and development. Also, funding for proof of concept or technology validation, productization, and pre-commercial business case validation work from public sector funding resources has typically been quite limited in most Asia-Pacific economies.

Private funding for innovation and enterprise development allows for the direct commercialization of scientific findings. This gives novel technologies and ideas a chance to prove themselves in the marketplace. It is being increasingly recognized that privately funded research and development efforts are not competitive but are essentially complementary, and potentially synergistic, with publicly funded research. There is substantial room for public–private cooperation in identifying and investing in life science innovation and enterprise development. Collaborations between government and academic institutions, entrepreneurs, and major corporations for mutual benefit are common in more developed countries. Such collaborations in the Asia-Pacific region are likely to increase the efficiency and success in translating research effort to viable products, services, and technologies in the marketplace. Done right, this has the potential to create a virtuous cycle, bringing high value-added job opportunities and economic benefit to Asia-Pacific economies, while enabling investors and entrepreneurs to generate substantial wealth.

It is crucial, in seeking to identify worthwhile specific initiatives or projects for public–private partnerships that the products, services, and technologies being developed respond to real market interest and demand – and that there exists a clear demand from customers and consumers who are able to pay for it; that the products, services, and technologies being developed can be protected; and that the quantum of funding needed can be realistically obtained from public and private funding partners given limited resources. Also, the initiative should be able to lead to revenue generation in a reasonable time frame to be of real interest to private players.

If the technology cannot be protected, or if the end-users and consumers are not able to pay for it (as with many public health products and technologies such as vaccines and therapeutics for the poor, or agricultural technologies to enhance future income of farmers), the innovation development initiative can still be entrepreneurially driven provided that local, national, or international public sector players are prepared to finance the development and implementation effort. Clearly, if the business case for the initiative does not meet the usual investment criteria and demands of private investors, it might still be worthwhile to private players eager to contribute to local development especially if there is strong government commitment to providing resources, facilities, expertise, funding, and facilitation support.

Mitigating Investment Risk While Incentivizing Performance

In today's investment climate, especially in Asia, the old 1980s biotechnology model of pouring funds in search of the "blockbuster molecule" with no revenue generation for a number of years is neither attractive to short-term and mercantile-minded investors, nor is it a model for business success in the region. There is strong interest in quickly and efficiently driving product and technology development through the innovation development pipeline so investors can see revenue generation within a few years.

As has been shown throughout this book, there are many opportunities across the BioBusiness landscape to capture the value of low-hanging fruit so revenue can be generated sooner rather than later, and longer-term and higher value-added "Summit" opportunities can be supported over the medium to long term (see Box 18.2, pg 280).

Not everything we do will work – there are bound to be occasional failures. Still, a strategic focus will minimize execution risk substantially. Companies that are most likely to develop into sustainable businesses will be those that have innovative products responding to market interest and demand, experienced management teams, and a financing plan that is realistic with respect to the amount of capital that will be required over time.

For example, it may make little or no sense to pour, say, US$30 million or more into a start-up (as does happen from time to time in the US and even Europe) where there has been little or no technology validation or proof of concept. Experience suggests that it is better to make long-term funding commitments while providing funding in tranches tied to the achievement of objective phase-related milestones. To incentivize performance by the entrepreneurial management team, it can be very beneficial to tie financial rewards to the achievement of agreed performance objectives and milestones. Such structuring requires creativity and flexibility from both the investors and the investee, but can prove mutually very beneficial in the long run.

Upon satisfactory achievement of each mutually agreed milestone (say, completion of "proof of concept" studies, or completion of product registration in at least three markets of interest), the next round of funding can be triggered (at appropriate higher valuation to incentivize performance by the entrepreneurs and innovators), and so on. If the milestone is not achieved, subsequent funding will be modified accordingly, and losses are therefore limited. In general, the value of an innovative technology or enterprise tends to increase as products, services, or technology platforms progress along the development pipeline (see Figure 4.3, pg 55) toward market entry. Hence, failure to validate the concept would mean reduced or no further funding beyond that stage, and the investment would then be limited to whatever amount was agreed for, say, the "proof of concept" stage (perhaps, US$1 million, for example). Risk for investors is limited with such an approach, but it does require proactive involvement by investors to understand what it takes to move things forward, while working closely with investee companies to ensure win-win deals so that entrepreneurs are incentivized to succeed while they receive commitment for on-going funding upon achievement of milestones. This enables them to focus on building long-term value rather than spend all their time and energy trying to raise money.

Conclusion

The Asia-Pacific region is well-poised to capture the value of life science and biotechnology investment opportunities. The region has invested heavily in developing its base of science and technology over the last several decades, and has established a growing range of world-class scientists and institutions.

Efforts to commercialize life science and biotechnologies have been relatively slow, but have been accelerating in recent years. Still, the region already has nearly as many life science and biotechnology companies as Europe and the US (see Table 10.2, pg 150). While the market capitalization of these companies is still less than 10% of the top 25 US companies, a substantial increase in valuation and market capitalization can be anticipated as the innovative products, services, and technologies developed by these companies come to market over the next several years.

The region has more than its fair share of "raw diamonds" that are waiting to be mined, shaped, and polished through the innovation development pipeline. There is opportunity and need for smart money investment to drive this technology and product development.

Asia-Pacific countries collectively possess most of the critical factors for success in biotech innovation:

- ***Smart people.*** Not just in the region, but smart people from the region in major centers of excellence around the world. A growing proportion of these people are keen to contribute to life science and biotechnology development in Asia.

- *Smart ideas.* There is no shortage of smart and creative ideas in the region that are waiting to successfully traverse the innovation development pipeline.
- *Smart money.* This is the greatest stumbling block in the region as the lack of smart money to support early-stage technology validation, productization and commercialization of innovative products, services, and technologies has led to a much slower rate of translation from concept to marketplace reality than is the case in other hotbeds of innovation around the world. More and more economies in the region have recognized this problem, and have started to make the necessary input to open up this bottleneck so the region can contribute to substantial value creation through innovation and entrepreneurship development.
- *Smart alliances and partnerships.* Growing awareness of the value of managing and licensing intellectual property to accelerate value creation has enabled several institutions and enterprises in the region to begin to apply state-of-the-art technologies to address problems and concerns in the region. This is already beginning to generate a range of products, services, and solutions that will bring substantial value and benefit.

The Asia-Pacific region stands to be a very significant player in life science and biotechnology innovation and value creation over the coming decades. Close collaboration and partnership amongst government, academia, entrepreneurial companies, and investors — both within and across national boundaries – will contribute substantially to enable countries in the region to capture the value being created.

Key Points

1. Research has traditionally been funded by governments and commercialization by private industry.
2. There is a growing opportunity for privately funded smart investment to support innovation and entrepreneurship development. Working closely with the public sector, such strategic investment can potentially drive substantial value creation by facilitating the commercialization of publicly funded research.
3. Private funding for innovation and entrepreneurship development is complementary and is not in competition with public funding.

Chapter 20
Conclusion: Realizing the Potential

Do not follow where the path may lead.
Go instead where there is no path and leave a trail.

Muriel Strode

Understanding the Potential

The potential impact of recent scientific breakthroughs is becoming increasingly clear, including:

- ***The mapping of the human genome and those of other organisms.*** The implications of these initiatives are far-reaching and will have a myriad of social and economic effects in the coming decades, ranging from better and faster disease diagnosis, improved drugs, individually tailored medical treatments, genetic modification of humans (through gene therapy) and other organisms, and improved disease prevention.

- ***The growing field of bioinformatics*** and increasing application of information and communications technology (ICT) to the life sciences provides a marriage of cutting-edge information technology with frontier science that would enable scientists to make better sense of the data and information being generated by various fields of life science research, and accelerate the translation of new insights to practical application.

- ***The genetic modification of animals, plants, and microbes*** can potentially impact disease management, food production, environment protection, and even conservation efforts. The identification of new genes associated with traits of interest in economically important organisms can potentially also bring additional benefits – including the creation of transgenes that promise to bring improved quality of agricultural products with higher yields, more nutritious foods, and environmentally friendly crops and livestock, among other benefits.

- **The ability to grow human tissues from stem cells** (from skin to blood vessels to whole organs) for surgical replacement is beginning to create a whole new life science industry sector. In time, it is not inconceivable that we will be able to apply tissue engineering technology to grow and replace entire organs as needed.
- **The deepening relationship between microelectronics, nanotechnologies, and the life sciences sector** which is responsible for creating novel technologies such as gene chip and lab-on-a-chip technologies (with potential use for disease diagnosis and management) and automated natural product screening.

The rapid evolution of the life science sector, the leaps in scientific and technical knowledge, and the wide-ranging commercial and social applicability of these discoveries promise to fuel economic growth and development for those societies that have the vision to invest in developing the infrastructure to capture the value and potential of life sciences and biotechnology, and to bring substantial returns to those who are smart and savvy enough to invest early and strategically in innovation and entrepreneurship development in the life sciences and technologies.

There is need for an enlightened vision, for a willingness to take calculated risks to invest in potential winners in the life sciences and biotechnology. The efforts of governments in the region to attract big pharma and to import biotech talent should be applauded – their efforts will bring substantial benefit, and increase the scope for strategic cooperation, collaboration, and partnership between public and private players and between local, regional, and international players. There is also substantial opportunity to recognize and support indigenous skills and talent, and to provide them with the opportunity to test and validate their ideas, and to bring them to fruition.

Asia-Pacific governments have done many things right. Still, we need to find the right balance between paternalistic support and creating a fertile environment that respects innovation and creativity, and provides the freedom and space to incentivize innovators and entrepreneurs as they work to capture the value they are creating for society.

What Holds Asia Back?

The factors that most hold us back, interestingly enough, tend to be self-imposed, mindset factors that have little to do with our actual capabilities.[1]

---

[1] The implicit assumption here is that all infrastructure, policy/regulatory, human resource, and financial needs are in place, and that there is already commitment to applying best practice approaches (including attention to the four "smarts": smart people, smart ideas, smart money, and smart alliances and partnerships).

BioEnterprise Asia describes these as:

- The "post-colonial" mindset
- the "crabs-in-the-basket" syndrome

The "post-colonial" mindset is a throwback to colonial times when many former colonies in Asia simply took it for granted that they were second-class and not as good as their colonial masters. This appears to stem from a curious lack of belief in ourselves and our capabilities that manifests today in tremendous respect and authority being given to US and European players, and to ideas coming from "Western" parts of the world, while equally good ideas from players in the country or region are not given the consideration they deserve. Recognizing that Asians are our own worst enemies when we allow ourselves to ignore our own talent in favor of talent from more developed countries is critical. This is particularly striking, and amusing, given that some of the best talent in US and European institutions and corporations are of Asian origin.

The "crabs-in-the-basket" mindset appears to be a curiously Asian phenomenon where people refuse to acknowledge the value and benefit that other locals bring – and seek to downplay and even raise doubts about the credibility and value of the contribution being made by their peers. Every time someone gets ahead, the others feel the need to rein them in, to pull them back into the basket, as it were. The "crabs-in-the-basket" syndrome is particularly insidious and destructive when it manifests itself in a refusal to allow another person or group to achieve their objective with the mistaken belief that the success of the other person or group somehow spells our failure – sometimes, individuals afflicted with this syndrome go so far as to undermine or sabotage the efforts of others.

The reality is that we need to break the stranglehold that these self-imposed mental prisons have on us and on our societies (see also Box 11.2, pg 169). There is a lot to be gained by all if we manage to succeed. The talent and capabilities to make things happen are scarce enough in Asia-Pacific economies – it makes much more sense to work together for common goals and ideals than to pull apart. We need to shift toward being societies that recognize and celebrate our winners and our heroes, and work together to encourage our best minds to achieve their best potential. The success of one makes success for others infinitely easier.

Asians need to stand up and be counted as the leaders in science and technology that we are, and have the potential to be if we only had a little more self-belief. We should take the reins to promote the development of indigenous enterprises even as we encourage the tremendous benefits of bringing in established international players into the region – and facilitate the exchange of ideas, people, and technology across institutional, national and regional barriers.

Conclusion: Translating Dreams to Reality

We have chosen, in this book, to address the BioBusiness issues and opportunities from the perspective of three very different but key sets of stakeholders in the Asia-Pacific region:

- The policy-maker keen to promote jobs and economic value-added to his/her society (Chapter 17)
- The entrepreneur eager to translate his/her bioenterprise dream to reality (Chapter 18)
- The investor keen to invest in the sector and eager to see his/her investment dollars grow from making such an investment (Chapter 19)

While these stakeholders are important, they are not the only potential partners who are needed in the enterprise if we are to capture maximum value from the life science revolution.

As has been emphasized throughout this book, success in BioBusiness depends on the coming together of a range of multi-disciplinary and diverse skill sets and capabilities – not just to drive innovative new products, services, and technologies through the innovation development pipeline and thereby increase the efficiency of R–D–A translation (see Figure 4.2, pg 54 and Figure 4.3, pg 55); but also to provide necessary support in a range of related activities including: intellectual property protection and management; technology partnering and licensing; training and education; technology business incubation and acceleration; marketing and distribution chain management; branding and public relations; ensuring access to state-of-the-art equipment and technology resources, access to financial management and resource mobilization capabilities; and so on (see also Figure 11.2, pg 177).

Also, it should be pointed out that the roles and activities undertaken by each key player across the BioBusiness landscape – from healthcare and biomedical sciences to agriculture to environmental and industrial sciences to entirely novel areas of life science and biotechnology application, will be essentially similar in spirit and approach, but very different in application because of the wide diversity of unique factors, and the different drivers operating in each sector.

The fundamental question for anyone who recognizes the potential of the life sciences and biotechnology to create "Summit" opportunities in BioBusiness is: How do I capture a piece of the value and wealth that this high growth sector is already creating and will create over the coming decades? Clearly, the answer to this question would vary according to who you are and where you fit among the various stakeholders who will be either winners or losers in capturing the value proposition of life sciences and biotechnology. Once you have an idea as to how you want to make a difference, you will likely find many of the insights and perspectives in this book helpful in getting you going.

Given time and space constraints, we opted to provide a strategic overview on where things stand, where they are likely to go, and what needs to be done to capture the value rather than attempt to get into encyclopaedic detail into every possible direction and option.

Our mission has been to act as your guide in helping you to understand the BioBusiness landscape, and to identify key landmarks and routes for exploration. Whichever way you choose to go, we promise you one thing: you will have an exhilarating and challenging experience – you will learn a tremendous amount about yourself, and the world around you.

And, if you choose your course well and identify the right guides and partners to help you along, you may well end up reaping more wealth, and bringing greater benefit to humankind and the environment than you ever dreamt possible. It is up to you now to decide which way you want to go, and how you wish to make the journey.

Key Points

1. Countries throughout the Asia-Pacific region have invested heavily in life science education and research over the last several decades. Such investment has resulted in a growing base of internationally recognized scientists and academic centers of excellence, and a substantial portfolio of intellectual property and know-how. There has, thus far, been relatively little crossing over of knowledge and expertise in the region into commercial application despite the obvious potential of some lines of research.

2. There is great need in the Asia-Pacific region for expertise in identifying and nurturing the development of high potential technologies and business opportunities through to the

establishment of sustainable life science start-up companies. Hence, a proactive market-oriented stance is vital to explore new business directions; to establish exciting new companies around innovative market concepts or technologies; or to adopt promising existing companies and technology concepts in response to identified market opportunities and demands.

3. A large market demand is foreseen for companies that are able to supply technologies and/or supporting infrastructure for the emerging private and public sector agricultural, healthcare, environmental, and industrial initiatives in Asia and beyond, and consequently good investment opportunities.

4. While governments can and should do their best to create infrastructure and fertile ground for innovation and value creation, true economic benefit and wealth will only come when entrepreneurs are prepared to roll up their sleeves to set up and establish enterprises that build on innovation, and to translate great ideas from the bench to bring value and benefit to the marketplace. Enlightened investors who are prepared to help finance and support the effort can greatly facilitate making dreams come true.

The future of life sciences and biotechnology in the Asia-Pacific region and beyond lies firmly in our hearts, our minds, and our hands.

Glossary of Abbreviations and Technical Terms

abiotic: Non-living.

accelerator (business accelerator): A business partner that accelerates the rate of output, value creation, and profitability of a business enterprise by providing such strategic inputs as knowledge, insight, infrastructure, business systems, skilled human resources, business development input, strategic alliance and partnership relationships, and/or capital investment.

ADB: Asian Development Bank.

adjuvant: A substance added to a drug or vaccine to enhance its effect.

A-IMBN: Asia-Pacific International Molecular Biology Network.

allele: One of a number of different forms of a gene. Each person inherits two alleles for each gene – one allele from each parent. These alleles may be the same or may be different from one another.

allergen: Any substance inducing an allergy, for example, pollen and house dust mites.

amino acids: The building blocks of proteins. There are about 20 different amino acids used by the cell to make proteins.

amplification (of genes): The process of increasing the number of copies of a particular gene or chromosomal sequence.

anemia: A condition in which the amount of hemoglobin and red blood cells in the body is lower than normal.

antibody: A protein produced by the immune system in humans and higher animals, which binds to a specific antigen. When antibodies bind to corresponding antigens, they set in motion a process to eliminate antigens (and antigen-bearing cells).

antigen: A foreign substance that, when introduced into the body, can stimulate an immune response. *See* **antibody**.

apoptosis: Controlled cell death.

autoimmune disease: A disease where an individual's immune system mounts an attack on a portion of its own tissues. Tissues undergoing such an attack are characteristically damaged in the process (for example, the thyroid gland in Grave's disease and joint tissue in rheumatoid arthritis).

bacteriophage: A virus that lives in and kills bacteria; also termed phage.

bacterium: A class of single-cell organisms.

base: A component of DNA made up of nitrogen and carbon atoms in a ring structure. There are two classes of bases: purines (adenine and guanine) and pyrimidines (cytosine and thymine). The bases pair in the DNA double helix.

base pair: Two nucleotide bases on different strands of the nucleic acid molecule that bond together. The bases can pair in only one way: adenine with thymine (in DNA) or uracil (in RNA), and guanine with cytosine.

BIO: Biotechnology Industry Organization.

bioassay: The determination of the effectiveness of a compound by measuring its effect on animals, tissues, or organisms in comparison with a standard preparation.

BioBusiness: Commercial activity based on an understanding of life sciences and life processes.

BioBusiness landscape: A conceptual framework for describing the range of BioBusiness activities in terms of a rugged and dynamic terrain with "Valleys," "Summits," and "Clouds."

BioCamp: An innovative life science and biotechnology education and enrichment program for school-age children developed by BioEnterprise Asia.

biocatalyst: An enzyme or micro-organism that activates or speeds up a biochemical reaction.

biochemistry: The study of chemical processes in biological systems.

biocluster: A concentration of life science- and biotechnology-related institutions, laboratories, and businesses.

bioconversion: Chemical restructuring of raw materials by using a biocatalyst.

biodegradable: That which is capable of being broken down by the action of micro-organisms or enzymes.

biodiversity: Biological diversity. This is usually defined in terms of the number of species per unit area.

bioeconomy: Activities related to the production and distribution of BioBusiness-related goods and services in any particular geographical region.

BioEnterprise Asia: An Asia-Pacific life science technology enterprise focused on working with future leaders in BioBusiness to build value together in the region.

bioethics: That branch of philosophy pertaining to how we should decide on what is morally right or wrong in relation to issues and concerns in the life sciences and biotechnology.

biofilms: Mixed microbial communities typically in an extracellular polysaccharide or slime matrix and attached to an environmental surface where sufficient moisture and nutrients are present.

biogas reactors: Reactors that generate energy from the combustion of methane and other combustible gases produced when bacteria degrade bacterial material in the absence of oxygen (anaerobic digestion).

biogeneric: Generic biopharmaceutical.

bioinformatics: The study of genetic and other biological information using advanced computer and statistical techniques.

bioinnovation: Life science or biotechnology innovation.

bio-IT: The application of information and communication tools in the life science and biotechnology arena. This includes the use of hardware and software tools and applications for R&D, genomic and proteomic analysis, computational biology applications, knowledge and database management, molecular modeling and simulations, and other related applications.

biologicals: Biological products.

biology: The understanding of life and its various processes.

biomass: The mass of biological material, for example, microbial cells or plants, commonly used to refer to agricultural feedstocks. In microbiology, this refers to the mass of microbial cells in growth studies.

biomonitoring: The monitoring key body functional parameters.

biopartnering: Working together with strategic partners to build value for BioBusiness enterprises. BioEnterprise Asia views biopartnering in terms of three dimensions: technology partnering; service partnering, and financial partnering.

biopharmaceuticals: Pharmaceutical products of biological origin.

biopharming: The agricultural cultivation and rearing of genetically modified multi-cellular organisms (typically plants or animals) to produce biological pharmaceutical substances that may be medically useful to humans.

bioplastics: Characteristically biodegradeable plastics produced by creating polymers from biological molecules.

biopreneur: A life sciences and biotechnology entrepreneur or BioBusiness entrepreneur.

bioprospecting: The research, collection, and utilization of biological and genetic resources for the purpose of applying the knowledge derived for commercial purposes.

bioremediation: The process by which living organisms act to degrade hazardous organic contaminants or transform hazardous inorganic contaminants to environmentally safe levels.

biosensor: A device in which powerful recognition systems of biological chemicals (enzymes, antibodies) are coupled to microelectronics to enable low-level detection of substances such as sugars and proteins in body fluids, pollutants in water, and gases in air.

biosphere: The regions of the Earth and its atmosphere where life exists.

biosurfactant: A surfactant of biological origin.

biotechnology: The application of insights from the life sciences to economically and industrially productive processes. This is generally recognized to include any technique that uses living organisms, or parts of such organisms, to make or modify products, to improve plants or animals, or to develop micro-organisms for specific use. It ranges from traditional or classical biotechnology, as in yoghurt-, bread-, and beer-making, to advanced modern or molecular biotechnology that builds on our understanding of molecular biology.

biotic: Pertaining to life.

brand equity: The holistic value of a brand identity as an asset belonging to its owner.

burden of disease: The impact and significance of a disease, typically measured in health, quality of life, social impact, or economic terms.

cancer: A term describing a broad range of diseases, all characterized by uncontrolled cell growth.

cell: The basic subunit of any living thing typically containing genetic material, an energy-producing system, and other components, all surrounded by a wall and/or membrane.

CGIAR: Consultative Group on International Agricultural Research.

chromosome: The DNA in a cell is divided into structures called chromosomes. Chromosomes are large enough to be seen under a microscope. In humans, all cells other than germ cells usually contain 46 chromosomes: 22 pairs of autosomes and either a pair of X chromosomes (in females) or an X chromosome and a Y chromosome (in males). In each pair of chromosomes, one chromosome is inherited from an individual's father and one from his or her mother.

clinical trial: A process in which drugs or therapies are tested extensively for safety and efficacy before being marketed for public use. There are generally four phases – I, II, III, and IV.

clone: A term which is applied to genes, cells, or entire organisms which are derived from, and are genetically identical to, a single common ancestor gene, cell, or organism, respectively. The cloning of genes and cells to create many copies in the laboratory is a common procedure essential for biomedical research. The "cloning" of organisms from embryonic cells occurs naturally in nature, for example, with the occurrence of identical twins.

cloning: The process of producing a genetically identical copy, or clone.

CMO: Contract manufacturing organization.

code: The sequence of DNA bases which forms the instructions for a given characteristic or trait.

codon: A sequence of three nucleotide bases that specifies an amino acid or represents a signal to stop or start a function.

complementary DNA (cDNA): DNA synthesized from a messenger RNA rather than from a DNA template. This type of DNA is used for cloning or as a DNA probe for identifying specific genes in DNA hybridization studies.

composting: Utilizing bacteria and fungi to break down waste into natural fertilizers.

computational biology: The development and application of data analysis, mathematical modeling, and computational simulation techniques to the study of biological systems.

cosmeceutical: Cosmetic products with therapeutic or health promoting effects.

cost-benefit analysis: An analytical approach for comparing the costs associated with taking a specific course of action to the benefits that such action will generate.

critical mass: In physics, the minimum amount of fissionable material required to sustain a chain reaction. In the context of bioinnovation and value creation, the minimum level of infrastructure development, capabilities, and resources to enable the establishment of a sustainable life science and biotechnology industry in any given environment.

CRO: Contract research organization.

cryopreservation: The process involved in freezing, storage, and thawing of biological materials.

CSF: Colony stimulating factor.

cultivar: A plant or animal maintained under cultivation.

culture: The cultivation of living organisms in a prepared medium.

culture medium: Any nutrient system for the growth of bacteria or other cells, usually a complex mixture of organic and inorganic materials.

cytokines: The generic name for a family of low molecular weight proteins that can modulate interactions between cells.

cytoplasm: Cellular material that is within the cell membrane and surrounds the nucleus.

demographic transition: The shift from high birth and high death rates in traditional societies, through high birth and low death rates in transitional societies, to low birth and low death rates in modern societies as a consequence of economic, technological, and social development.

diagnostics: The use of molecular characterization to provide more accurate and quicker identification of a disease.

differentiation: The process of biochemical and structural changes by which cells become specialized in form and function.

diploid: A cell with two complete sets of chromosomes.

DNA (deoxyribonucleic acid): The molecule that encodes genetic information. DNA is a double-stranded helix held together by bonds between pairs of nucleotides.

DNA fingerprinting: A quick way to compare the DNA sequences of living organisms.

DNA probe: A molecule (usually a nucleic acid) that has been labeled with a radioactive isotope, dye, or enzyme and is used to locate a particular nucleotide sequence or gene on a DNA molecule.

DNA sequence: The order of nucleotide bases in a given DNA molecule.

double helix: The physical structure of DNA, consisting of two parallel strands of DNA coiled helically.

downstream processing: The stages of processing that take place after the fermentation or bioconversion stage. It includes separation, purification, and packaging of the product.

ecosystem: The entire system of living organisms and nonliving environment and geographical factors in a given area.

embryology: The science that studies the formation and early development of living organisms from the ovum stage till the adult stage.

emerging disease: A new or existing disease whose incidence has increased in recent years or whose incidence threatens to increase in the near future.

environmental impact assessment (EIA): An analysis of likely environmental consequences of a proposed human activity at the earliest possible stage in the development of the project, program, or policy.

enzyme: A protein that facilitates a biochemical reaction in a cell. In general, these biochemical reactions would not occur if the enzyme is not present. For example, an enzyme can facilitate (also called "catalyze") the destruction of another protein by breaking the bonds between amino acids. An enzyme of that type is called a protease.

EPA: Environmental Protection Agency (US).

epidemic: An outbreak of a disease (usually refers to infectious diseases).

epidemiological transition: The changing pattern of diseases as societies undergo development. Characteristically, traditional societies tend to experience a high burden of infectious diseases while chronic diseases and cancers tend to predominate in modern, developed societies. Transitional societies tend to have a mixed pattern of disease.

epidemiology: The study of the occurrence and distribution of diseases, and the factors that govern their spread.

epitope: Any part of a molecule that can act as an antigenic determinant that is capable of stimulating production of a different specific antibody.

erythropoeitin (EPO): A naturally-occuring glycoprotein, normally produced by the kidneys, that stimulates red blood cell production in the bone marrow.

ES cells: Embryonic stem cells. Cultured cells derived from the pluripotent inner cell mass of blastocyst stage embryos.

Escherichia coli (E. coli): A bacterium that inhabits the intestinal tract of most vertebrates. Much of the work using recombinant DNA techniques has been carried out with this organism because it has been genetically well-characterized.

ethnopharmacology: the study of differences in response to drugs based on variations in ethnic and pharmacogenetic origin

eukaryote: A cell or organism containing a true nucleus, with a well-defined membrane surrounding the nucleus. All organisms except bacteria, viruses, and blue-green algae are eukaryotic (*compare with* **prokaryote**).

evolution: The process of heritable change in any given biological population over many generations.

exon: In eukaryotic cells, the part of the gene that is transcribed into messenger RNA and encodes a protein (*compare with* **intron**).

expression: In genetics, the manifestation of a characteristic that is specified by a gene. For example, a person can carry the gene for a hereditary disease but not actually have the disease. In this case, the gene is present but not expressed. In industrial biotechnology, the term is often used to mean the production of a protein by a gene that has been inserted into a new host organism.

extracellular: Outside the cells (of an organism).

FAO: Food and Agriculture Organization.

FDA: Food and Drug Administration (US).

feedstock: Raw material used for chemical or biological processes.

fermentation: The growing of micro-organisms for the production of various chemical or pharmaceutical compounds. Large tanks, called fermentors, contain micro-organisms or other cells and the nutrients they require.

Fermentation has been used for hundreds of years in beer, wine, and cheese production.

food security: Ready access to nutritionally adequate and safe food for an active, healthy life.

functional genomics: The study of the functions of specific genes and groups of genes in both normal and disease states.

GCP: good clinical practice.

gene: The segment of the DNA molecule made up of linear sequences of four nitrogenous bases that carry the structural information for a protein. These proteins make up the cell's structure, mediate its metabolism, and control all cellular functions.

gene chip: Analogous to a computer chip, a gene chip is an array of thousands of independent but simultaneously functioning analysis units. In this case, each unit is a small sequence of DNA, a probe, immobilized in a defined position on a solid surface. Unknown DNA sequences applied to the chip will interact with various probes in a pattern that will characterize the previously unknown gene. Gene chips can speed up identification of DNA, enabling earlier clinical diagnostics and more targeted disease management.

gene mapping: The determination of the relative locations of genes on a chromosome.

gene sequencing: The determination of the sequence of nucleotide bases in a strand of DNA.

genetic code: The mechanism by which genetic information is stored in living organisms. The code uses sets of three nucleotide bases (codons) to make the amino acids that, in turn, constitute proteins.

genetic engineering: The technique of removing, modifying, or adding genes to a living organism; also called gene splicing, recombinant DNA (rDNA) technology, or genetic modification.

gene therapy: Gene therapy involves the insertion of normal genes into cells in an attempt to create a beneficial genetic change, for example, to correct for a genetic trait associated with disease. If a change is introduced via germ line gene therapy, that change may be present in the offspring from birth in every cell in the body.

genetic fingerprinting: Broadly, the assembly of data from genomic analysis into accessible forms.

genetic testing: The analysis of an individual's genetic material. Among the purposes of genetic testing could be to gather information on an individual's genetic predisposition to a particular health condition or to confirm a diagnosis of genetic disease.

genome map: The description of the order of genes and the spacing between them in all chromosomes of an organism.

genome sciences: The integration of life science disciplines that build on an understanding of the genetic make-up of entire organisms.

genome sequencing: The determination and description of the entire linear sequence of the entire DNA (all genes and chromosomes) that makes up an organism's genome. This descriptive knowledge must be augmented by functional genomics research to characterize the role of these DNA sequences.

genomics: The study of genetic information – how it is structured, stored, expressed, and altered.

genotyping: A range of technologies that will produce a description of specific individuals at the genetic level. These technologies enable the diagnosis of genetic traits and genetic predisposition for various diseases in plants, animals, and humans. These technologies are also central to functional genomics because one of the current methods to identify gene function is to conduct gene mapping in patients and families likely to bear a variant gene that predisposes to a particular disease.

GLP: Good laboratory practice.

GMP: Good manufacturing practice.

gross domestic product (GDP): The total market value of goods and services produced in an economy in a given period (usually a year).

hemoglobin: The protein involved in oxygen transport in our bloodstream.

high-throughput DNA sequencing: The automated approach to sequencing large DNA segments such as chromosomal regions containing a disease gene or the entire genome of a micro-organism.

HIV: Human immunodeficiency virus.

homeostatis: The ability of an organism to maintain a constant internal environment (for example, body temperature, fluid content, and so on) though compensatory regulatory mechanisms.

human development: The process of maximizing human potential and enlarging the range of choices for personal growth and fulfillment.

immune system: A biological defence system that has evolved in vertebrates to protect them against the introduction of foreign material (such as pollen or invading micro-organisms) and to prevent the body from developing cancer.

immunotherapeutics: The immune molecules used for therapeutic purposes.

industrial enzymes: The enzymes used to catalyze commercially important processes.

initial public offering (IPO): The first offering of shares in a company on the stock market.

innovation development pipeline: The process pipeline for translating promising concepts through the R&D process into the marketplace. BioEnterprise Asia defines five discrete phases in the innovation development pipeline: concept, technology validation or proof of concept, productization, business case validation, market entry and growth.

insulin: A hormone produced in the pancreas that is essential for regulating the metabolism of blood glucose.

intellectual property (IP): The commercially valuable output of the human intellect.

intellectual property rights (IPR): The legally enforceable power to exclude others from using the intellectual property (to set terms in which it can be used). IPR include trademark, copyright, and patent rights, as well as trade secret rights, publicity rights, moral rights, and rights against unfair competition.

interferons: A family of small proteins that stimulate viral resistance in cells.

interleukins: A family of low molecular weight proteins that can modulate the growth and activities of certain white blood cells.

intron: In eukaryotic cells, a sequence of DNA that is contained in the gene but does not encode for protein.

in vitro: Literally, "in glass." Performed in a test tube or other laboratory apparatus.

in vitro **fertilization (IVF):** The fertilization of an egg cell by sperm cells performed "in glass," that is, in a laboratory procedure. This process is often used to achieve pregnancy if the mother's fallopian tubes are damaged or missing.

in vivo: In the living organism.

IRRI: International Rice Research Institute.

ISAAA: International Service for the Acquisition of Agri-biotech Applications.

IVI: International Vaccine Institute.

lead compound: A compound that could potentially be converted to a new drug by optimizing its beneficial effects and minimizing its toxicity and side effects.

library: A set of cloned DNA fragments.

life sciences: The understanding of life and its various processes. Characteristically involves the integration and application of biology, engineering, chemistry, and information technology to such fields as agriculture, pharmaceutical development and manufacturing, food technology, medical devices, and healthcare services.

ligase: An enzyme used to join DNA or RNA segments together. They are called DNA ligase and RNA ligase, respectively.

linkage: The tendency for certain genes to be inherited together due to their physical proximity on the chromosome.

locus: The position on a chromosome of a gene or other chromosome marker; also, the DNA at that position. The use of locus is sometimes restricted to mean regions of DNA that are expressed.

lymphocyte: A white blood cell that is important in the body's immune response. Because they contain nuclei, lymphocytes serve as an easily accessible source for genomic DNA.

lysis: The breaking apart of cells.

microinjection: The injection of minute amounts of a substance into a microscopic structure such as a cell.

micro-organism: An organism that can be seen only through a microscope. Micro-organisms include bacteria, protozoa, algae, and fungi. Although viruses are not considered living organisms, they are sometimes classified as micro-organisms.

milestone event: A significant accomplishment; intermediate goal.

mitochondria: Organelles in cells responsible for energy production.

MNCs: Multinational corporations.

molecular biology: The understanding of biological or life processes at the molecular level.

monoclonal antibodies: Mass-produced antibodies against very specific antigens.

morphology: Form and structure.

mutation: A heritable change in DNA sequence.

nanotechnology (also described as molecular technology): The design and manufacture of extremely small electronic circuits and mechanical devices built at the molecular level of matter – typically 100 nm or smaller.

NCE: New chemical entity; new candidate drug molecule.

nucleotide: A building block of DNA and RNA, consisting of a nitrogenous base, a five-carbon sugar, and a phosphate group. Together, the nucleotides form codons, which when strung together form genes, which in turn link to form chromosomes.

nucleus: The membrane-bound region of a eukaryotic cell that contains the chromosomes.

nutraceuticals: Food-based products with therapeutic or health promoting effects (sometimes also described as "functional foods" or "pharmafoods").

oncogene: This refers to a type of genes that can help make a cell become cancerous. Typically, it is a mutant form of the normal gene.

organ: A fully differentiated structural and functional unit in an animal that is specialized for some particular function.

organelle: "Little organ;" a specialized part of a cell, analogous to an organ.

pandemic: An outbreak of disease (epidemic) that is widespread across several different geographical locations.

PCR: Polymerase chain reaction; a technique for amplifying a piece of DNA quickly and cheaply.

peptide: Two or more amino acids chained together by a bond called a "peptide bond." A protein is a long chain of amino acids joined together in this way, and, therefore, is sometimes referred to as a "polypeptide." Some proteins contain more than one polypeptide chain.

pharmaceuticals: Drugs.

pharmacogenomics: The science of understanding the correlation between an individual's genetic make-up (genotype) and their response to drug treatment. Some drugs work well in some patient populations and not as well in others. Studying the genetic basis of patient response to therapeutics allows drug developers to design more effective therapeutic treatments.

phenomics: The study of phenotypes and phenotypic expression patterns based on knowledge of genomics and genotypes.

phenotype: The observable structural and functional manifestation of a genotype which may be expressed physically, biochemically, or physiologically.

phytoremediation: An innovative technology utilizing the natural properties of plants in engineered systems to remediate hazardous waste sites, and remove, destroy, and detoxify environmental contaminants.

plasmid: A small piece of DNA found outside chromosomes in bacteria. Plasmids can be tools for inserting new genetic information into micro-organisms or plants.

poverty: A state of deprivation and destitution with inadequate income and insufficient resources to meet basic living and personal or family development needs, all too often defined narrowly in economic terms alone.

poverty trap: The situation wherein a combination of factors tend to operate as a vicious cycle to keep a person in poverty including indebtedness; lack of educational, skill enhancement, and employment opportunities; as well as lack of access to capital.

productization: The process of translating a product, service, or technology platform concept that has been technologically validated into a commercially ready product, service, or technology platform.

prokaryote: A unicellular organism having cells lacking membrane-bound nuclei. Bacteria are the prime example but also included are blue-green algae and actinomycetes and mycoplasma.

proteomics: The study of the identities, quantities, structures, and functions of proteins in an organism, organ, cell, or organelle, and how these properties vary in space, time, and physiological state. The focus is on improving the understanding of the pathways by which genes affect structure, function, and activity (since genes typically express themselves through proteins). Proteins present "targets" for the development of drugs designed to affect tissues or cells containing those proteins.

R–D–A translation: The process of translating insights and understanding arising from Research (R), through the Development pipeline (D), into practical Application in the marketplace (A).

Receptomics™: Natural ligands and drugs act in natural systems by interacting with active sites or receptors. Receptomics™ refers to the understanding of the structure and function of such active sites, and the application of this understanding for drug design, molecular physiology, and other purposes.

recombinant DNA: Genetically engineered DNA that has been altered by joining genetic material from different sources.

reproductive biology: The study of processes involved in, or related to, reproduction.

ribosome: The organelle responsible for protein synthesis in the cytoplasm of a living cell that is composed of proteins and RNA.

RNA: Ribonucleic acid.

SMEs: Small- and medium-sized enterprises.

somatic cell: A somatic cell is any cell of the body except for germ cells (sperm cells and egg cells) and their precursors.

stem cell: Undifferentiated, primitive cells in the bone marrow with the ability both to multiply and to differentiate into specific blood cells.

strategic alliance: An understanding between individuals or entities to act in concert to build on complementary strengths and capabilities for mutual benefit.

systems biology: The integrated approach to studying life processes in biological systems including intracellular pathways, cells, organs, functional biological systems, and even the entire organism.

tissue engineering: The science of growing human tissues and ultimately organs for transplantation and repair. Cells and biocompatible scaffolds are usually used.

tongkat ali (*Eurycoma longifolia*): Malaysian name for a root traditionally known for its aphrodisiac and medicinal properties. Also known as *pasak bumi* in Indonesia.

toxicogenomics: A scientific subdiscipline that combines the emerging technologies of genomics and bioinformatics to identify and characterize mechanisms of action of known and suspected toxicants. Currently, the premier toxicogenomic tools are the DNA microarray and the DNA chip, which are used for the simultaneous monitoring of expression levels of hundreds to thousands of genes.

transformation: The introduction of single genes conferring potentially useful traits into plants, livestock, fish, and tree species.

transgene/transgenic: An organism whose genome has been altered by the inclusion of foreign genetic material. This foreign genetic material may be derived from other individuals of the same species or from wholly different species. Genetic material may also be of an artificial nature.

translational biotechnology: The process of translating promising concepts in the life sciences and biotechnology to practical application.

UNDP: United Nations Development Programme.

vaccinology: The science of vaccine development.

virus: Viruses consist of a piece of nucleic acid covered by protein. Viruses can only reproduce by infecting a cell and using the cell's mechanisms for self-replication, which, as a result, causes disease. Modified viruses can also be used as a tool in gene therapy to introduce new DNA into a cell's genome.

WHO: World Health Organization.

WTO: World Trade Organization.

xenotransplant: The transplantation of tissue or organs between organisms of different species, genus, or family. A common example is the use of pig heart valves in humans.

yeast: A general term for single-celled fungi that reproduce by budding. Some yeasts can ferment carbohydrates (starches and sugars), and thus are important in brewing and baking.

Index

309

About the Author

A mover, shaker and communicator [in the vaccine world],
whose intellect and organizational skills superbly served the
development of the [International Vaccine] Institute during its
formative years.

United Nations Development Programme's Frank Hartvelt, referring to the
author's contribution in the effort to establish the International Vaccine
Institute, 1992–1997

Gurinder S. Shahi is a physician with training in molecular biochemistry and international health policy and management. He is a leading expert on change management and strategic program implementation in healthcare and the life sciences. His experience includes work on life science technology assessment; strategic business planning; R&D and work process improvement; performance analysis of joint ventures and strategic alliances; market strategy development; economic and policy analysis for health intervention; evidence-based decision-making for investment and implementation; life science technology innovation and bioentrepreneurship.

Dr Shahi has played a role in institution-building and the development of several major international initiatives including the International Vaccine Institute and the Asia-Pacific International Molecular Biology Network, and has served as advisor and consultant to leading international organizations, governments, corporations and foundations. He has been actively involved in establishing and operationalizing a range of start-ups in Asia including Lynk Biotechnologies (a drug design and development company, and one of Singapore's first home-grown biotech companies) and DNA Phenomics Asia-Pacific (a cutting-edge company focused on translating insights from gene expression toward understanding the genetic basis of disease susceptibility, pharmacogenomic diagnosis, forensics application, and the development of new therapeutics).

Dr Shahi is deeply committed to education and the promotion of bioliteracy. In addition to working with children through school-based science enrichment programs (including BioCamp), he is involved with organizing executive education courses for non-life science professionals. Among other commitments, he holds an adjunct appointment at the Singapore Management University where he teaches a course on *Technology and World Change*, and is working to develop research and training programs on biobusiness and bioentrepreneurship in collaboration with leading academic and research institutions in the region and beyond.

Dr Shahi has authored over 50 articles, refereed journal papers and conference presentations, and served as lead editor for *International Perspectives on Environment, Development and Health: Toward a Sustainable World*.[1]

[MBBS, PhD – National University of Singapore; MPH – Harvard University; Warren Weaver Fellowship – The Rockefeller Foundation]

About BioEnterprise Asia

[*Note: Many of the concepts and ideas outlined in this book were developed in the course of projects and initiatives led by Gurinder and colleagues at BioEnterprise Asia over the years.*]

BioEnterprise Asia (www.bioenterprise.org) was established and inspired by the realization, in the course of work with governments and corporations in the region to support life science and technology development, that the Asia-Pacific region faces a fundamental dearth of effective "managers of science"– people who understand both the impact and potential of new life science technologies, and how to capture their commercial potential.

Building on this observation, and recognizing the need to help fill the gap, BioEnterprise Asia focuses on three primary business areas where knowledge and understanding of the management of science and scientific enterprises, and translation of scientific insight into practical social and commercial application are critical:

- *The consulting and advisory practice* – dedicated to working with leading international and regional life science technology players to establish and successfully expand high growth operations and effective strategic alliances in the region. Focused on building sustainable economic, commercial and social value in the region through

---

[1] GS Shahi, BS Levy, A Binger, T Kjellstrom and RS Lawrence, Springer Publishing Company, New York, 1997.

exploitation of new advances in life science and biotechnology, facilitating technology transfer and partnership, and building market and business development opportunities

- **The technology business acceleration practice** – dedicated to facilitating the development of innovative products/services/ technologies and of high growth technology enterprises in the region
- **The education/market research/events management practice** – dedicated to helping to raise awareness and understanding of the potential and opportunity that the life sciences and biotechnology offer for catalyzing economic and social development in Asia and beyond; helping to train future leaders in BioBusiness; and to promoting interaction, networking and biopartnering. BioEnterprise Asia has, among other activities, pioneered BioCamp (an innovative life science education experience for school students), as well as Executive Education programs for life sciences and biotechnology, and for Bio-IT and bioinformatics

The BioEnterprise Asia network of associates and affiliates consists largely of colorful, passionate individuals with strategic/management expertise and vision, and with domain knowledge and insight of the core competencies critical to successful life science enterprises in Asia – from product/technology development, to market development, to intellectual property management, to technology licensing, to strategic alliances and partnerships, to financial management, to media/investor relations management.

BioEnterprise Asia has been actively involved in working with governments, investors and established international corporations as well as start-ups to capture the potential of "Summit" opportunities in the life science landscape – in the region and internationally. The organization is committed to working with future leaders in healthcare, the life sciences and related areas of biotechnology to help translate their dreams into reality.

We warmly welcome your feedback and perspectives. Please write or e-mail:

BioEnterprise Asia
c/o Dr Gurinder Shahi
e-mail: gurinder.shahi@bioenterprise.org

For book reviews, updated information and analysis, discussion forums, and access to related links, check out:

http://www.bioenterprise.org/biobusinessinasia